Bernie or Bust Pioneers of Electoral Revolt

by
@BernieOrBust
with Patrick Walker

DORRANCE PUBLISHING CO
EST. 1920
PITTSBURGH, PENNSYLVANIA 15238

The contents of this work, including, but not limited to, the accuracy of events, people, and places depicted; opinions expressed; permission to use previously published materials included; and any advice given or actions advocated are solely the responsibility of the author, who assumes all liability for said work and indemnifies the publisher against any claims stemming from publication of the work.

All Rights Reserved
Copyright © 2018 by @BernieOrBust

No part of this book may be reproduced or transmitted, downloaded, distributed, reverse engineered, or stored in or introduced into any information storage and retrieval system, in any form or by any means, including photocopying and recording, whether electronic or mechanical, now known or hereinafter invented without permission in writing from the publisher.

Dorrance Publishing Co
585 Alpha Drive
Pittsburgh, PA 15238
Visit our website at *www.dorrancebookstore.com*

ISBN: 978-1-4809-4885-3
eISBN: 978-1-4809-4908-9

This book is dedicated to the millions of people Senators Sanders woke up to the need for a political revolution in the United States and to the many millions more who will have to rise and shine if we are to outlaw oligarchy and legalize a free and fair, democratic order.

Bernie or Bust Pioneers of Electoral Revolt

Table of Contents

Introduction

"I don't think I ever let you know that your #bernieor-
bust pledge was a lifeline to me. One dark night, I
thought, of course I'll vote for HRC over Trump as the
four walls closed in. I found the RAP pledge, and it gave
me strength and hope. Thank you."
~Meggie Rodgers

Bernie or Bust: Pioneers of Electoral Revolt is, in part, a documentary of that
movement as a first-hand account of what exactly the strategy was about.
Who was behind it? What is their agenda? How did they gain a following,
and what does "or bust" actually mean? The story of this movement will answer these and many other questions. I will also share our mistakes, so that
the strategy, encompassed by the words "or bust," will work better when it's
undertaken again.

Before starting this overview of our revolutionary strategy, I have a favor
to ask. Readers, who were members of our Bernie or Bust army, know I often
asked people to do something on behalf of our group's efforts to help Senator
Sanders win the nomination. I try to never forget the most important word of
all when making a request of online allies or, in this case, book readers: **please**.
The favor: if you stop reading this story and see it gathering dust, please give
it to someone else to read. Share this with someone you love, like or anyone
else who is involved in politics regardless of their party affiliation but preferably supporters of Senator Sanders and registered Democrats.

A longtime working subtitle for this project was Lessons Learned Undertaking a Labor of Love. Instead, we will convey our mistakes as part of the story and count on the reader to learn about our blunders as we recall and convey them. One reason for publishing this story is to share what we did wrong, so other revolutionaries can learn from our mistakes.

Some of the chapters of this book include the actual contents of quarter-sheet fliers, emails, our Philadelphia billboard, and an important committee discussion which are all indented. This book is part narrative, part documentary, part manifesto and part memoir. Another reason we tell this story is to provide readers with the truth about how the mainstream and even much of the alternative media did an amazing job of ignoring and/or distorting the strategy of this movement. The most ambitious goal of this book is to explain why revolution or bust is a necessary strategy in the current political order in the United States. Chapter 1 explains why the United States needs a revolution, and the rest of the book describes the how and why "or bust" was and can be used again.

Another subtitle we considered was going to mention the "establishment" Senator Sanders referenced time and again. The establishment is also called the "Washington Consensus" and neoliberalism. Our revolt is not limited to "plutocracy." What's that? Every "Bernie or Bust" argument we made on our website leading up to and during the primaries began with a definition of plutocracy. Plutocracy is a society or government run by and or for the wealthy few. Our movement for a political revolution is not limited to support for solutions to abolish plutocracy because the plutocratic order we live in is buttressed by establishment politics that run on large donations from the neoliberal corporate order. Our movement is at war with that order.

We will describe neoliberalism's 14 major characteristics in Chapter 10 and use them to evaluate President Trump, Secretary Clinton, President Obama and Senator Sanders. We also recommend a free, online pamphlet which describes that political philosophy. We tell the story about the Bernie or Bust movement and the revolution its founders and untold numbers of other Americans continue to support in order to expose and undermine the neoliberal agenda. Sanders' campaign showed that millions of citizens are ready for another American revolution, this time against the neoliberal establishment and their puppets in government. A key aim of this book is to help build an understanding of neoliberalism and to foment continued revolution against that dangerous, anti-democratic ideology.

We use the phrase "corporate globalization" a lot. An entire book could be written about the subject. For readers, who are online, we recommend a YouTube video lecture titled "Michael Parenti – Globalization, the New Imperialism."[1] Parenti states "globalization is being forced upon us through a series of secret, international trade agreements."[2] We will describe the threat posed by the Trans-Pacific Partnership "free-trade" agreement sufficiently well to give readers without access to YouTube a good understanding of corporate globalization without drilling down into boring and technical details. The Trade in Services Agreement is still under negotiation, and the United States remains involved with the process under President Trump.

Senator Bernard Sanders and Donald J. Trump attempted to win major party nominations running as outsiders. Bernie's strategy for his political revolution was unprecedented, using a major party's structure to attempt to capture the presidency as a democratic socialist. The Bernie or Bust movement, started by Revolt Against Plutocracy co-founder Patrick Walker and myself, was also unprecedented, using the threat of not voting for the party nominee unless it was Bernie Sanders and his political revolution. The latter, not the man, is what motivated our strategy and activism and continues to do so.

Trump, of course, was successful; and he is the insider in the White House for now. Bernie's revolution and our attempt to use the leverage we ended up calling "or bust" (specifically "we'll either write-in Bernie's name or vote Green Party on Nov. 8th") was not the reason Trump won. However, it could be the reason he will win re-election. We understood the Democratic Party was rigged against insurgent candidates like Sanders and others before him. Superdelegates, Super Tuesdays, super PACs and mainstream media were and remain nearly insurmountable obstacles, so we believed a grassroots movement to let the Party voters and superdelegates know they would lose the general election unless Sanders was the nominee was not only necessary but the "miracle" (to use Chris Hedges' word) Bernie needed to overcome the obstructions he was faced with. The 2016 primaries were a "swing and a miss, strike one" for the deployment of this strategy.

The Democrats either didn't know about Bernie or Bust, especially early on, or they just preferred Hillary Clinton, despite her long list of flaws as a candidate and politician, including the ongoing FBI investigation into her private email server throughout the primary season. The superdelegates certainly did know about the Bernie or Bust movement by the time of the Democratic National Convention, and they chose to nominate Clinton and divide the party anyway. They knew Sanders polled better against Trump than Clinton did. They also knew Bernie or Bust was not "Party Unity My Ass." They may have thought Bernie or Bust was Bernie or bluff, but we made it as clear as we could to them that we were not bluffing. We tried to defeat Secretary Clinton and Donald Trump because hawkish, neoliberalism is at least as dangerous as Trump's nationalistic fascism. Donald Trump may be a careless hawk, but Hillary Clinton has been a reckless hawk.

Chapter 1 provides background information as to why we understand a revolution is needed. It includes a reprint of my post from New Year's Day 2015 titled "Standing on the Edge of the Next American Revolution" and touches on corporate globalization.

Chapters 2-9 tell the story of the Bernie or Bust movement that continued to function right up to the general election for a revolution the nation and the planet's climate need. The "or Bust" strategy we call leverage was actually sparked the weekend before Sanders declared his candidacy. The Bernie Sanders write-in idea began during a street corner conversation in April 2015. The strategy we launched as a website in June 2015, received media recognition after 50,000 voters had taken the Bernie or Bust pledge in March 2016 and culminated in Philadelphia during the Democratic National Convention.

In the post-election blame game underway as this was being written, almost nobody was pointing at the superdelegates, which were put in place originally to override the popular will if they felt another candidate had a better chance of winning the general election. By 2016 they had become largely part of the neoliberal establishment. They neglected their duty and voted for a candidate many progressives and the public throughout the rust belt did not trust, like or believe. Every superdelegate, who voted for Secretary Clinton at the Democratic National Convention, should lose their position. They failed because when they could have united the Party behind Senator Sanders, they voted for the establishment candidate in a year of anti-establishment sentiments. Despite all the signs that people wanted change, they allowed Secretary Clinton to run and campaign as the candidate of the neoliberal status quo.

Chapter 10 addresses their culpability in the election of Donald Trump. Chapter 11 covers our manifesto for revolutionary change in the United States, and the Conclusion outlines a strategy Trump's opponents can use to undermine his political fortunes and help preserve the climate at the same time. It also touches on foreign policy, terrorism and the leverage strategy. Unless you're a history buff or a movement revolutionary, chapters 2 through 9 are not as important to read as chapters 1, 10, 11 and the Conclusion.

The media did a horrible job at covering the Bernie or Bust movement unless you are a supporter of Secretary Clinton. In that case, they, especially MSNBC, did a splendid job of ignoring the movement and insuring as few people knew about it as possible. There were several misleading and flat-out inaccurate reports printed in articles about the Bernie or Bust movement. This book is an attempt to correct the record by telling the story of relevant background information from its inception to the last chapter announcing our plans going forward. The hope is to provide readers with a quick understanding of where the Bernie or Bust movement came from, how we built and deployed it and to offer lessons for future, revolutionary electoral revolts.

The Bernie or Bust movement took on a life of its own. Some people held local Bernie or Bust meetings. A dozen or so Bernie or Bust Facebook groups and Twitter accounts arose. Some people, even citizens who took our explicit pledge, committed themselves to vote for Trump against our wishes. Rarely did my counter-arguments in support of casting a revolutionary vote instead serve to change their minds. About 4% of our Bernie or Bust pledge–takers ended up voting for Donald Trump.[3] 10% of those, who took our pledge, voted for Clinton. "Or Bluffers" we call them ("bluffers" for short).

This story describes how the corporate media collaborated with Secretary Clinton to keep Bernie or Bust (and Sanders himself) out of the news. It will convey the movement's successful tactics (Democratic Party caucuses) and its failures (burning through Clinton's southern "firewall"). What worked and what didn't work will be described and explained throughout the story of Bernie or Bust from the founders' perspective.

The individuals cited in this story either gave me permission to do so, or they wrote articles that are public and cited. Where I discuss an unnamed person, who worked with or against us, that person did not give me permission to use his or her name. Because of blocking on Facebook, some people referenced anonymously were not notified their words were to be included in this story.

It's not hard to figure out who the revolutionary candidates are in a general election for President. Trump is part of the system. He's not a corporate tool like Clinton; he *is* a corporation. Winning the election means his sons will be that corporation until he's out of office. The establishment may use his unwillingness to place his business empire in a blind trust as a good reason to impeach him and make free-trader VP Pence the Puppet-in-Chief.

We're telling this story, warts and all. Bernie or Bust ultimately failed to help get Sanders the nomination or help get the Green Party the 5% they need to become a formal minor party. There were mistakes made, and we hope this will help non-violent revolutionaries in the future. As we started and proceeded with movement building, we had no guide. We had no history book to go by. We were pioneers forging a new strategy. This story offers a guide for future revolutionary, grassroots movements confined and bound by a first-past-the-post voting system and perhaps for candidates themselves. Answering the first question of the first Republican primary debate, Trump said he'd consider running as an independent if he didn't secure the nomination. "I'm talking about a lot of leverage," he said.[4]

We stressed in Bernie or Bust pledge narrative after pledge narrative, "or bust" was leverage. Either get behind our candidate, or you're going to lose the general election. The 2016 election was the dawn of leverage strategy progressives can deploy until the establishment changes first-past-the-post elections and implements run-off elections across the United States. People need to be able to vote their consciences before having to choose between two unacceptably horrible candidates, the proverbial "two evils," a concept we reject. Faced with a choice between Secretary Clinton and Donald Trump, a lot of people just didn't bother voting.

I don't usually explicitly point out a lesson learned describing how we undertook this strategy. I hope it's clear, when I'm describing a mistake, that it's about learning a lesson, sometimes alone, other times with friends, family or foes and other times *for* other people. There is a lot to learn about how to successfully undertake a non-violent revolution.[5]

I am using @BernieOrBust instead of my name as the author because I own the Twitter account and want to direct attention away from the person behind the movement I started. I'm not using it because I own the movement; if anything, it's the other way around now. It doesn't matter if people don't know my name because I am not the important part of this story. The ideas themselves are what matter.

Unlike Senator Sanders' book about his campaign, *Our Revolution*, there are not many policy issues discussed in this story. However, we make the argument that Hillary Clinton was more dangerous than Donald Trump, so of course we must explain why we believe that to be the case. The mainstream, corporate media, from Fox to MSNBC to the BBC, do not want the American public to understand what transnational corporations are attempting to do to our very system of government. The "fundamental transformation" of the United States then-Senator Obama promised five days before he was elected in 2008 was at least set aside for now largely because Hillary Clinton did not win the election. That is a huge relief to our cause that neither Senator Sanders nor Noam Chomsky seemed to appreciate. For now, the Framer's experiment still holds power over corporations, but that is slipping away even under NAFTA.

Trump's view toward "free-trade" policy played a significant role in his victory, and, along with the United States' relationship with Russia, explains our desire to objectively understand what must be "bizarre" and/or "stupid" from the perspective of the pro-Clinton, liberal American. Avoiding a hot or cold war with Russia with the potential of having nuclear weapons exchanged is relatively easy to everyone except, it seems, to Clinton's supporters to understand.

Trade policy has the tendency to put people to sleep. It's boring, and it can be arcane [understood with difficulty and necessarily after the study of international law.] The agreements are written in legalese, using many terms only lawyers and law students can really understand. There is a big difference between free-trade and President Obama's Trans-Pacific Partnership (TPP). I keep the fundamental concerns about the TPP that profoundly concerned me to a minimum of understandable paragraphs and stick to only three transformative features of the TPP. The loss of American jobs is not one of my concerns as a political philosopher who is secure in technical employment. Overseas labor is very inexpensive and is one of the major reasons the corporate elite want these so-called "free-trade agreements." Luckily, the loss of

American jobs was a good enough reason in the rust belt for Clinton to have lost the general election, but my distress about the TPP focused on the "handcuffing" of our representatives in government, trade tribunals and the assertion of corporate rights.

Nationalist Trump may have stopped, for now, so-called "globalization," our new world order that is unfolding and already deeply established. Neoliberals are ushering in a new global order that is of, by and for transnational corporations. If that corporatist agenda is allowed to advance, democratic order in the United States as we know it will be sharply curtailed. When it comes to regulating the behavior of corporations based in another country, it will not matter whether you vote Blue, Red, Green or Libertarian. The TPP would have prevented any politician from controlling corporate greed that is based in another country. On this issue, the Breitbart wing of Trump's support is largely in agreement with real progressives. Neoliberals are coming after our sovereignty by going over it using supranational tribunals. By the way, the Libertarian candidate for President in 2016 largely supported this agreement. That should not be too surprising as neoliberalism supports state-enforced arrangements that suit the laissez-faire, corporate agenda which largely characterizes their political philosophy. 2% of those who took our pledge voted for hyper-neoliberal Governor Johnson (L).

The Green Party's candidate for President, Jill Stein, would have also abandoned the TPP without the warmongering, sexism and apparent racism[6] that accompanies Trump. Mike Lofgren and Bill Moyers pointed out, "If authoritarian populism is the wave of the future, its midwife is neoliberal economics turned punitive and illiberal."[7] We cannot give in; we cannot give up. We're not just fighting for human freedom; climate preservation and even survival of the human species depends on this revolution ultimately succeeding.

The Bernie or Bust movement made it into two documentaries, one about the Sanders' campaign, "Bernie Sanders Documentary"[8] and another devoted an entire section, part 4 of The Revolution Televised,[9] to this movement. What follows is a written documentary from the perspective of the two "nobodies" who initiated and, along with increasing numbers of other people, promoted Bernie or Bust for over a year on social media, websites and even offline in some cases.

We are confident our critics will dismiss Patrick and me as part of the "far left." We are not Marxists or anarchists. I don't even like the label "socialist" because it suggests state-run enterprises and a fully planned economy. We support a mix of private enterprise and public services, of market activities and state spending. We're politically aligned with former Secretary of Labor under President Clinton Professor Robert Reich for the most part. However, Reich's loyalty is to a party whereas our loyalty is to the revolution. We are mainstream progressives, and we see our country moving away from a barely democratic order into, not just a plutocratic order, not just an oligarchic order, but an order characterized as an oligarchic, corporate state. The United States is a nation in desperate need of a revolution to rescue it from the tyranny of neoliberals like Secretary Clinton and fascists like President Trump.

As stated earlier, chapters 2-9 are a detailed description of our movement, our failures as well as our successes, limited as they were. Whereas chapters 2-9 will be of interest to history buffs and movement revolutionaries, chapters 1, 10, 11 and the conclusion delve into the urgent need for an American revolution and should be interesting to all concerned citizens. And again, please share this book; it is vital that Americans of all political stripes know and understand what is going on and, as a consequence, what will be going away if the neoliberal agenda is advanced. If either Trump's fascism or the neoliberal status quo he campaigned against continues to hold political power in the United States, we will lose freedoms or national self-determination and U.S. democratic self-government on all levels of government respectively. We need a revolution as a matter of life or death for cities around the world, an issue that unified Trump, Clinton and Gov. Johnson on one side of the climate change spectrum with Dr. Stein positioned on the other side in the general election of 2016.

The cities at risk are by the ocean or sea. If you believe or suspect climate change is a hoax and you have access to a computer, go to YouTube and search for "The Most Terrifying Video You'll Ever See." It's less than 10 minutes long, and I cite it in chapter 1 at the end of the first bullet point which ends "logic of worst–case scenarios." It provides a common sense understanding of the risks associated with doing nothing about climate changes that actually will take place in the future on one hand and committing resources to do something about global warming that is not taking place on the other. It has less than 10 million views, but every climate change skeptic needs to watch it. The

Internet is a vast source of both information and misinformation. Before sharing something, do a search of the fact(s) you discover. When we are the media, we should follow standard journalistic standards. Find a second source before you "publish." Revolutionaries do not need to be dishonest in any way.

Chapter 1:
Revolution Before Bernie

"We still need some Paul Revere of conscience to alert every hamlet and every village of America that revolution is still at hand."[10] ~Martin Luther King Jr.

The *Citizens United v FEC* decision in January of 2010 changed my life. When I listened to Keith Olbermann's monologue[11] on MSNBC that evening, I knew inaction was no longer a possibility. I had to get involved; I had to help stop the coming corporate takeover of our government that decision unleashed.

I began by finding out when the Supreme Court first granted corporations the constitutional rights of individuals. I queried on Facebook and was first led to Thom Hartmann's *Unequal Protection: How Corporations Became "People"—And How You Can Fight Back*.[12] It is available on the *Truthout* website in its entirety free of charge. The first chapter, "The Deciding Moment,"[13] explains how the 1886 Santa *Clara County v Southern Pacific Railroad* set the stage for future decisions to grant, initially, the rights of the Fourteenth Amendment, "due process" and "equal protection under the law," to corporations.

Further inquiries let me to a video of a talk[14] by David Cobb, co-founder and national spokesman for Move to Amend. They were organizing grassroots efforts to build a movement to eventually have Congress pass and the states ratify a constitutional amendment to overturn the *Citizens United* and all related decisions. Central in the Court's reasoning was the *Buckley v Valeo* decision, which protected the money spent on electioneering communications (campaign ads) as if it were the content of the ads itself. The amendment would have to make it clear to legislators, citizens, PACs, candidates and Supreme Court judges money is not speech and corporations have no rights under the Constitution. Both political money and corporations should be regulated, or else the United States is not a democratic order. Unregulated political money leads to a plutocratic order, and unregulated corporations lead to a greed-driven corporate-state. The *Citizens United* unleashed corporate money in 2010, and the corporate capture of the federal system was completed in the 2014 midterm elections. After hearing Cobb speak locally in August of 2011, I worked with other members of the community to form a chapter of Move to Amend. I also got the attention of a like-minded person I knew from comments he and I were posting on the Mediaite website, Paul Westlake. He joined Move to Amend and started the online publication *The Amendment Gazette*.[15] I joined him as the "senior columnist" writing posts about corporate personhood (rights granted to corporations by the Court) and about how money became equated with speech.[16] He and I alternated deconstructing articles by defenders of these illegitimate Court decisions.

We were able to arrange video interviews with Ben Cohen[17] of Ben and Jerry's Ice Cream, Martin Kirk,[18] author of the free, online 60-page political pamphlet, "One Party Planet,"[19] and Chris Hedges,[20] a columnist with *Truthdig* (an online, progressive publication) and the pre-eminent writer describing the United States as a corporate state.

David Cobb came back to Ithaca[21] on another speaking tour of New York in June of 2014. During that talk, he asked a room of over 100 people, "Who here is a revolutionary?" Slowly, after quickly thinking about it, I raised my hand. I was one of maybe 25 to do so. Was I a revolutionary? By year's end, I came to the conclusion that no progressive legislation or constitutional amendment was going to come of out a Congress controlled via campaign finance anarchy by corporate actors (CEOs, COOs, Wall Street bankers, lobbyists, etc.).

Martin Gilens and Benjamin Page published a study in September of 2014 entitled "Testing Theories of American Politics: Elites, Interest Groups and Average Citizens."[22] It concluded, "majorities of the American public actually have little influence over the policies our government adopts." I reluctantly came to realize the only way to deal with the problem of the corporate state was to do what I could to spark and perhaps mobilize a peaceful revolution against it.

Revolution

On New Year's Day of 2015, Westlake and I published "Standing on the Edge of the Next American Revolution."[23] It begins with a quote, apparently from the online hacking group Anonymous:

The Activist

It starts like an itch. Something happens in our lives that causes us to question what we know. We open our eyes and seek the truth. The more we uncover the hungrier we are for understanding. But the world isn't perfect and there's a lot of pain and deception. We have the burning desire to do more. We read, a lot. We start protesting. Our family labels us as too negative, our friends start to pull away, our spouses reject us. We are labeled as hippies, anarchists, angry kids, conspiracy theorists and terrorists. We are beaten by police and mocked by the news. Yet, we have become obsessed with spreading the truth. It becomes a very solitary journey.

And it continues:

The R Word

Readers are no doubt familiar with the first American Revolution which had been building for sixteen years before the violent war of independence from the British Empire. The Second American Revolution[24] occurred at the ballot box in 1800 with the election of Thomas Jefferson. The President described his election "*as real a revolution in the principles of our government as that of 1776 was in its form.*" Of course, he never gave up his slaves, which makes that democratic "revolution" partial and flawed at best. Still, "Jefferson believed his election was a peaceful revolution by the American people overturning an elitist faction that was stamping out cherished constitutional rights and trying to transform our young democracy into an authoritarian state. It was a transfer of power back to the people, not a change of parties."[25] The 40th president is said to have brought about the "Reagan Revolution."

Crises Galore

Today the United States political system has been corrupted[26] by the Supreme Court decisions *Buckley v Valeo*,[27] *Citizens United v FEC*[28] and *McCutcheon v FEC*.[29] Congress is under the thumb of its wealthiest citizens; therefore, a number of urgent problems will not be dealt with in the coming session of Congress, perhaps never. Almost certainly it will not without a mass movement of resistance.[30] Most urgent among these critical issues are:

- Climate change. Time is running out[31] if we're going to keep the planet comfortable, not to mention habitable. Climate change skeptics need to understand the logic of worst–case scenarios[32]
- Money in elections (legalized corruption[33]), a bipartisan rigging of the game[34]
- $17 + trillion dollar and growing national debt[35]
- Vast inequality of wealth,[36] increasing poverty and decreasing demand for goods is bad economic practice
- Reckless financial deregulation just enacted[37] (again!) in the Cromnibus bill
- Endless war[38] by the American Empire[39]
- NSA/corporate scrutiny of Americans[40] which undermines the Fourth Amendment[41]
- An increasingly militarized police state,[42] impacting people from all walks of life[43]
- American citizens are murdered on orders from the President with no due process, a "post-constitutional" act[44] with no check from Congress
- Structural classism[45] in the justice system
- A "war" on whistleblowers,[46] the life blood of investigative journalism
- Increasing authoritarianism by police[47] in the land of the "free"
- Corporate constitutional rights[48] which undermine public policy[49]

To address these issues and solve critical problems — when running for office has been priced beyond the reach of talented and worthy outsiders and all third party candidates who are not self-funded — another American Revolution is required. *Revolution* is a frightening word for most Americans, but the Second and the last American Revolutions indicate that weapons are not required, blood need not spill. Minds need to change.

Republic Lost

This revolution has already begun[50] for many, not most, people. The Next American Revolution will not be a solitary journey—far from it. Demonstrations, protests, marches and disruption of business as usual have already shaken the nation, but the movement for racial justice has not yet reached the momentum and visibility of either Occupy Wall Street or the tea party in their heydays. The list of critical issues above strongly suggests that the United States is sliding toward fascism.[51] Genuine democrats and republicans who believe in self-government in a democratic republic must support a revolutionary movement and come to distrust the elites in both major parties who back the corporate interests (profit and survival) over the public interests (peace, democratic policy making, keeping the Earth habitable, etc.). What, then, will spark a revolutionary movement to outlaw plutocracy, abolish the corporate-state, establish political equality and save the world from the ravages of war and predatory, transnational corporate capitalism,[52] i.e., the neoliberal world order[53] we call corporate feudalism?[54]

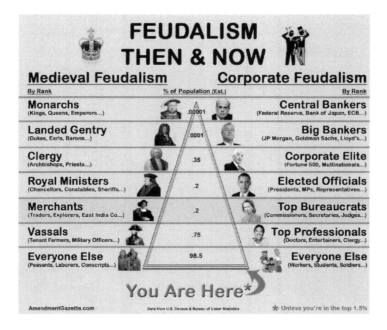

That question is impossible to answer. It could come from an article on a blog; but were it that simple, the Next American Revolution would have been sparked by Chris Hedges' essays on *Truthdig*[55] by now. Perhaps it will be triggered by another Wall St.–induced financial crash. Perhaps a flood of independent politicians will somehow manage to win office, including the White House, a pipe dream in this era of legalized corruption and multimillion dollar campaigns. Perhaps a public space will be occupied again (Occupy Congress?), or enough people will come to realize that the Framers' republic has been transformed into an oligarchic, corporate-empire and rise up in rebellion in time. Perhaps the left will learn to work with the right on the issues of mutual agreement.

How this revolution will be waged is open to tactics employed by the dispossessed, the oppressed, the disgruntled and the rest of those involved. The revolutionaries must be non-violent,[56] or else they risk pushing the U.S. government into full-blown, fascist police state in reaction to them. In all likelihood, any violence will be initiated by the police.[57] Revolutionary activists can use the freedoms we still have left: assembly, petition, speech, theater, the ballot box and civil disobedience — all employing a variety of tactics. "What Makes Nonviolent Movements Explode?"[58] reviews the tactics of disrupting business as usual and need for "personal sacrifice." Will enough folks sacrifice some time they normally spend watching television, exercising, reading, etc.? It's worth taking the time to read as a companion piece to this call for civil participation. Revolution must become part of many more people's lives until the American corporate-state is returned to We the People.

Hope

The anti-fracking movement in New York waged a six-year struggle for a ban on hydrofracking of natural gas, and its success demonstrates when enough people work together in a disciplined and consistent manner, the corporate agenda can be stymied. Certainly, much more activism across the nation is needed. Thomas Jefferson believed every generation should have its own constitution and considered revolution and rebellion the lifeblood of republican governance. Many more Americans need to rediscover these Jeffersonian ideals and join the effort to shake off oligarchy, oppose the corrupted Democratic/ Republican political duopoly and peacefully forge a new path toward a genuine, democratic form of a government of, by and for all the people, not just the 1%. To be clear, there are a few, good public servants in Congress.

Suggested Principles for Democratic Revolution

"One just principle from the depths of a cave is more powerful than an army."[59] ~Jose Marti, Cuban revolutionary

Any serious revolutionary movement must have principles to confront the serious problems and drift toward fascism we are confronting. Political equality[60] must be a primary, key revolutionary demand to legalize democratic order. The following are *proposed democratic* principles to address the list of "critical issues" above:

- Long-term human survival trumps short-term corporate profits, sustainable and green energy sources[61] have been developed
- Political equality: one person/one vote *and* $X.00 maximum/person[62] per election cycle
- The federal budget should be in the black via fair taxation and wise spending
- Equity, not equality, should be based on advancing human rights and quality of life for all
- Corporate behavior, especially large financial institutions, should be under democratic regulation

- National self-determination: all non-emergency military interventions should be consistent with international law and be approved by Congress
- Terminate scrutiny of Americans' activities without a warrant
- Demilitarize domestic police
- Police should protect and serve all citizens
- Abide by the Constitution and impeach all presidents, regardless of ideology or party, when they appear to have committed any high crime or misdemeanor
- Equal justice for all
- Respect and protect whistle blowers' First Amendment rights
- Citizens should be free to pursue happiness, protest, dissent, etc. in a democratic order
- Rights are for natural persons only; associations should have privileges that can be protected, revoked and/or regulated depending upon the class of association

Become a Revolutionary Patriot

"We have it in our power to begin the world over again."[63]
~Thomas Paine

Minds need changing; therefore share this article. Take some time out from watching television, reading or shopping to copy and paste http://wp.me /p2BCCS-1e9 onto news sites reporting war, corruption, racist police tactics, etc., on political blogs, on social media, in emails, anywhere possible online. The revolutionary conversation needs to begin, and it's not coming from corporate media, not Fox News, not MSNBC, not CNN and not on the network news sources. Initially, Gil Scott Heron was right, "the revolution will not be televised." The Internet is the movement's best, perhaps our only hope to rescue democratic order. Billionaires have the money; revolutionary patriots have the inexpensive Internet. The latter needs to make the Internet their revolutionary machine before the government or corporate interests usurp it for their private agendas of holding government power, corporate greed and corporate-state control. To that end, we must preserve net neutrality as part of the revolutionary, democratic agenda.

Edge of a Revolution

"When we tune out politics, when we abandon hope, we aren't being cool or hip or ironic or even realistic—we are being played."
~Robert McChesney

The author of *The Authoritarians* (below) summarizes his essay with words that serve to conclude this article with one word added:

Research shows most people are not in this [revolutionary] movement. However, Americans have, for the most part, been standing on the sidewalk quietly staring at this authoritarian parade as it marches on. You can watch it tear American democracy apart, bit by bit, bite by bite. Or you can exercise your rights too, while you still have them, and get just as concerned, active, and giving to protect yourself and your country. If you, and other liberals, other moderates, other conservatives with conscience do, then everything can turn out all right. But we have to get going. If you are the only person you know who grasps what's happening, then you've got to take leadership, help inform, and organize others. One person can do so much; you've no idea! But time is running out, fast, and nearly everything is at stake.[64]

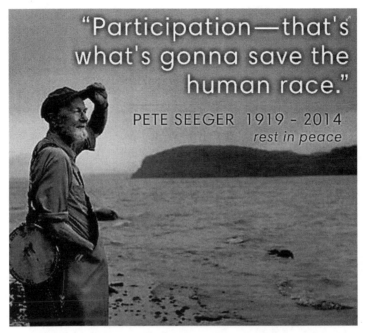

"Participation—that's what's gonna save the human race."

PETE SEEGER 1919 - 2014
rest in peace

Well, neither the conversations about having a revolution nor the revolution itself took long to begin. In early February of that year I spoke to an adult education class at the local Unitarian Church, and during my talk[65] I said, "Senator Sanders is saying that we need a political revolution in the United States." Much to my delight, he framed his candidacy for the White House as a political revolution. Little did I know, when I gave that talk, I would be initiating a movement a few months later that would come to reverberate in stadiums and coliseums, both inside and outside of Sanders rallies, by April in 2016 as the chant that came to haunt the Democratic Party elite: "BERNIE OR BUST."

Corporate Globalization

There is a topic I omitted in that essay, but I addressed it in my speech at the Bernie or Bust rally in Philadelphia. The so-called "free-trade agreement" formally referred to as the Trans-Pacific Partnership is something I did not know much about on New Year's Day in 2015, but a series of conference calls over the course of 2015 and much of 2016 served as the equivalent of a graduate class in "free-trade." I owe a debt of gratitude to the organizers of those calls and the experts on them for my understanding of globalization gained over that 18-month period.

These agreements, the TPP, the Trans-Atlantic Trade and Investment Pact, and the Trade in Services Agreement are agenda items for Wall Street banks and other large, American transnational corporations. They are significant threats to our system of government, an argument I'll elaborate on in other chapters. They are a key part of the neoliberal agenda.

In my Philadelphia speech and again in the last chapter, I recommend a free, online pamphlet that addresses neoliberalism. Instead of providing goods and services to people, neoliberals intend to corporatize the legal order of as many states as possible including the United States. While their agenda is bigger and broader than that, defeating neoliberalism and corporate globalism must be a fundamental goal of revolutionaries everywhere. Neoliberalism is not your grandfather's post-WWII regulated capitalism. Transnational {based in one country with outposts in other countries} corporate executives and lawyers want to write their own rules and regulations for their behavior regarding the environment and the people, create rights for themselves, use a "tribunal" system that national courts cannot overrule and render democratic self-government obsolete.

President Trump appeared to be disrupting that order during the campaign, but he's filling his cabinet with corporate and military elites. He's replacing the swamp monsters. After Obama named Wall Street insiders to his cabinet I rationalized why he might want to do that, as a transitional step to his "fundamental transformation" he promised five days before he was elected in 2008. Almost seven years later, we were on the edge of revolution; but we ended up with Donald Trump instead. *Bernie or Bust* is our progressive perspective on how that happened. This may anger a lot of Obama's supporters, but his political philosophy—neoliberalism—helped birth Trump's success. Trump seemed to oppose that neoliberal order, and Chapter 10 offers a simple analysis to indicate how well he "scores" as a neoliberal.

Chapter 2:
From Revolution to Bernie or Bust

"In fact, it is always because of one person that all the changes that matter in the world come about. So be that one person."[66] ~Buckminster Fuller

Citizens United Against the Supreme Court

In the winter of 2014 the movement to overturn *Citizens United* and related decisions was bracing for another Supreme Court decision on the *McCutcheon v FEC* case. An organizer in the Washington-based group Public Citizen suggested activists create Facebook community pages as a tool of communication for the protests we were preparing if the Court ruled in favor of more money in politics. I started a community Facebook page called Citizens Against Plutocracy.[67] Plutocracy is a government or society ruled by the rich. It is government for and by the proverbial 1%.

On April 2, 2015, the Court decided in favor of Alabama coal baron Shaun McCutcheon and his fellow plutocrats. Instead of citizens of the 1% being limited to $46,200 per election cycle that individuals could previously donate to candidates for federal office across the country, now they are allowed to contribute $2,700 (maximum/candidate) times 536 (congressional candidates and a presidential candidate) times 2 (primaries and general election): a cool $2.89 million! The decision also broadened the Court's perverse and dangerous interpretation of money as speech. Before *McCutcheon*, money spent on electioneering (advocacy by super PACS and nonprofits for or against a given candidate, uncoordinated with any candidate's official campaign) was protected by the First Amendment. Now money donated to campaigns is also protected as a First Amendment right. Once again, the Supreme Court had imposed a highly debatable interpretation of the First Amendment that favors wealthy Americans' excessive—and growing—influence on government.

Contrary to our Founders' intentions, this amounted to *legislating* by the Supreme Court—which, unlike Congress, was intended purely to *interpret* the Constitution. And worse yet, it was legislating on behalf of plutocrats who *already* held too much power. Like other informed citizens, I strongly feared the Court was undermining the checks-and-balances thinking our Founders had favored to keep any one faction from gaining excessive power. Representative government itself was under threat by plutocrats and by courts and politicians too favorable to their interests.

I began inviting local people I knew on Facebook to "like" the page and posted articles about plutocracy, campaign finance, etc., along with the time and location of the protest for the day of the decision. We held our rally at 4:00 P.M. on April 2 with about 30 people in attendance, and no one from the local mainstream media covered it even though they had received a media alert and a phone call that afternoon.

Shortly later that year, a like-minded friend I knew from another Facebook group, Patrick Walker, joined Citizens Against Plutocracy as a page administrator. Since Bernie or Bust evolved largely from the interplay of my views and Patrick's (as well as our complementary skill sets), it is important to briefly sketch Patrick's views at the time, as well as the activist experience that shaped them. Understanding Patrick's slant will help readers grasp not only his unique role in shaping the movement, but the conflicts with me and other members of our committee that later caused him to leave it—not once but twice! Like most significant political movements, Bernie or Bust involved both headstrong personalities and considerable conflict.

But the tale of our conflicts lies ahead; I will focus now on Patrick's views and contribution in the early days of our harmony.

Like me, Patrick was appalled by the *Citizens United* and *McCutcheon* decisions and how they tipped the scales further in favor of plutocrats. But, though as hostile to plutocracy as I was, he was not specially focused on the direct attempt to reverse those decisions. Rather, he was preoccupied with what he considered a more basic problem: finding politicians free enough from plutocratic corruption that they would actually *want* to overturn those decisions—or work against plutocracy in any other way.

Enter Patrick and His "Democrat Problem"

Patrick's essential contribution to Bernie or Bust—as well as his heated quarrel with the movement as it took shape—is best viewed through the lens of his perennial (and perennially frustrating) attempt to solve "the Democrat problem." For Patrick, today's Democratic Party, populist or progressive in rhetoric but corporatist and warmongering in policy, is not just *a* problem, but *the* central, lynchpin problem of U.S. politics. In a political system (technically termed a *duopoly*[68]) where only two major parties are viable, that both should serve corporate and plutocratic interests is a *major* problem. This problem had become Patrick's Gordian knot, and the strand of rope that his activist sword needed to "sever" was clearly the Democratic Party.

But how? Neither reforming Democrats from within nor just leaving the party en masse seemed like a viable solution. On the one hand, the annals of recent political history were littered with the wreckage of attempts, usually starting as populist presidential campaigns, to give Democrats a progressive or populist "makeover." Once the relevant presidential candidate was duly (and predictably) defeated in the primaries, the shattered hulk of his "movement" did not disappear altogether; instead, it lingered as a largely toothless political organization that fostered the illusion of progressives having a voice in the Democratic Party. Thus did Jesse Jackson's campaign spawn the Rainbow Coalition; Howard Dean's, Democracy for America; and Dennis Kucinich's, Progressive Democrats of America. But plutocrats' iron grip on the party did not lessen in the least.

On the other hand, neither did a movement to leave the party altogether seem viable. In close collusion, Democrats and Republicans had placed *formidable* obstacles in the way of third party ballot access and debate participation, and stymied by those obstacles, third parties reliably posted dismal electoral results. Of course voters, eagerly prodded by mainstream media with a stake in both major parties, predictably responded with skepticism toward the electoral viability of third parties. Citing a comparison economist J. M. Keynes used in relation to picking stocks, Patrick maintained that successful movement building was like guessing the winner of a beauty contest, where what counted was *not* objective beauty itself, but rather what the contest judges would *perceive* as beautiful. And in the beauty contests known as U.S. elections, third parties were clearly America's ugly ducklings. Therefore, a *direct* attempt to lure disgruntled progressive Democrats away to third parties would simply not suffice.

What was needed was something like a Tea Party of the left, but adapted to the aim of fighting plutocracy and doing so within the Democratic Party. On the plus side, an overtly anti-plutocratic movement, hostile to plutocratic aims, would not lend itself to cooptation by plutocratic patrons like the Koch brothers, as the Tea Party clearly did. But that plus was offset by a *gargantuan* negative: the left-wing Tea Party could simply not muster the money to "primary" any Democratic incumbent who displeased it. It became obvious to Patrick that the prospective "Tea Party of the left" needed a different main weapon, one that could compensate for its inability to readily oppose corporate Democrats in primaries. What Patrick hit on was a scheme of electoral *extortion:* If organized progressive voters couldn't make their preferred candidates win, they could surely make their political enemies *lose*. From Patrick's logic of electoral extortion—and my passion for overthrowing plutocracy by any moral means necessary—was born the movement that became Bernie or Bust.

From Theory to Practice I: The True Blue Democrats Blunder

Patrick had grappled with his "Democrat problem"—and its potential solution by electoral extortion—long before joining my Facebook page. In fact, one fairly painful reminder of his rookie mistakes in movement building lingers on as the Facebook page True Blue Democrats: A Progressive Revolt.[69] Whether from sheer laziness, Patrick's wanting yet another Facebook outlet for his political writings, or a vague sense that the page might someday have historic value (as documenting a precursor of more viable movements), Patrick never bothered to take the page down. Even today, its "blue donkey kicking a red donkey" banner reminds him how mind-numbingly he was seduced by a clever marketing idea—without considering the tastes of the leftist audience to whom he initially needed to appeal.

For sure, the name "True Blue Democrats" may evoke misty memories for disgruntled Democrat loyalists who fondly remember the New Deal party of FDR, but for leftists nauseated by mere mention of Democrats, the name was a poison pill. How strange of Patrick to choose it, considering he himself was far from a "true blue Democrat" (*never having* voted for Obama) and as an avid daily reader of *CounterPunch* (later to be published there) much closer to leftists' jaundiced view of America's "jackass party." But above all, Patrick needed support from the harder left, since for anyone who really understood it, his scheme of political extortion definitely menaced the electoral prospects of the Democratic Party. When veteran political activist John Stauber, who had kindly lent Patrick a sympathetic ear, suggested he hook with up with Progressives Democrats of America, Patrick acutely felt how little he had made his own radicalism understood.

Perhaps all of Patrick's originality lay in his insistence that, due to the peculiar, duopoly-related dysfunction of U.S. politics, any successful progressive movement needed to be an uneasy *dance* with Democrats, taking place neither entirely within nor entirely outside the party. But in dubbing his first invitation to the dance "True Blue Democrats," Patrick had definitely emphasized the *wrong* partner in the dance for his intended audience. In translating his voter extortion theory to practice, it was a rookie mistake he planned never to repeat.

Patrick made other rookie mistakes with True Blue Democrats, but they are not especially relevant to the Bernie or Bust story. What is especially relevant is that he had a solid political idea—a sculpture lurking inside the stone— that had to wait on, among other things, his acquiring both able helpers and more skillful use of his political sculptor's tools. But perhaps above all, it had to wait on better political circumstances. Those better circumstances (along with able helpers) were soon to come, and their arrival is the next episode in the story of this movement.

From Theory to Practice II: The Perfect Bernie Storm

It is late 2014, and Patrick Walker and I, two avowed enemies of plutocracy looking to stir up trouble for the high and mighty, are in frequent communication. Both of us are Facebook mavens and writers with bully pulpits, I as a columnist at the *Examiner* and *The Amendment Gazette*, and Patrick as a regular contributor to *OpEdNews*, where he has become a popular author. Both of us view Barack Obama as a major betrayer of progressives (to say nothing of the Constitution), and see Democrats' "inevitable" nominee Hillary Clinton as guaranteed to double down on Obama's betrayals. Indeed, like most leftists and even some traditional conservatives (paleocons, not neocons), we regard Clinton as the pin-up girl or poster child for the deep plutocratic evil befouling our political system.

Alongside these common threads, Patrick has a theory of movement building—of subjecting Democrats to political extortion—looking for implementation. Besides his extortion theory, Patrick has a certain marketing flair—the same one that tricked him into choosing a clever idea unsuited for his audience with True Blue Democrats. (Indeed, Patrick's college rhetoric professor expected him to make a fortune in advertising, a fate Patrick perhaps wisely avoided by considering the cocaine habit he would probably need to live with himself—and, as a money maker for plutocrats, could probably easily afford. But marketing flair is just as valuable in political organizing; what "Mad Men" lost, we later gained as angry activist.)

It was probably in our stars for Patrick and me to collaborate (and for me to let him give my Facebook page a makeover in line with his theory.) Seeking to jazz up the page, Patrick convinced me to change the name of the page to Pitchforks Against Plutocracy. This stemmed from Obama's reported statement to Wall Street bankers in the White House. "My administration is the only thing between you and the pitchforks," he told them[70] in April of 2009.

We continued posting articles about plutocracy and campaign finance anarchy on the page, and I continued my work as a local amendment organizer and writer/researcher for *The Amendment Gazette*. On New Year's Day 2015 I posted our piece on revolution in that publication.

Meanwhile, Patrick used the Pitchforks page (and many other Facebook pages) to popularize his *OpEdNews* articles, where he explored the merits of our different options for confronting Democrats with an ultimatum: Either support candidate X and his or her policies, *or else* our organized voters will cost you the 2016 election. With 2016 being a *presidential* election—the kind where most U.S. voters actually pay attention—it seemed especially important to choose and organize around a progressive presidential candidate. In my speaking of "candidate X and his or her policies," the "his or her" part wasn't merely to honor the principle of inclusive language; we were utterly torn between the potential Clinton-challenging candidacies of Bernie Sanders and Elizabeth Warren. Patrick's *OpEdNews* pieces in the early Pitchforks Against Plutocracy days clearly reflect our vacillation.[71] Eventually, the candidates themselves (by Warren's refusal to run and Sanders' choice to do so) would decide.

Two points about Patrick's pieces on the Pitchforks ultimatum—one concerning its "either" term and the other concerning its "or else" term—bear emphasis.

As regards our "either" term—the candidate we demanded Democrats nominate for president—it is important to realize that the Pitchforks leaders considered *neither* Bernie Sanders nor Elizabeth Warren ideal. Rather, we were trying to gain as much *actual* power for opponents of plutocracy as we could, and that involved supporting the candidates (with minimally acceptable policies, in our view) who could actually win the nomination.

Our criteria for minimal acceptability involved a willingness to fight plutocrats on at least *some* issues, and from that standpoint Bernie Sanders seemed the preferable of the two. Among other things, he had a much clearer record of standing up to fossil fuel plutocrats on climate change and the closely related issue of fracking. Additionally, not being a *de facto* Democrat, he seemed potentially freer in his ability to criticize the party leadership for its lackey service of plutocrats. (Though not all that free, as his undue "chivalry" toward Hillary Clinton eventually proved.)

But from another standpoint—prospective electability—Elizabeth Warren seemed the superior choice. Being the Democrats' progressive "rock star," Warren was simply much better known than Bernie and had the added credibility for Democratic voters of actually *being* a Democrat. Whereas it was unclear at that point whether Bernie, should he actually choose to run, would even run *as* a Democrat. Patrick, at least, considered that the politically savvy choice and expected Bernie to make it; he even suspected Bernie's exploratory probing of which party he should run in was largely seeking affirmation for a choice he had already made. Provided, of course, that he chose to run at all. What appears true is that Bernie, as Patrick did, rated Warren's chances of winning the nomination as better than his own and substantially preferred her candidacy to throwing his own hat in the ring. He also probably realized, as we all did, that (rock star status aside), Warren's gender would annul Clinton's "woman card"—the one her supporters in the media so sleazily played against him from the bottom of the deck by stigmatizing his supporters as sexist "Bernie Bros."

Turning our attention to the "or else" term of our ultimatum, it is interesting to note that Patrick's initial leaning toward a punishment for Democrats refusing to nominate our preferred candidate was to vote Green. In retrospect, given the role that writing in Bernie's name eventually played in our pledge, this should clear up any misconception that we were Democrat lackeys or "sheepdogs." In fact, the idea of writing in Bernie, so long associated with our pledge, was something of an accident, as I'll now relate.

On Saturday mornings I join a small group of peace activists on a street corner, the intersection of Meadow St. and the very end of—I'm not making this up—Clinton St., downtown Ithaca, NY, to protest drone strikes that kill mostly innocent people. On April 25 it was clear Senator Sanders was preparing to launch a campaign for the White House. (He did so the following Wednesday.) I struck up a conversation with Garry Thomas about whether or not Bernie would run as a Democrat. I was hoping he'd lead an American Syriza, a coalition of radical left parties. My personal fear was he could win a national election, but for the fact that the Democratic Party was so rigged against insurgents like Sanders that he would fall short in the primaries. I reasoned we could not nominate and get him on the ballot for the general election as a minor party candidate because he could sue to get his name taken off the ballot.

"What about a write-in campaign?" Garry asked. I thought that sounded like a brilliant idea. There would be nothing Senator Sanders could do to stop us because we have the right to free association. Without researching the idea, I set out to find collaborators.

First I knew we'd need a PAC. If we didn't raise money to tell Democrats on the radio and television they had better nominate Bernie "or else," all we'd be doing is undermining the Democrats and helping elect the Republican. I reached out to the coordinator of the Binghamton Move to Amend chapter I had been working with. She is a retired accountant who immediately embraced the idea of organizing a national write-in strategy and agreed to become the PAC treasurer.

Next, I reached out to Patrick by email. He quickly warmed to the idea and embraced the strategy. By Patrick's current account, this was a mistake on his part, but a lucky one. He now judges it a mistake from two standpoints: 1) his overestimation of Bernie's willingness to fight for his agenda and 2) his failure to research state laws regarding write-in votes. As regards point 1), Patrick wrongly calculated that Bernie would use the frightening prospect of running as a write-in candidate to gain leverage for his platform. While he fully expected Bernie, in the likely event of his losing the nomination, to keep his promise to endorse Clinton, he expected Sanders (given how much his supporters *disliked* Clinton) to extract a bigger chunk of policy flesh before doing so. With respect to point 2), Patrick readily admits his ignorance at the time of laws in most states that would have required Bernie to register as a write-in candidate in order for his write-in votes to have counted at all.

However, Patrick's assessment of the write-in pledge as a mistake does not end there. He considers it crucial, in correctly telling our movement's tale, to note that it was a *lucky* mistake. Indeed, probably a *very* lucky one. Again citing the "beauty contest" principle of movement organizing, what matters in organizing movements is not the absolute, but rather the *perceived* value of what you are offering. On an objective analysis, Green Party policies—especially on war-and-peace issues—are arguably superior to Bernie's. However, for U.S. voters, the Green Party is an especially hard sell, whereas Bernie, for his supporters, was an easy one. It is even fair to say that many overrated his merits and had "Bernie on the brain." So, in Patrick's plausible assessment, our movement grew much bigger with an intellectually unsound write-in pledge than it would have with an intellectually flawless Green one. Just as Christian theologians consider sin the *felix culpa*—the "happy fault"—that caused God Himself to enter our world as its redeemer, so a write-in pledge we later judged unsound was the "happy fault" of the Bernie or Bust movement.

Thus we wound up not merely with a flawed pledge—but thanks to Warren's refusal to run—with a flawed pledge supporting an electorally inferior candidate. Yet, from the standpoint of a movement pioneering a scheme of electoral extortion, this combination proved almost ideal; our scheme was about to profit from a "perfect Bernie storm." For, as much as Bernie's being an outsider to the Democratic Party hurt his electoral chances, it offered unique advantages to a movement seeking to inflame disgruntlement with the Democratic establishment and its neoliberal frontrunner, Hillary Clinton. Bernie's outsider status was destined to make him a virtual demigod with voters prone to distrust and even loathe the political establishment. The write-in pledge itself seemed delightfully anti-establishment, and making it on behalf of a burgeoning demigod to the young (and young at heart) political rebels only deepened its appeal.

Additionally, not being a Democrat probably made Bernie less apt to shut down our pledge. Unsurprisingly, we wondered from the get-go how the Sanders campaign might react to our pledge, and felt some anxiety on that score. But it eventually became clear Bernie and his campaign would treat us with benign neglect. As a result, we reached a sort of unspoken agreement to go about our business without drawing our movement to Bernie's attention. With Warren or some other progressive Democrat, constantly fearing for party unity and wishing above all to remain a Democrat in good standing, we might not have been so lucky.

But probably what served our purposes best—what made outsider Bernie our "perfect storm"—was the danger the Democratic establishment was courting in letting him run at all. To put matters at their most cynical, a Help Wanted ad for progressive Democrats could easily read, "Wanted: Political Castrati to Sing Sweet Progressive Tunes." Now, if the progressives in question are actual Democrats, their good standing in a party dominated by neoliberals is a strong guarantee they've been well and duly politically castrated. But since political castration isn't as easily verified as actual, recruiting political outsiders runs the risk that those sweet tunes might be accompanied by stirrings of political potency. Or, to briefly switch the metaphor, that your gentle progressive-herding sheepdog may harbor ancestral strains of wolf. But castrato or stud, sheepdog or wolf, Bernie bayed out one tune that was absolute music to our movement-organizing ears: political revolution.

You'll hear a lot about political revolution in these pages, since from our standpoint, it was Bernie's #1 Top of the Pops smash hit. That Democrats were willing to let outsider Bernie sing such an edgy, ambiguously worded tune— one so easily prone to subversive interpretations—was an index of their sheer desperation, their inability to fill concert seats for the tuneless Hillary Clinton. And Bernie's chance obsession with that deeply subversive phrase (however tame his own interpretation of it) was probably the ultimate "gust" that transformed him into our movement's "perfect storm."

The First Days of the Pledge

Having laid our bets on Bernie, we realized the organization, whose strategy depended on supporting a mainstream candidate, needed a softer, less militant-sounding name. Since Bernie himself spoke of "revolution" (though qualifying it as "political"), we imagined the word "revolt" would not offend. Instead of Pitchforks Against Plutocracy, we debated between Revolt Against Plutocracy and Progressive Revolt Against Plutocracy. I pushed back against the latter because I didn't want to exclude anyone who wasn't a progressive. I knew from my work in the amendment movement many moderates and conservatives didn't approve of having so much money involved in our elections. After some debate, he agreed with me; and we renamed our Facebook page Revolt Against Plutocracy a week before we launched the website.

Seeking to share the movement labor, Patrick brought in his friend and fellow *OpEdNews* writer Robert Becker, and we held a conference call to discuss the strategy. A grave concern was this strategy could backfire and help elect the Republican which would certainly be a disaster for climate change. Once Clinton came out during the primaries as an advocate for hydrofracking of natural gas, however, it was clear that she would be nearly as disastrous for climate change as the eventual Republican candidate.

We quickly decided on a pledge to write in Sanders as a tool to convey support for this idea. That idea was borrowed from Move To Amend, which asks citizens to pledge to vote for candidates who support a constitutional amendment. Another Facebook friend and ally, DeNeice Kenehan, suggested we call it the WIN pledge, Write-In November. We added Bernie's last name, and we initially called it the WIN-S pledge.

From about mid-May of 2015 until much later in the year, I took my hand-held digital voice recorder to work with me. I do a lot of driving, and jotting down "to do" notes was dangerous if not impossible on the road. Almost every weekday for a few months, I would record reminders to myself to do something that evening after I arrived at home.

Revolution: Our Manifesto

After changing names from Pitchforks Against Plutocracy to Revolt Against Plutocracy, I set out to build the website to serve as our pledge platform. I had been using WordPress, the free blog domain with many advanced features, as columnist with The Amendment Gazette. Making it look like a website rather than a blog required tutoring from another ally in the amendment movement. I composed the home page narrative, and Patrick wrote our manifesto, "Revolution."[72] I added a Frequently Asked Questions page, a "Bernie who" page, an "About us" page and an HRCC page for Hillary Rodham Corporate Clinton. Two of our early hashtags were #CorporateClinton and #SheepNoMore.

The early knock on Senator Sanders was he'd lose the primary and serve as a sheepdog to corral progressives into the neoliberal fold.[73] That is, in the end, what happened; but the write-in campaign was a way to tell the establishment we would not be herded because we are not sheep.

From "Revolution" (as modified after the DNC in Philadelphia):

> Bernie Sanders had a *campaign* to run—a thing he does extraordinarily well—and we should all be deeply grateful to him for running it. We at Revolt Against Plutocracy feel we best express that gratitude by doing the one thing his campaign shackles him from doing—and which only grassroots activists can do anyway—organize his *revolution*. "Grassroots revolution isn't just BS" is one slogan we pray becomes a meme, and as ardent believers that our disintegrating political system *screamed* for Bernie's revolution, we're writing to announce it. And to recruit for it.
>
> But to do so effectively, we must demolish the crippling misconception that his revolution's the same thing as his campaign. It's *not;* as just noted, the revolution's not really *his* at all. It's *ours,* and dangerously overdue. His campaign simply provides our ideal springboard for launching it.
>
> You've probably heard the familiar revolutionary slogan, "To make an omelet, you've got to break some eggs." In the vivid contrast between "breaking eggs" and "walking on eggs"—the latter expression implying a tortuous, torturous effort to *avoid* cracking the shells one is forced to tiptoe among—we glimpse the most compelling reason Sanders' called-for revolution *can't* be the same thing as his campaign.
>
> In a political system that's now a hollow shell of representative government, our eggshell metaphor couldn't be

better chosen. Where virtually the sole *real* purpose of government is to shove the will of plutocrats—whether Wall Street, fossil fuel, Big Ag, Big Pharma, or military-industrial-surveillance complex plutocrats—down the sane majority's throats (to the planet-threatening detriment of the common good), the chief purpose of most political campaigns is to maintain the *trompe-l'oeil* solid appearance of representation's hollow shell. In other words, most campaigns amount to *propaganda* touting the lie that our existing political system is still serving *us*. It's clearly *not*—to the extent that even such a sold-out tool as today's Democratic Party must allow more radical voices bent on serving the common good, like Bernie Sanders or Elizabeth Warren, within its ranks to maintain the faintest illusion of legitimacy.

Given the extreme betrayals of faux-progressive presidents like Bill Clinton and Barack Obama, political leftists have earned an incontestable right to distrust: above all, to distrust of soaring campaign rhetoric high on promise and devoid of detail. Considering the global catastrophe for economy, democracy, and peace that was George W. Bush's presidency, Obama's betrayal of urgently needed progressive reform is especially unfortunate. But amidst its well-earned distrust, the left makes a serious mistake by tarring the likes of Bernie Sanders and Elizabeth Warren with the same incriminating brush as Obama and the Clintons, punishing them for their mere association with Democrats. As regards the treachery of Democrats' party leadership and its favored minions like Clinton, the left is incontestably right, as the analysis of honest veteran operative Bill Curry[74] or a little research into the sleazy trickery of its corporatist leadership[75] should make clear.

But by two powerful litmus tests—speaking in detail and speaking in season—politicians like Sanders and Warren prove they *shouldn't* be tarred with the same accusatory brush as Hillary and the DNC. Just contrast the detail of Sanders' economic platform and the timeliness of his TPP opposition with Clinton's detail-allergic vagueness and cowardly equivocation on the same two matters. Besides, as the Democratic leadership well knows, Democrats' legitimacy among progressives is so near-moribund that only the strong medicine of real sincerity, and not the placebo of fake, can restore its vigor. That the party is tolerating a lifelong independent and self-professed socialist (one calling for political revolution, to boot) as contender for the top spot on its ticket underlines the sheer desperation of Democrats' quest for lost legitimacy.

So, leftists should regard Democrats' *desperate* need for legitimacy as vouchsafe of Bernie's sincerity. But his personal sincerity provides *no* evidence whatsoever we should trust the substantially bought-off party he's running in. Nor does it free him from the delicate, eggshell-walking task of ardently fighting plutocracy while maintaining the illusion of legitimacy for a party whose leadership has made plutocrats' wettest wet dreams their own. (Again, witness TPP.) Clearly, Democrats' acute crisis of legitimacy opens a vulnerable flank for attack by Sanders' revolution. And it makes our battle plan equally clear: to hammer the message that *all* legitimacy lies with Bernie and his sympathizers, and *none* with Hillary and the party leadership. Responding to the facts on the ground, Bernie's revolution must treat his candidacy as a hostile coup against Hillary and the corporatist party leadership. Clearly a job for Bernie's revolution and *not* his campaign, since his campaign must—at peril of shutdown by the DNC—diplomatically avoid cracking the same eggshell of legitimacy his revolution needs to smash.

Revolutions don't walk on eggs; they smash the eggshell of phony legitimacy. But phony legitimacy is *exactly* what today's Democratic leadership and Hillary Clinton seek: legitimacy without fundamental reform. As *fundamental reform* is what Bernie's political revolution seeks—why the hell else start a revolution?—the Democratic Party leadership, Hillary Clinton, and her political allies, who clearly intend to go on forever feeding like pigs at the plutocrat trough, must remain squarely in our crosshairs as our revolution's determined enemies.

But the illegitimacy of today's Democrats hardly implies today's Republicans are legit. In fact, the urgency of political revolution in a nation saddled with a malfunctioning two-party system strongly implies that both parties *suck*. And it's hardly going on a limb to say that today's know-nothing, science-denying, vote-repressing, proto-fascist Republicans suck. In fact, today's Republicans are a blasphemy on everything that's sane, civilized, and (ironically, given their religious bent) even Christian—strong candidates for the title "whore of Babylon" if not that of "Antichrist." But their utterly perverse badness—for which, as we argued, superdelegates bear *sole* responsibility—hardly implies that Democrats are acceptable. The TPP and Clinton's uber-hawkish and mistake prone foreign policy experience, coupled with her support for corporate-fascistic "free-trade agreements," make Secretary Clinton the greater of two dangerous, revolting plutocrats. Nothing in the notion of a two-party system logically implies that *both* parties can't be unspeakably bad. Indeed, given a two-party system, that's *precisely* what one would expect in circumstances demanding political revolution.

Which brings us to the Democrat's sleazy, "lesser-evil" con game. Now, what should be clear is that both major parties serve roughly the same corporate puppet masters. What differs is that Republicans serve somewhat more evil ones,[76] and serve them with greater unanimity and stronger fealty; it's as if the party had made taking Voldemort's Dark Mark[77] a litmus test for membership. While Democrats certainly are somewhat different, they're certainly not *different enough*—different enough, that is, for responsive, responsible governance meeting the grave emergencies of our society and planet.

Not only do corporatist Democrats differ little from evil, bought-off Republicans; they're actually *criminally* culpable for condoning and perpetuating Republican evil. Nowhere can we see this more clearly than in Obama's failure to investigate and prosecute major war criminal[78] George W. Bush and his henchmen, and in Democrats' utter refusal (a refusal imposed even on plain-spoken Bernie Sanders) to label Jeb Bush "the war criminal's brother." Considering Democrats' obvious self-interest in using that label—it would be the instant death blow for Jeb's campaign—their refusal to apply it proves just how much Democrats are part of the same evil game. For applying it would raise embarrassing, unanswerable questions for Democrats, like why Bill Clinton imposed genocidal sanctions[79] on Saddam Hussein's innocent people, why Democrats overwhelmingly joined the bandwagon[80] for Bush's wildly imprudent criminal war or why Barack Obama decided to continue Bush's universal spying and even expand his unending ill-advised war on terror[81] (albeit in proxy form)? But perhaps the worst instance of Democrats and Republicans playing the same evil game is Obama's and Mitt Romney's criminally irresponsible "gentleman's agreement" never to mention climate change[82]—a life-or-death issue for humanity, but politically inconvenient for both—throughout their series of 2012 presidential debates.

All of which convincingly proves that Democrats' "lesser-evil" argument, blaming reform-minded voters for enabling Republican evil when in fact no one deserves blame for enabling it more than the Democratic Party itself, is a *sleazy con game. CounterPunch* writer Andrew Levine has insightfully argued that "lesser-evilism" is a political race to the bottom,[83] but he didn't go far enough in explaining its sleazy dynamic. In fact, it's rather simple: both Democrat and Republican teams playing for the same plutocrat owners, both operate under severe constraints controlling what they may say and do. Ditto for consolidated mainstream media, owned by an ever smaller number of corporate media giants. So among the three "parties" (Democrats, Republicans, and media), there's a common conspiracy—that Republicans' worst misdeeds—generally embarrassing to Democrats and media, since they're complicit—should disappear down the memory hole. Their worst misdeeds never properly denounced, Republicans are emboldened for ever-worse coups against the common good.

A Democratic Party *not* complicit, and holding the moral high ground to denounce Republican evil, could have stopped the GOP's worst misdeeds long ago. With Democrats, so deeply to blame for Republican evil, *no* reform-minded voters should be duped by the sleazy blame-shifting con of voting for Democrats as the lesser evil. In fact, Democrats simply hide beneath the ground cover of Republican evil to perpetuate their own plutocrat donors' preferred brand. What voters should in fact feel guilty for is enabling *that*.

…what we plan to do is *rigorously* apply our slogan "Show Us the Anti-Money" to the whole pack of 2016 presidential candidates. Plutocrats' purchase of our government is the root of *all* our political evils, and as the *only* major party candidate who's called for a political revolution against plutocrat money, Bernie Sanders is the *only* adult in the room, the *only* candidate virtually free from the influence of that money, and the *only* one with a viable platform for ridding us of it. Therefore, he's the *only* major party presidential candidate worth voting for. As solicitors of billions of plutocrat dollars, Hillary Clinton and Jeb Bush don't even register on our radar as serious candidates. And we have a strong bias against other Democrats and Republicans, because their party leadership makes it virtually obligatory for them to accept oligarch dollars. As a lifelong independent scarcely funded at all by corporate dollars, strategically forced to run as a Democrat, Bernie *alone* has our trust. If he doesn't win the Democratic nomination—and if he fails to, it will be due simply to party propaganda we aim vigorously to counteract—we plan to write him in in the general election. In states where write-in votes aren't counted, we plan to simply vote Green.

As the political revolution Bernie called for but can't as a Democratic candidate lead—and perhaps must disavow—we passionately believe Bernie can't be a sheepdog[84] if his ever-growing legion of supporters aren't sheep. In fact, we're insulted that the likes of Chris Hedges—who shares our belief in the moral imperative of revolt—considers us such and, therefore, can't imagine a political revolution *based on* Bernie's candidacy. For those who do, who "feel the Bern" so strongly its sparks could ignite revolution, please consider joining ours. For more information, visit our Revolt Against Plutocracy Facebook page; to take the ultimate revolutionary plunge, take our #BernieOrBust pledge on our Revolt Against Plutocracy homepage.[85] By refusing the con of lesser-evilism, you'll show RAP's revolutionary movement truly deserves the nickname "Sheep No More."

HRCC

There were many articles written by progressives that were critical of Secretary Clinton before and during the primaries. These along with videos that came out during the primaries were added to the HRCC page as I found them. The following is a sampling of what we listed on that page:

- "Barack Obama: Hillary Clinton 'is just like Bush'," *The Telegraph*, 1/01/2008.
- "Hillary Clinton's Unapologetically Hawkish Record Faces 2016 Test: Burned by Iraq in 2008, but still a strong voice for military action" by Michael Crowley, *Time Magazine*, 1/14/14.
- "President Hillary Clinton Would Be Far More Conservative Than You Think," by H.A. Goodman, *Huffington Post*, 6/24/2014.
- "Hillary Clinton – The Perfect Republican Candidate," by Farron Cousins, *Ring of Fire* (video), 8/14/2014.
- "Gary Hart: Billion-dollar Clinton campaign should 'frighten' Americans," *Politico*, 4/05/2015.
- "Hillary Clinton Helped Sell Weapons To Hostile Nations To Enrich Defense Funders," by Farron Cousins, *Ring of Fire*, 5/28/2015.

- "Hillary Helps a Bank—and Then It Funnels Millions to the Clintons," by Conor Friedersdorf, *The Atlantic*, 7/31/2015.
- "Hillary Clinton Presidency Would Not Be A Victory for Women," by Debbie Lusignan, *Sane Progressive*, 8/31/2015.
- "The Insiders: Nixonian Clinton strikes again," by Ed Rogers, *Washington Post*, 9/28/2015.
- "Why No True Democrat Should Support Hillary Clinton," by Michael Blecher, *Op-Ed News*, 10/07/2015.
- "Corporate Media Won't Tell You Hillary Clinton is a Lying Fascist," by Jack Bawkwill, *Dissident Voice*, 10/22/2015.
- "Hillary in Blackface: The Blaxploitation Politics of Identity Democrats," by Patrick Walker, *Nation of Change*, 1/24/2016.
- "Hillary is the candidate of the war machine," by Jeffrey Sachs, *Huffington Post*, 2/05/2016.

We kept adding more articles as we found them and eventually listed over 200 articles highly critical of Secretary Clinton. By the time the DNC came around, I was able to and did make the argument that Hillary Clinton was more dangerous than Donald Trump.

The treasurer, meanwhile, filed the paperwork with the FEC to register our PAC, the Citizens Against Plutocracy super PAC. We chose a super PAC for two reasons: 1) the rules were easy to understand and follow and 2) it was easy to apply for. We didn't want to be seen as agents of plutocrats, however. Another conversation with Garry Thomas led to the idea of limiting total donations to $1,000.00 per person. This was to be a grassroots PAC.

Over the weekend of June 20-21 in 2015, we finalized preparations of the website. I had the Google spreadsheet set up to record the pledges, a skill I had learned from amendment organizing. I didn't know how much data one Google doc would hold, but I planned on replacing a full spreadsheet with a fresh one as more pledges came in.

I came up with the idea of using the tactic of network marketing to build the movement. The pledge had two parts: commit yourself to writing-in Bernie Sanders on November 8, if he's not the Democratic Party nominee, and find two more supporters of Sanders to take the pledge as soon as possible. The math behind that idea, if people actually recruited others to take the pledge, is an expediential curve. If only one person took the pledge on the first day and recruited just two more to take it and they each recruited two and so forth, in a month, if everyone understood this movement-building tactic and acted quickly, we'd have over a million pledges.

n	2^n	n	2^n	n	2^n
0	1	11	2,048	22	4,194,304
1	2	12	4,096	23	8,388,608
2	4	13	8,192	24	16,777,216
3	8	14	16,384	25	33,554,432
4	16	15	32,768	26	67,108,864
5	32	16	65,536	27	134,217,728
6	64	17	131,072	28	268,435,456
7	128	18	262,144	29	536,870,912
8	256	19	524,288	30	1,073,741,824
9	512	20	1,048,576	31	2,147,483,648
10	1,024	21	2,097,152	32	4,254,967,296

Patrick and I published in alternative media outlets we used to report and promote this strategy. He contributed to progressive Internet magazines *Op-Ed News* and *Nation of Change* and, during the primary season, *CounterPunch*, and I had been a reporter and writer for *Examiner*, a pro-am outfit, since 2010. On June 22, we formerly launched the WIN-S pledge strategy. Patrick and I published news stories about this strategy. That day 71 people took the WIN-S pledge.

Patrick, the treasurer and I promoted our website on Bernie Facebook groups. Patrick shared the task of asking other organizations to join our primary campaign strategy by asking their members to take the pledge for a period of time, but I had to drop that effort once data management became a time consuming effort. I had asked the Democratic Socialists of America and Progressive Democrats of America, an organization started by Congressman Kucinich (D), a failed candidate for President in 2000. DSA never replied to my queries and the director of PDA claimed he didn't have the "bandwidth" to ask their members to consider taking the pledge. I replied they would end up endorsing Clinton, but he insisted they would not.

Our Petition

Having administered a change dot org petition for the amendment movement, I understood its effectiveness in building a large list of email contacts of more or less like-minded people. I couldn't think of an idea that would garner support from Bernie supporters, but Patrick did. He suggested a petition to Senator Warren and everyone in the Congressional Progressive Caucus asking them to endorse Bernie Sanders. Patrick crafted the bulk of the petition text:

Endorse Senator Sanders for President[86]

Senator Warren and Congressional Progressive Caucus members,

Founding member of the CPC, Senator Bernie Sanders is the only true progressive and the only CPC member running in the Democratic Party primaries.

Unlike Secretary Clinton, Senator Sanders strongly opposes the corporate-crafted Trans-Pacific Partnership which is detested by progressives of every stripe. Only Bernie Sanders has a convincing plan to kill the anti-reform payola that gave us fast-track for the TPP—the very political bribery that stains Secretary Clinton and her Foundation. Deeply understanding that such money is a malignant cancer on our body politic, Sanders alone has dared call for a desperately needed "Political Revolution" against its electoral and legislative domination.

Author Naomi Klein, echoed by Pope Francis, has stressed that humanity's very survival now depends on peace-minded grassroots progressives taking control of policy from greedy, militaristic neoliberals. Knowing the dire urgency for a progressive to capture Executive Branch control over national policy, how can Congressional progressives for one second consider entrusting U.S. policy to corporatist hawk Hillary Clinton rather than exemplary progressive Bernie Sanders?

Grassroots progressives expect congressional progressives to "walk your talk" and support your fellow progressive, Bernie Sanders. We, the undersigned implore you, Senator Warren and members of the Progressive Caucus, to publicly endorse Senator Sanders for President.

From that we eventually garnered nearly 24,000 signatures and around 16,000 email contacts we could reach out to using updates on the Change.org petition itself. They were asked three times before and during the primaries to take the voter pledge. Only two members of the CPC ended up endorsing Sanders, the two chairmen, Rep. Raul Grijalva and Rep. Keith Ellison. Grijalva was not addressed in the petition distribution list because I could not locate his email address.

Patrick wrote about RAP's two fists, an iron fist—the petition—and a steel fist—the pledge itself.[87] As a writer, he was deemed our knife, cutting Hillary Clinton to pieces; and I was the hammer—pounding her on flip-flops, dishonesty, trade and her neoliberal ideology. He wrote "Hillary in Blackface: The Blaxploitation Politics of Identity Democrats" from the list of articles on our HRCC page above along with:

- "Climate Judge Hansen "Profiles" Clinton's Democrat Criminals,"[88]
- "Whitewashing Hillary–By "Redwashing" Progressive Critics,"[89]
- "Sanders Correctly Rattles Sabers—at the Climate Change Enemy,"[90]
- "Clinton's Updated Tammany Hall: Destroying Democracy AND Climate Too,"[91]
- "The Thugs Are Taking Over: Bernie or Bust Is Effective Tool of Revolt."[92]

Neoliberalism is not your grandfather's capitalism, and the so-called "free-trade agreement," the Trans-Pacific Partnership, is far more dangerous for the American experiment in democratic self-government than what the vast majority of Americans understood based upon surveys at the time. In an *Examiner* column I predicted Secretary Clinton would lie about her support for it. After speaking in favor of it 45 times as Secretary of State, calling it the "gold standard of free-trade agreements" at one point, she did come out against it. Asked by a reporter if she would use her "power" to lobby Democrats in Congress against the agreement, she replied "no." (The question presumed she would have power as President-elect without stating "if elected." It wasn't until the WikiLeaked emails in the run-up to the general election that we discovered the collaboration between the Clinton campaign and the "news" media.[93]) I wrote an *Examiner* column "Hillary Clinton: sex, lies and videotape." The video used in the column showed candidate Senator Clinton claiming in 2008 she opposed NAFTA and earlier clips of news reports and her directly as First Lady promoting NAFTA.

@BernieOrBust

Once the website was launched, one of my next tasks included the establishment of the Twitter account. Initially, the application used my Gmail account name. I couldn't think what to use for the account address, so once again I asked our idea guy, Patrick. He made a couple suggestions that were already taken. His next suggestion was something he saw as a comment on a Facebook post. "Try Bernie or Bust," he wrote. To my surprise, it was available. I told Patrick in a reply it was available and I used it adding, "That's perfect." Patrick suggested in a June 29th email renaming the write-in strategy from WIN-S to the Bernie or Bust pledge:

> The only thing I've been wondering is whether we should take my Facebook friend's suggestion and change the pledge campaign name to "Bernie or Bust." It strikes me as both catchier and a LOT clearer. And it's very much in the fighting spirit of a revolution that gets "in your face." I also like the suggestion that our government will BE a bust without Bernie.
>
> I thought WIN-S was clever when I first heard it, but I hadn't heard Bernie or Bust. For our purposes—and given the vibes I'm picking up on Facebook, "Bernie or Bust" captures how people feel and blows everything else I've heard out of the water…I think "Bernie of Bust" would VASTLY facilitate our efforts to push the pledge.

I didn't need persuading. That night, the WIN-S was gone; and we were promoting the Bernie or Bust pledge strategy.

Chapter 3
Movement Building and Adaptation

"Leadership is the art of getting someone else to do something you want done because he wants to do it."[94]
~ Dwight D. Eisenhower

One month after we launched the Bernie or Bust write-in strategy, we had fewer than 2,000 pledges. The idea of having people take the pledge and recruit two more people to take the pledge clearly was not working as hoped. We decided to post a new pledge narrative on our website on the lunaversary date of our launch, the 22nd, and to create a new Facebook community page to help build this strategy into a movement. We also reached out to everyone who had left an email address and asked for volunteers to help promote the pledge online.

We started with very little money in our PAC account, $250.00 I donated and about $20.00 from our treasurer. We used some of that money to establish an account with the bulk emailing service SendInBlue. We also applied for credit card vendor status, thinking we'd be raising money right on our website. Once we realized how much easier it would be to use the Act Blue website for that purpose, our treasurer asked for and received a refund for the application fee several months later.

Logo:
We also needed a logo, and we were not going to pay to have some company create one for us. I got the idea of coming up with something that would serve as a counterpoint to Secretary Clinton's logo, which featured an arrow pointing to the right:

Our logo's arrow would point to the left. My idea was to have a blue R and to use the U.S. flag as the backdrop with the word "Revolt" underneath it. My wife, a Photoshop artist, created the drafts which I shared with committee members. Patrick suggested placing the word "Revolt" across the arrow rather than underneath the R, an idea we ultimately adopted. After nearly a month of debates and discussions on five mock-ups of a logo to use, we finally settled on one no one was enthusiastic about.

Building Support

By this time we had a few more people working with our RAP committee. I had asked a number of my Facebook friends to take the pledge, and one of them, Charlie Hobbs, took the pledge on June 30. He was a true believer in the strategy, and I asked him to join the RAP committee in early July. I could tell from email notifications received from Facebook group posts, Charlie did more to promote the pledge on Facebook than anyone else, and I will be forever, especially grateful for his inexhaustible energy and enthusiasm. He has told me, "I worked so much to promote it because doing so helped me to feel like I was really contributing something significant to a radical cause far bigger than myself. Working to promote the pledge was incredibly meaningful for me, especially in the wake of losing my other vocation." (Teaching philosophy at the college/university level).

Another committee member set up a new Facebook page called Bernie or Else. "Or else" meant "or else the Republicans will win the general election." It was a threat, a promise and a strategy we called #leverage. We used that page to help recruit more pledge-takers. We pinned a Bernie or Bust pledge narrative to the top of the page and asked selected pledge-takers to become administrators of the page. As such, they could use an "Invite" feature of the page to ask their Facebook friends to "Like" the page. It took me two to three hours to invite all my Facebook friends at the time (around 1,300 people), and I spread the process out over three days. At one point we had around 20 volunteers inviting their Facebook friends to "Like" our Bernie or Else page.

Since May, when it was clear we were going to attempt this strategy, I had been sleeping about five hours a night and working on this strategy 45–50 hours/week on top of my day job. That work load continued until after the Democratic Party Convention in late July of 2016. Early one morning, when I was on Facebook, a little message popped up in the lower left-hand corner of that browser tab indicating someone had requested deletion of the Bernie or Else page. I immediately canceled the request and asked the guy why he did that. Someone had made him a page administrator, and he didn't want to be. I removed him as an administrator and downgraded everyone but a few trusted allies to Editors of the page because clearly people were making Sanders' supporters administrators who didn't want to be: a lesson learned. Editors still had the access to ask their friends to "Like" a community Facebook page, but they don't have the ability to make anyone else a page administrator or to delete the page.

Facebook Promotion

Apart from our own Facebook pages, we promoted the Bernie or Bust pledge by a number of us posting "hooks" and the URL to our website on the many Bernie-supporting Facebook groups and pages and elsewhere online. The hooks, otherwise known as "click bait," were written to entice readers to click on the post. We would type, copy and post—for example, in a Bernie Facebook group:

> Sanders needs a miracle called Bernie or Bust to secure the nomination. Won't you join us?
> http://citizensagainstplutocracy.org/2015/07/22/bernie-or-bust-pledge-is-the-miracle-senator-sanders-needs-to-secure-party-nomination/

Then volunteers would go to another Bernie group and paste it again, over and over going down the list of Bernie Facebook groups that I supplied our volunteers. I joined every Bernie group I could find throughout the primary season. This tactic was and remained to the last days of our recruiting efforts the most effective manner of driving traffic to our website. In 2015 55% of the traffic came from Facebook, and in 2016 36% of our website traffic derived from Facebook. This was a social media–based, revolutionary movement.

I work for a company that provides a laptop computer to use. They block many sites from us, but for some reason we have access to Facebook and Twitter. I would spend idle time and breaks promoting the pledge and spent a good deal of time after arriving at home responding to comments on my posts. I often had 150–250 emails to deal with after my day job.

Clintonbook

When I was writing for *The Amendment Gazette*, I used to spend 30–60 minutes nonstop posting my articles on Move to Amend Facebook groups. During the primaries, many people found themselves blocked by Facebook from posting or leaving comments on groups for some period of time. Facebook suddenly claimed we were posting too much, too fast. I was blocked 3–4 times for short periods. It wasn't just people promoting Bernie or Bust; a number of Sanders' supporters reported to me they were blocked from posting information about his campaign by Facebook. I wrote a column for *Examiner* entitled "Is Facebook Clintonbook now?" It became apparent to many of us that this was the case.

America Online

Meanwhile, as new pledges came in, I continued to email the pledge-takers in groups using BCC from my AOL account, reminding them to recruit two more people.

This tactic continued whether I used AOL or SendInBlue later on—after AOL in early June suddenly required the time-consuming insertion of a comma between email addresses—until after the DNC in July of 2016, but for whatever reasons, pledge-takers were not finding two more people to take the pledge. In September of 2015 my wife rewrote the reminder email, but the following message did not work to motivate most people to find just two Bernie supporters to take the pledge either.

> **The Bernie or Bust pledge you took will not work unless....**
> ...you fulfill the second part of their pledge. It's urgent now and *easy.*
>
> Bernie or Bust pledge-taker,
>
> Thank you for taking the Bernie or Bust pledge. In our effort to support Senator Sanders' political revolution, we must keep in mind that *only* strength in numbers can change the course of history. The pledge was designed to grow exponentially. The second part of your pledge to Bernie is easy to fulfill.
>
> Just highlight, copy and paste:
> > Will you take the Bernie or Bust pledge?
> > http://citizensagainstplutocracy.org/

...into emails and/or social media messages to friends and relatives. Only when only two people reply that "yes," they will take the pledge, will your two-part pledge be completed. 14% of Democrats[95] will not vote for Hillary, so we need your help to find them for us.

However, the volunteers we recruited to help build this strategy into a movement did work hard to promote the pledge. One comment left by a volunteer on a *Huffington Post* story about the primary race generated over 1,000 views of the pledge narrative; she directed them to using a short comment and the URL for that webpage. This information was available to me as the website administrator. Roughly half of the people visiting our website would go ahead and take the pledge.

Every month on the 22nd I would publish a new narrative. The August narrative stressed the need for Sanders to have leverage in order to secure the nomination. A recommended hook and URL for that narrative might have been:

> Think Bernie can secure the nomination without leverage? Think again.
>
> http://citizensagainstplutocracy.org/2015/07/22/bernie-or-bust-pledge-is-the-miracle-senator-sanders-needs-to-secure-party-nomination/

Less Is More

If you transcribe that URL into your browser, you won't find that webpage. I have taken down the pledge narratives. One of our pledge-takers had emailed me explaining he is a social media professional. He recommended keeping our "hooks" short, less than three seconds to read. More than that, he explained, and people stop reading. We are in the Twitter Age. After he offered that advice, my instructions to volunteers was to keep the hooks very short.

In October of 2015 I sent another blast out to recent pledge-takers asking them to volunteer to promote the Bernie or Bust pledge online. Many more signed up. By then we had a platoon of online activists helping promote the Bernie or Bust pledge. It wasn't until early 2016 when I recorded a video[96] to demonstrate how to quickly paste and post "hooks" and the URLs for our website on Facebook groups. I also recorded a video demonstrating how to use a dedicated browser tab to tweet or message followers on Twitter.[97]

Needless to say, we got a good deal of pushback from Clinton supporters and some of Bernie's supporters. The former often accused us of being right-wing operatives in cahoots with the Koch brothers or Karl Rove. On one particular post was a series of comments centered on Clinton's political philosophy, neoliberalism. (After she claimed to be "a progressive" during the primary debates, I composed an *Examiner* piece entitled "Who is advising Secretary Clinton, Joseph Goebbels?") One of our allies fired off a comment I copied and pasted into a document I always kept open to use for copying and pasting of website URLs, tweets, tutorial URLs, etc. I modified the comment slightly to suit my particular story and copied to paste it any time I was accused of working with some Republican or right-winger:

> <someone's name>, if I'm a conservative, Koch Brother–loving, right-winger or anything of the kind, you can have my vote for Hillary. Unfortunately, what you'll discover is that I'm a life-long progressive who, like Sanders, has fought against corporate control of the country, racism, imperialism, and the destruction of the poor and middle class for decades. In other words, I'm not guilty of what you are groundlessly accusing me of. If I gave a shit, I'd say you owe me an apology. But from what I've seen in this particular go-round of HRC's vaulting ambition, her supporters are instructed to accuse all her critics of being Tea Party members, Republicans, shills for the radical right wing, etc.
>
> I don't know who or what you are. I do know what Hillary Clinton has stood for and done over the last 50 years. It's not liberal, it's not progressive, and it's only "Democratic" thanks to what she and Bill and their allies have been allowed to do to the Democratic Party. The fact that there have been multiple and evolving definitions of "neoliberal" is irrelevant. The current meaning is clear and it fits the Clintons and the "New Democrats" to a tee. Live with it. Own it. Embrace it.

But don't tell me or any critic of HRC that we're right-wingers. That's a cheap and transparent trick that fools no one but you and your fellow Kool-Aid drinkers. http://citizensagainstplutocracy .org/hrcc/

After I added this to my document of URLs, tweets, etc., I sent it to the volunteers for their modification and use. Often, a supporter of Senator Sanders would express fear of our pledge strategy. Our reply was simple: Be afraid; be very afraid. We understood fear as a factor when people voted, and we realized our pledge both fed fears of a Republican victory in November and potentially benefited from it. Vote for Bernie Sanders, or else we will end up with a conservative in the White House starting January 20, 2017.

From when we launched the strategy forward, I was looking for two people to assist our movement: a trustworthy, famous person who would join our committee, and someone in a major market to serve as our spokesperson. We never found anyone famous to join our committee, although later on Susan Sarandon became the unofficial spokesperson for our movement.[98] We needed someone famous and trustworthy to assist with our fundraising efforts, but we never recruited a celebrity.

One early Bernie or Bust pledge supporter and volunteer was a former bodyguard for famous musicians. I messaged him on Facebook asking if he knew anyone famous who might be willing to join our movement. He was indignant and replied, "Yeah, me." He immediately blocked me on Facebook. He also demanded to be removed from our list of volunteers. Apparently, I was supposed to recognize his name.

I continued to ask people to be the spokesperson for our organization and our growing list of pledge-takers. People either didn't feel comfortable or they were not in a major media market. My intention was to remain behind the scenes because I did not wish to become the face of Bernie or Bust.

Early on in the summer of 2015, someone suggested we come up with a shorter URL to use instead citizensagainstplutocracy.org. I checked bernieorbust.org and found it landed on a Bernie website in FL. I was able to contact the site owner and asked him if he would sell us that URL. He was a strong supporter of our campaign strategy and simply redirected the URL along with bernieorbust.com to our website without charge.

On August 6, the Republicans held their first primary campaign debate. The first question the candidates were asked was whether they would commit to supporting the eventual nominee. All but Donald Trump raised his hand. Asked why he would not, he explained he would use the threat of an independent candidacy as "leverage." *Business Insider* reported "Donald Trump kicked off the GOP debate with a dramatic threat to the Republican Party."[99] The next day I published "Corporate media covers Trump's threat to run as independent but ignores RAP's idea." The closest Senator Sanders came to anything like Trump's threat was to warn the DNC that "the huge crowds of supporters he has drawn may not vote for Democratic candidates in 2016 unless he is at the top of the ticket." That happened during the DNC's summer meeting on August 28. He told them as they listened in silence:

> "In my view, Democrats will not retain the White House, will not regain the Senate or the U.S. House, will not be successful in dozens of governor races across the country, unless we generate excitement and momentum and produce a huge voter turnout."[100]

Offline Promotion

When I found out Bernie was going to be speaking in some city, I would email people from that state asking them, if they were planning to attend his rally, to please print out as many of an attached quarter sheet flyer (depicted below) as they could afford, arrive at the venue early and hand them out to people in line to go in. Later on, the flyer was changed to reflect the modified meaning of "or bust," but the first flyer we encouraged volunteers to hand out to Sanders supporters was designed for us by Ricky Cherry, owner of Culture Mix:[101]

BERNIE ⊕R BUST !

"Revolt Against Plutocracy"

Is building a list of voters pledged to write-in Bernie Sanders - 2016
in order to apply leverage during
the Democratic primaries
and help him secure the nomination.

You can read the explanation of this innovative strategy
and get all of the details, answers to frequently
asked questions, etc. at their website:

citizensagainstplutocracy.org

Take the pledge for democracy today

Bernie

REVOLUTION

I never knew if pledge-takers actually undertook this effort on any kind of large scale. I would monitor pledges coming in, and there never seemed to be a surge of pledges in the aftermath of a Sanders campaign event from that state.

Ad Campaign

We had to create ads for our campaign to run on television and the radio. A "Mad Man" I am not, and neither was anyone else on our committee. One day, when pasting pledge-taker email addresses into the BCC of my reminder (to recruit two more people to take the pledge) email, I noticed one of our pledge-takers had an email address "marketmaven." I reached out to her for help creating an ad script. After a few back-and-forth email exchanges, Linda finally admitted she doesn't create ads; she just works in the business. She recommended an ad man. I reached out to him, and after a long phone conversation he suggested I compose a creative brief to give him guidance for writing our script. It read in large part:

> **1. Overview:**
> Senator Bernie Sanders is attempting to undertake a "political revolution" using a major party he does not belong to. If successful or not, we believe his strategy to be unprecedented. No mainstream pundit believes he has a chance, and

the far left is accusing him of being a sheepdog, herding progressives back into the Wall Street-corrupted neoliberal order. Revolt Against Plutocracy supports Sanders' decision to run within the Democratic Party for tactical reasons, and we bring four "weapons" to this fight his campaign can or will not. RAP is convinced that the revolution will fail if Sanders loses the nomination, so we're employing all legal means to aid and abet his revolutionary campaign with revolutionary primary campaign strategy: the Bernie or Bust pledge, our most potent, dangerous and frightening "weapon." We also have a petition and our CAP Political Action Committee.

2. The Objective:

Liberals and Democrats must support Bernie Sanders, or the progressive, revolutionary pledge-takers are walking away from the Democratic Party in the general election. Most polls indicate Secretary Clinton to be the formidable favorite that virtually all mainstream pundits believe will be the nominee, but she is not ahead of all Republicans in the polls by very much. Senator Sanders needs three elements to come together to pull off an upset: 1) a ground game, based on volunteer political activism, which he is building. His revolution also needs an all-of-the-above Internet strategy, **and** the Bernie or Bust pledge strategy: the revolutionary, innovative, grassroots insistence that Bernie is the only nominee the Democrats can offer if they expect 1 million + pledge-takers to vote Democrat in the General Election next year.

RAP intends to compel Democrats to support Bernie Sanders or else they're on their own in the general election. We're not saying "please."

3. Target audience:

CAP PAC's ad will strike fear in the minds of voters who want a woman in the White House, as we do too, but know that

Clinton is under FBI investigation and may face charges. They may not really trust Clinton and have never read a political book or essay in their lives. They are vulnerable, weak, low-information voters, who don't pay that much attention to politics, have no idea what a dangerous, corporate *coup des lois* [corporate power grab] the TPP [would] foist upon our system of self-government. They just need to understand one thing after seeing, hearing or learning about the ad: If they do not vote for Bernie in the primaries; the Democrats may well lose the election.

This strategy is as unprecedented as Bernie's campaign strategy, and we know his campaign knows about us, could contact us, but has not yet. The campaign does not know that we intend to scare the uninformed voters as an ad tactic, but we make no secret of it either. We insist on our website that the only way to deal with their fear we're seeing expressed a lot on Facebook is to support Senator Sanders in the primaries and caucuses. Only in this way can they relieve that fear.

We plan to communicate with these voters with press releases to major state media outlets announcing the number of pledges so far, state by state; and by paid newspaper, radio, magazine and free online sharing of the two scripts using targeted social media before each contest if Clinton/Biden leads in the polls. The Internet will be key in our ad campaign, and most of it will be voluntary. We also hope to afford putting the video of the script on television a couple of days before the primary.

We believe this approach is so radical and threatening that the nation will know about the Bernie or Bust primary campaign strategy before we pay for advertising. Because we have a grassroots "super" PAC, it seems to RAP that Sanders is going to be asked by someone in the press to address CAP PAC. Sanders does not want super PAC support. His answer could make or break the strategy. We hope he reiterates his support for the nominee and refuses to denounce the pledge strategy. We will not stop until after we receive a cease-and-desist order from him, if then. It is our right, according to *FreeSpeechPAC v FEC*, to establish and use CAP PAC.

Our targets are busy and terrified of another Republican picking Supreme Court judges or defunding Planned Parenthood. They believe Clinton is the most qualified, the way Hillary was compared with Obama in 2008, and it's time to break the glass ceiling.

Psychographically, this audience is more conservative than Bernie. We want the Reagan Democrats to support Bernie because … well, Donald Trump.

At the same time, they want a woman in the White House and believe, quite correctly, that Clinton is more qualified. These people do not have a clue as to why we need a political revolution or just how corrupt the Democratic Party has become. This audience may not have strong opinions or beliefs about the topic of politics. They may be conservative on taxes but support liberal positions on some social issues: slightly liberal, sometimes conservative. They are busy housewives and dads, and their family gets their "news" from CBS, ABC, CNN or NBC if at all. Many remain "undecided" until almost primary day, or they want Clinton only because she would be the first woman in the White House.

4. Focus:

We want the message to convey that the election will probably be lost to the Republicans without Bernie Sanders as the nominee. "Do you want Donald Trump choosing the Supreme Court nominees next year? If not, #UniteBehindBernie."

5. Reasons why: what is in it for the voters?

If not Bernie, then Donald Trump with VP-nominee Senator Cruz a distinct possibility.

1) **Fear**. New, legal strategy could lose the election for Democrats, just like in 2000….

After discussing payment, he declined to write for us, but the document served its purpose. With the help of people who read our Revolt Against Plutocracy Facebook page, we would write the ad script. I came up with a draft and posted it on our page for suggestions on refinement and changes. A number of good suggestions came in. This is the script we used for our 60-second spot.

> Fellow Democrats, we are **genuine** progressives pledged to either write-in Bernie Sanders in the general election or vote Green if he is not the Party nominee. Why would we do this?
>
> We will not accept another Wall Street-backed candidate for President. While we want a woman in the White House, the United States needs a political revolution to bring an end to our plutocracy which is a government by and for wealthy people. Therefore, we cannot and will not vote for Hillary Clinton, an untrustworthy establishment candidate funded by billionaires.
>
> If you support anyone but Senator Sanders in the primaries or caucuses, you will divide Democrats, and you will be on your own in the general election. Let's not have a repeat of the disastrous 2000 election.
>
> We must # UniteBehindBernie, an honest and principled Senator, or you'll risk having Donald Trump or Senator Cruz nominating the next Supreme Court judges.

My original intention was to have a local organizer with a great baritone voice read the ad, but I read a post sometime in November stating voters were sick and tired of white men telling them how to vote. I needed a woman with a pleasant voice to read the script, and I knew the perfect person for this job: my wife.

Once she recorded the three 15-second, 30-second and 60-second scripts, we needed someone to sync the audio to images for video ads to run on television. At *Progressive Examiner* I had interviewed Miles Disney, aka MC Moneypenny, a musician who had written a rap song called "Bernin Down Da Haus." I reached out to him asking who produced his ads, and he put me in touch with Adrian Atwood. He did a great job with them, and they can be viewed on YouTube:

- 15-second ad: https://youtu.be/I7HdSoytYqg
- 30-second ad: https://youtu.be/tQOPRV-s0tY
- 60-second ad: https://youtu.be/QxjIDa5Ezq0

We would need to raise a lot of money to run these on television, but we were not Bernie Sanders for President or anyone famous. Meanwhile, we needed to get more people taking the Bernie or Bust pledge.

#BustExit1

My Revolt Against Plutocracy and Bernie or Bust pledge co-creator Patrick, meanwhile, had continued to promote the pledge in the way that best suited him: writing. From his initial base at *OpEdNews*, Patrick gradually expanded to writing for *Nation of Change*, *CounterPunch*, and *Dissident Voice*. At *OpEdNews* and *Nation of Change* in particular, he had become a popular writer, often landing a top headline and a featured spot in their daily newsletters. Patrick would routinely write a timely opinion piece on some current issue, using misbehavior by the Clinton campaign, for example, as a reason to take the pledge, to which he'd link in his article.

Patrick not only used Facebook extensively to promote his own pro-pledge writings, but he became quite adept at concocting framing introductions to other authors' pieces he posted there as a means of promoting the pledge. Or, promoting it indirectly, he used his framing intros as means of stirring up disgruntlement or even outrage with Clinton, putting readers in the right mood to take the pledge. Patrick joined many Facebook groups to post his own articles or his framed versions of others' pieces. Like the rest of us, he sometimes paid the price for posting too much too rapidly: a few days in Facebook "prison."

In September Patrick informed us that due to pressures at home associated with a move from Georgia to New York and disagreement over our unwillingness to negotiate over issues with the Clinton campaign should she secure the nomination, he was stepping down from the committee. He thought we should use the strength of our movement to essentially make policy demands of Secretary Clinton, but I could not imagine doing so. Sometime between the Party Convention and the general election, we'd have to ask people, who took the Bernie or Bust pledge, to vote for her on Nov. 8 if we had our demands met.

Patrick, by contrast, made a calculation. He reckoned on Clinton's huge lead in superdelegates and the strong likelihood those superdelegates would never "flip" to Sanders. While our pledge numbers were gradually increasing, they struck him as likely to be too small, by Democratic convention time, to persuade superdelegates either sharing Clinton's taste for donor money or fearing reprisals due to the Clintons' clout in the party and their known vindictiveness. Since he thought our pledge would very likely not succeed at nominating Sanders, he felt we should use it instead as leverage to gain platform concessions from the Clinton camp. And he hoped Sanders himself would use it that way; recall from Chapter 2 that the prospect of Sanders using our pledge as platform leverage was Patrick's chief rationale for agreeing to make it a write-in rather than a "vote Green" pledge.

Patrick felt, in short, that using our pledge solely as leverage to nominate Bernie would make our movement irrelevant after the Democratic convention. He felt we could apply platform leverage even after the convention, especially if the race between Clinton and the Republican nominee got tight. But Patrick acknowledges that the pressure of his family's long-distance move also played a role in his decision to quit at that moment. I had a phone conversation with him the next day and let him know, should he change his mind, he would be welcome to rejoin the RAP committee.

Consequently, after he was settled into a new home in early November of 2016, Patrick rejoined us for the upcoming primary season fight ahead. He calculated that the potential leverage from the pledge was a good thing, whether it was used to nominate Sanders or to force platform concessions. While maintaining his reservations about the value of the pledge in actually nominating Sanders, he decided to bury his differences with us for the moment and simply work for the pledge. As readers will see, those differences came back to haunt us later.

But, with everyone content for the moment, Patrick was introduced to new committee members, who had been recruited to our committee since his departure, on wiggio. Wiggio is a type of list-serv where members can start a conversation and then reply to it either on the website or by email. A sample of one discussion is pasted into Chapter 10, "What's Next?"

Decision Making

The RAP committee typically operated with between five and seven members. Voting on decisions on raising and spending money was done with simple majority unless we had an even number of committee members. During those periods we used a super-majority to make decisions, 4 to 2 when we had six members or 5 to 3 the rare times we had eight members on our committee. All expenditures of PAC donations were authorized unanimously by the committee.

Campaign and Bernie or Bust

Most of the RAP committee members were assisting offline with Sanders campaign efforts. Although I didn't spend as much time as I had originally planned to, I gathered signatures on a ballot petition. We never discouraged volunteers from helping out with the Sanders campaign. If fact, we encouraged it. Our primary campaign strategy was not in competition with what the formal campaign was doing; we saw our strategy as complementary and, we hoped, synergistic to what the Sanders campaign was undertaking.

On our FAQ page,[102] we quoted Harold Meyerson from the *Washington Post*. Writing about Sanders' campaign as a "political revolution," he wrote, "Movements are built from the bottom up, not the top down." We understood Bernie or Bust to be one of the bottom up, grassroots revolutionary movements supporting his top-down campaign. Other independent, bottom up movements supporting Sanders' campaign included Movement4Bernie (now Movement for the 99%[103]) and The People for Bernie.[104] We asked the latter to join our strategy, to have the people in their movement take the Bernie or Bust pledge; but no one ever replied to our queries on Facebook or Twitter.

We Are Not Sandernistas

In early August, Patrick authored a column at *CounterPunch*, another outlet he gained access to after we started the voter pledge movement. A long-time fan of *CounterPunch*, Patrick had been delighted to get published there, but he was distressed that the die-hard leftist staff—especially chief editor Jeffrey St.

Clair and managing editor Joshua Frank—had failed to notice the Bernie or Bust movement, let alone grasp its real radicalism. Accordingly, Patrick wrote St. Clair and Frank, asking if *CounterPunch* would publish his rebuttal to their articles pooh-poohing the Sanders revolution. Wanting to host an honest leftist debate on the value of Sanders' campaign, St. Clair and Frank readily agreed to publish Patrick's rebuttal. To this day, he thanks them for their fair-mindedness in doing so.

Patrick's article, "We're Not Sandernistas: Reinventing the Wheels of Bernie's Bandwagon," addressed Sanders' critics on the left and made it clear we were going to criticize Sanders when appropriate:[105]

> Regular *CounterPunch* readers will recognize in my title allusions to recent articles by two top CP staffers, chief editor Jeffrey St. Clair and managing editor Joshua Frank, pooh-poohing Bernie Sanders' presidential candidacy. Namely, "Bernie and the Sandernistas"[106] by St. Clair and "The Wheels Fell Off the Bernie Sanders Bandwagon"[107] by Frank. Though intended to rebut both, my response here is *not* the sort of Bernie-awed talkbalk CP readers might expect; it's certainly *not* the spittle-flecked outrage of a Bernie-bedazzled "Sandernista."Instead, I strongly agree with St. Clair and Frank that the *conventional* ways of supporting Sanders, unaided by something sharper-edged, are doomed to failure, perhaps not even the *memorable* failure that would make Sanders at least a "beautiful loser" in Leonard Cohen's sense. But I, as both leftist and regular *CounterPunch* reader, sense the left is making a *tragic* mistake in not recognizing Bernie Sanders as a unique presidential candidate, running under unique historic circumstances, who could reap unprecedented gains for the left—*provided* our support is tailored to the singularity of both candidate and circumstances. Both conventional Sanders supporters and the Sanders-skeptical left suffer from a common fault: thinking "inside the Bernie box." Revolt Against Plutocracy, the revolutionary movement I represent, has concocted a viable way of supporting Sanders

while working "outside the Bernie box." *CounterPunch* readers deserve this chance to hear and assess our strategy.

As you'll quickly see, my rebuttal is light-years away from branding Joshua Frank a "fucking ass-wipe," as some Sandernistas apparently have, for daring to criticize their idol. Indeed, a certain criticism of Sanders is *implied* in our strategy, which repudiates his "friend" Hillary Clinton[108] to a *far* greater extent than he'll ever dare. Indeed, we'd rather *appeal* to the Sanders-skeptical left than middle-finger it, since our movement is premised on a fair bit of radicalism among Sanders supporters—considerably more than they've yet shown. Enlisting a larger sector of the left in support of Sanders is critical to increasing radicalism among his devotees. And that radicalism, in turn, is utterly essential to securing leftists "bang for our Bernie buck."

Finding Sanders Worthy—of "Critical Support"

As a *CounterPunch* habitué, I find much to agree with—and use for activist purposes—in its pages. For example, CP regular Andrew Levine has contributed a crucial concept to my present case. In a timely, insightful article,[109] Levine argues that the left should "dust off" the long-neglected concept of *critical support* for candidates. I couldn't agree more.

Given how much corporate and plutocrat agendas shape our candidate selection pool, and propaganda by consolidated corporate media shapes "mainstream" attitudes, the probability of leftists finding an *electable* candidate who is in all or most ways satisfactory now approaches zero. So the trick is to find an electable candidate who's satisfactory on one or two of the most crucial issues and to support that candidate's election, reserving the right to otherwise disagree openly with that candidate and to pressure him or her to adopt more of your views. Naturally, most of the disagreement should be expressed behind closed doors or after the election, since a candidate who's right about even one or two of society's most critical issues is probably already a considerable underdog.

Almost perversely, Levine applies his impeccable critical-support logic to unelectable Jim Webb (based on his intelligent, experienced-soldier's caution about U.S. militarism), when the most fitting subject for his leftist logic is *obviously* Bernie Sanders. Were I asked to title an "executive summary" of Levine's critical-support idea, I'd feel compelled to write "Brilliant Idea, Wrong Issue, Wrong Candidate."

Now, in asserting that U.S. militarism is the wrong issue, I'm decidedly *not* saying that war-and-peace issues are unimportant, either to me personally or to Revolt Against Plutocracy. Rather, I'm making the *obvious* point that they're not the "sexy" issue of U.S. political discourse and are unlikely to become so anytime soon. Why? The best way to explain this is by examining the last time war-and-peace *was* our nation's central issue: roughly the late 1960s and early 1970s, when protestors had successfully elevated the Vietnam War to the headline story of U.S. politics. Four significant differences between then and now *scream* for attention: (1) our military was *not* professional and was based on the draft; (2) the economic lot of the average middle-class person was, relative to the rich, *vastly* better and allowed the leisure essential to citizenship; (3) college education was *vastly* more affordable and less governed by business interests; and (4) the press was far less conglomerated, meaning that there was more adversarial journalism that opposed the interests of the rich and powerful. Perhaps a fifth difference should be added: that there were fewer of the escapist diversions—especially the electronic ones—that now divert people's attention from their comparative political impotence.

The key result of these differences for war-and-peace issues is twofold. First, lack of a military draft severely curtails Americans' interest in U.S. militarism, because they literally don't "have skin in the game." Secondly, without that skin in the game, today's Americans fighting militarism on disinterested, principled grounds is *far* less likely, because their lack of leisure (time untroubled by economic stress) and lack of unbiased political information (due to corporate takeover of media and college curricula) severely cripples their ability to act as free citizens devoted to the common good. So, unsurprisingly, the economic issues that thwart both life prospects and responsible citizenship, along with the endemic political corruption that thrives on economic inequality and mass political castration, move to the political front burner. And if Bernie Sanders generates an excitement that's simply inconceivable for Jim Webb, it's because he—and he *alone* among presidential candidates—has the central political issues of our times *nailed*.

And supporting Bernie pays an incredible dividend: beyond his solidity on the economic-inequality and political-corruption issues that form the lynchpin of all current political progress, he's the gold standard among current presidential candidates on climate change action. Precisely because he's uniquely unbeholden to corporate oligarchs—fossil fuel oligarchs *very* much included—he's uniquely positioned to heed the best science and not Shell's or Exxon-Mobil's bottom line when devising energy policy. By his impeccable resistance to corporate and plutocratic domination, he's empowered to protect humanity from an evil, entailed in corporate domination, latently *far* more dangerous than corporate domination itself.

So clearly, there's *zero* hope of success for candidates who make U.S. militarism their signature issue, and it's not even clear that Webb, now that he has entered the presidential race, will do so. Which strongly hints that the left, in rifling through prospective grounds for critical support, should get behind the most popular candidate who's solid on the lynchpin issues of economic inequality and political corruption—

and who's an unimpeachable climate hawk to boot. And even as regards U.S. militarism, Sanders' basic priorities (unlike those of Hillary Clinton and most Republicans, with their vested interest in U.S. imperialism) point by their inner logic toward peace. Funding for Sanders' costly proposed infrastructure makeover has to come from somewhere, and the metastasized cancer of our military budget (toward which he *has* expressed skepticism[110]) is the most obvious source. Moreover, a president who's *not* aggressively imposing corporate donors' will on foreign citizens has considerably less need of "boots and bombs." When an *indirect* peace dividend is the absolute best peace activists can currently hope for, Bernie's implicit offer of one seems yet more ground for critical support.

Our Strategy: Bernie as Dynamite for Democrats' Fault Lines

So crucial is Levine's notion of critical support to Revolt Against Plutocracy's support for Sanders that it's at the very heart of our Bernie-based political strategy. By operating in absence of that notion—by acting as if uncritical "Sandernista" support is the only type possible—both St. Clair and Frank miss the unique opportunity Sanders now offers the left. And in that they share common ground with many Sanders supporters, especially Democrat loyalists who simply prefer him to Clinton but will dutifully vote for "Madam President" should she beat Bernie for the party nomination. In truth, St. Clair, Frank, and conventional Sanders supporters share the common fault of thinking "inside the Bernie box." In other words, because Bernie, to cite Chris Hedges' words, "cut a Faustian bargain"[111] by running for president as a Democrat, they assume his supporters must act as Bernie does and accept the same Faustian deal.

Hedges, St. Clair, and Frank, in short, castigate Bernie for his Faustian bargain with Democrats, while *never* raising the serious question of whether, for Bernie personally, any better bargain was available. And frankly, I think their bias against Democrats (a bias Democrats *substantially* merit) has blinded them to the sheer impotence and futility Bernie would have embraced by running as an independent or for a third party. If there's now so much excitement over Bernie, it's precisely because Bernie, by running as a Democrat, gains instant ballot, debate, and media access he wouldn't otherwise have achieved; his election, while perhaps unlikely, certainly seems *possible*. And, while corporate mainstream media has certainly *not* been Bernie-friendly, it *has* been forced to cover him as part and parcel of typical "horse race" politics: the highly profitable creation of drama around a primary race. Contrast that with the deadly silence—or the "freak show" ridicule—with which mainstream media would have treated a Sanders Green or independent campaign. The best he could have hoped for was to be "Ralph Nader on steroids," and as Bernie astutely realized,[112] Democrats' resentment of him as a spoiler—and clampdown on his publicly valuable Senate career—would have been equally "steroidal."

Revolt Against Plutocracy, therefore, assesses Bernie's decision to run as a Democrat as an utterly sound one—the best of the universally *bad* options available in a deeply corrupt system. And in a sense, we feel Hedges, St. Clair, Frank, and the "hard-ass left" aren't cynical or hard-ass enough: they treat Sanders' candidacy as an undeserved legitimizing of Democrats and *not* as an opportunity to be *exploited*—by leftists with more radical agendas than Bernie. We feel that Bernie, in his utterly sincere opposition to domination of our nation by corporate and plutocrat money (a sincerity vouched for his refusal to take it) is sheer political *dynamite*. And we intend (whatever Bernie himself does) to *exploit* that dynamite in a revolutionary way: to blast open the *very* real fault lines between corporatists and populists in the Democratic Party.

Progressive Examiner

In addition to handling the pledge information as it came in, moving the email addresses over to our SendInBlue account, correcting obvious address typos, tweeting and posting articles on our two Facebook pages, I was writing and publishing columns in *Examiner*. On Dec. 13 I published "Who is more fascistic: Donald Trump or Hillary Clinton?" The answer was Trump, by a few of the 14 characteristics I used as a framework of comparison.[113] This exercise is repeated in Chapter 10.

On December 20 I published "Who is more electable, Hillary Clinton or Bernie Sanders?" I made the argument that Clinton's many scandals and lack of trustworthiness made Sanders the more electable candidate in the general election. *Examiner* has since gone out of business, and none of my stories or columns are available for reading. All that remains are the headlines on my *Progressive Examiner* Facebook page.[114]

By year's end we found out from a series of comments on Facebook posts our strategy had a serious problem, leading to what would be the most contentious decision the committee had to make. It turns out, a national write-in campaign is a bad idea.

Although we weren't getting nearly as many pledges as we would need to serve as leverage on voters, the strategy was gaining momentum. On September 24 I reported on *Examiner* we had reached 10,000 pledges, and three of us used a spreadsheet of Twitter contact information to notify about 100 members of the media of this threshold. Not one of them covered it as a story. By Thanksgiving I reported we had reached 25,000 pledges. Again, four of us used Twitter to notify people in the media of this accomplishment; and again we were completely ignored.

By then, we had recruited a platoon of over 50 volunteers to promote the pledge, and I was providing tips and ideas to them regularly. Facebook provides the option of receiving notifications of new posts on group pages, and I turned that off for most of the 200 Bernie groups I had joined to promote the pledge. At the time it was easy to use the Facebook groups listing to copy and paste them into emails. We encouraged our volunteers to join all of the Bernie Facebook groups. I could tell which volunteers were busy promoting the pledge and which "volunteers" were not by the email notifications I received of new group posts for the groups where I had not turned off the email notification.

On December 17, the DNC cut off the Sanders campaign access to the voter database because of a breach in the "wall" that blocked the campaigns from accessing each other's data. On the 18th and 19th, more people took the pledge than during any previous 48-hour period. On our wiggio communications account I wrote, "Thank you Debbie Wasserman-Schultz."

On December 9 I had reported on wiggio, "A blogger has written about the Bernie or Bust pledge quite critically over issues we're aware of. He recommends a #BernieOrGreen2016 pledge." We were reluctant to change the strategy name, Bernie or Bust, which was beginning to take hold in people's minds.

This Is A Really Bad Idea

Around that same time a comment from someone in California caught my attention. We had standardized replies to our critics, but this time I had no answer, no snappy come-back. I ignored it. I saw the same concern expressed two more times, each time by someone from California. People were claiming that write-in votes in California, for someone who had not registered as a write-in candidate, would end up having the entire ballot thrown out uncounted, even the down-ballot votes. After seeing this comment expressed three times, it dawned on me: write-ins are a really bad idea. It never occurred to me to call the office of the California Secretary of State to find out if it was true or not, at least not until October of 2016.

By the end of the month, we were ready to shift over to Bernie or Green in 2016. I wrote to the committee, "Starting on New Year's Day, I will rewrite all of the narratives to #BernieOrGreen2016. I'll mark the pledge sheets and store the addresses in new folders at SendInBlue." Then we hit the brakes on moving away from Bernie or Bust.

We knew the write-in strategy was not a smart idea. We had learned by then Bernie himself would need to register as a write-in candidate in most states, but we didn't want to give up on the slogan "Bernie or Bust." We spent two weeks debating what we should do about our stupid strategy. Our most active promoter of the pledge, Charlie Hobbs, wanted to keep "Bernie or Bust," but we believed it could harm down-ballot progressives, at least in California if not in other states as well.

After going back and forth, sometimes spending days just thinking about what we should do to fix this problem, Patrick suggested a compromise. Leave the pledge "Bernie or Bust," but add the option "or vote Green Party." No one on the committee dissented from that idea

We chose the Green Party for one reason. Their domestic party platform almost completely overlapped with Sanders' agenda. We planned to contact the pledge-takers after the Democratic National Convention in July and let people know we had abandoned the write-in option altogether.

One concern I had about this shift in the Bernie or Bust strategy was people might think we were members of the Green Party all along and used Bernie or Bust as a scheme to build support for that party. I remember asking all committee members before publishing a story about the change in *Examiner*, "are you or have you ever been a member of the Green Party?" The answer was no from everyone on the committee. On January 11, 2016 I published, "RAP modifies Bernie or bust pledge to include voting Green this November."

For a week after updating the home page and every other pledge narrative we had published up to that point to include the option of voting Green, I would count the number of pledges coming in. It soon became clear to me this was not slowing our momentum.

As usual, I posted my *Examiner* story on as many of the Bernie Facebook groups and tweeted it out. We asked people to leave feedback in comments on the Examiner website. While there was some dissent, most people seemed to take the option of voting Green in stride.

For now, problem solved; but the write-in strategy roared back again during the general election with another spin off strategy called #OpDeny270.

Chapter 4
The Treasurers Dropped Like Flies

"A new challenge keeps the brain kicking and the heart ticking."[115] ~E.A. Bucchianeri

The First

I know our first treasurer personally, and she was the first person I recruited understanding we'd need a PAC to pull this off. She was enthusiastic about this revolutionary strategy. She was also ill with a heart problem. She was generally able but was having difficulty getting around town on her bicycle. She was scheduled to go to New York City for open heart surgery in late July of 2015.

She went with me to the bank to open the checking account we'd need for the PAC. Before departing for New York, she made a few $5.00 deposits to the account to avoid a fee the bank would otherwise have charged us. She also dealt with the company that was going to provide us with credit card vendor status, so we could take donations on our website, an idea we abandoned in favor of the much simpler idea of using Act Blue. She also established our committee with the FEC: Citizens Against Plutocracy PAC.

Within a few days of registering our PAC, a reporter with Politico asked me for an interview. He questioned me on the phone for about 10 to 15 minutes. I explain to Aaron Mak that we were driving a stake into the progressive end of the political terrain and chaining ourselves to it. Politico never published the interview. It was the first unpublished interview of several more to come before this campaign strategy was over in July of 2016.

Shortly after the treasurer made the $5.00 deposits in our checking account, she departed for NYC. She remained down there for a couple months as she had severe complications. Five times, while in NY, she nearly died; but eventually she returned to Binghamton thrilled to be alive and feeling much better. During a conversation in her kitchen she told me she felt as if her entire life had led up to this opportunity to be part of our Bernie or Bust movement. I told her I felt the same about my life. By then I had donated around $250.00 to our PAC to cover expenses.

Sometime in October, she complained to me we should be appealing more to moderates rather than just leftists. "The work I agreed to do was not," she wrote, "the lefty losing approach." I thought it was strange since the obvious people to ask to take the pledge were Sanders' supporters who are progressive for the most part. Then, one day she abruptly resigned. I begged her to change her mind, but she refused. I told her she could write her own narratives targeting moderate supporters of Bernie Sanders, but to no avail. She complained someone had commented "steaming pile of shit" on Facebook, but she doesn't remember who. Until the day I wrote this chapter, I didn't fully understand why she quit as our treasurer.

Even though our agenda is posted on the website, I was essentially focused on the pledge's threatening characteristic: #leverage. Leverage is non-ideological. Supporters of a libertarian Republican candidate could use it. A voters' pledge is a revolutionary demand, and by October of 2015 I quoted Frederick Douglass in the monthly narrative: "Power concedes nothing without a demand. It never did and it never will."[116] Asking her again while I wrote this chapter she explained, "I resigned because I believed in an expansive Bernie campaign and your writing became increasingly narrow and off-putting. Also I was very offended by your reply to my input, that my one and only job was to do the books and take all responsibility as Treasurer. I would have been a fool to remain in that position as I perceived your message in stark contrast to my own."

In an email sent while writing this chapter I replied:

> "I need to apologize because I never meant to convey you should not if you wanted to do more. Because of your health, I wanted you to understand you had no other respon-

sibilities. You were doing what the committee needed, and other people were responsible for other activities. I would have appreciated everything you did to promote an inoffensive, moderate narrative. I don't know what more you wanted to do, but I would have appreciated anything more you wanted to take on, to take responsibility for. All volunteers were encouraged to promote the pledge on social media, and I think pursuing the moderate Bernie supporters makes complete sense as one of two or more target segments of Sanders' supporters.

It was a misunderstanding, and it's my fault. I'm sorry."

The Second

At the time panicked and desperate, I sent a blast out to everyone who had taken the pledge.

> Our PAC treasurer has resigned from Revolt Against Plutocracy. Without a treasurer, we have no grassroots PAC, and without a PAC, we will not be able to run newspaper, radio and television ads telling Democrats that their choice is Bernie Sanders or else they may lose the election next year. #BernieOrElse
>
> If you have accounting skills and a few hours/month you can offer to our Bernie or Bust strategy, please contact me using the email address below my name.
>
> Having a treasurer is essential to our success. If we cannot replace [her], we will have to give up on using leverage and providing insurance for Bernie at the Convention next year.

About a dozen pledge-takers replied. After a few of those volunteers fell through, a committee member stepped forward to offer her services. She had done this work at the state level. Perfect. I removed the original treasurer from the FEC committee and added Susanna Patterson. Because we hadn't raised $1,000.00 by the end of September, we weren't required to file a report for that quarter.

We had a quarterly report due on January 30th. Unfortunately, Susanna was in the intensive care unit of a hospital at that time. She recently told me during her nine days in the ICU, she was hallucinating about being a political prisoner. I downloaded the "Getting Started with FECfile User Manual" and the FECfile application. The FEC campaign finance reviewing analyst in charge of our account was extremely helpful getting a complete novice through the process. Between the tutorial videos and his assistance, I muddled through and submitted the report on time.

The Third

I reached out to one woman, who had written she would "be happy to help" in reply to the email blast I sent out in October. She replied she was still willing to help out. I let her know that the work involved a lot of data entry. She replied she enjoys doing such work. After vetting her, I sent her URLs to the FEC user manual and tutorial videos explaining how to download the FEC application and how to enter contribution and expense information. I made her the records keeper for CAP PAC, and when a filing deadline approached, I sent her the emailed reminder from the FEC.

About a week after the April 15th deadline, I got a notice from the FEC that our report hadn't been filed. I reached out to our "records keeper," and she never replied. She dropped the ball and never let me know. We were now in violation of federal campaign finance law. I called Susanna, who was out of the hospital and feeling a little better, and asked her to file the April report. She didn't want to, but I had a set of home projects my marriage required at the time and pressed her to file it. She agreed to do so. I sent her the spread-sheet of donations and a list of expenses.

Sometime after that, I received another notice from the FEC. Susanna had filed a written report, and they required an electronic report uploaded using their application, a program called FECfile. It was around that time Su-sanna submitted her resignation as treasurer and committee member, citing health issues. Once again, I had to file the report. This time there was a lot more donation and expenditure data to enter into the report. Only after a weekend of eight hour days entering every individual contribution (first and last name, 3 or 4 part address, employer and job title) did I call our reviewing analyst to ask if there was a shortcut. As it turned out, I could combine all the small contributions into one generic contribution which saved a ton of time preparing the remainder of that report and all subsequent report submissions.

I called our campaign finance reviewing analyst again to ask him about our potential fine. He showed me where to find on the FEC website the calculator to determine an estimate. Because we hadn't raised that much money and weren't very late, we are liable for approximately $140.00 in late fees. With the campaign finance violations by the Clinton and Trump campaigns and their obvious and illegal coordination between campaigns and their super PACs, it's doubtful the FEC will bother coming after us. They have bigger fish to fry, but don't hold your breath waiting for the FEC to take action and uphold campaign finance law for either major party candidate.

I've reached out to other pledge-takers who volunteered to serve as treasurer for CAP PAC. By this time we were prepared to offer the next treasurer a percentage of the donations for his or her efforts. In every case I explained the applicant would need to:

- Download the user manual
- Download the FECfile application
- Watch the tutorial on donations
- Watch the tutorial on expenditures
- Follow those instructions, enter the data and upload the quarterly report.

I offered my assistance and told potential treasurers how helpful our reviewing analyst is. No one stepped up and took on the role of treasurer.

After the DNC, we were hoping to raise a lot of money on our website to run ads on television and radio for the "or bust" candidate, Jill Stein (G). Because we were no longer supporting a Democrat, it seemed inappropriate to continue to use Act Blue to raise money. We hired a website builder to take care of this for us. He was assigned administrative rights to our website. He had us purchase certain software tools we needed, and then he told us we needed to obtain a dedicated IP for our website.

I called Blue Host, where I had the primary URL directed toward my political blog, and purchased a dedicated IP. CitizensAgainstPlutocracy.org was a secondary URL on my account. The website builder then told me I needed to have the dedicated IP assigned to the secondary URL. I called Blue Host back, canceled the original dedicated IP and had one assigned to the secondary URL. That didn't work either.

I needed to cancel that order and have the dedicated IP assigned to the primary URL, and then purchase more software to use that dedicated IP in order to take donations using credit cards from the secondary URL, citizensagainstplutocracy.org. I called Blue Host five times, but for some technical difficulty they could never assign the dedicated IP back to the primary URL. From that point forward, our fund-raising was limited to donors with PayPal accounts and checks made out to Citizens Against Plutocracy PAC mailed to my home.

During the general election, we had audio tracks recorded for 30 and 60 second ads we could use for radio. A video producer, recommended by one of two people, who served as our spokesperson, never came through to put images to the audio, so I contacted the guy who produced our video ads for Bernie. He replied he was tied up for the next three months.

For those three reasons (no treasurer, no ability to accept donations using credit cards and no video advertisements), we essentially halted our fund-raising effort. Our work for the "or bust" general election candidate would have to be done, like the recruiting effort for the Bernie or Bust pledge, online by volunteers.

No group in American history had previously attempted what the RAP committee undertook to support a revolutionary before. Revolutionaries have run outside of the major parties in the United States, people like Republican Abraham Lincoln, Socialist Eugene V. Debs (whom Senator Sanders admires), Party of Socialism and Liberation candidate, Gloria LaRiva, and Green Party candidate, Jill Stein, this year.

Bernie was doing what he deemed to be safer than running outside the two major parties. He didn't want to become a spoiler like Ralph Nader, but that's who we were explicitly reminding Democrats of in our ads even though we understand Al Gore lost in 2000 on his own. (If he had carried his home state, for example, he would have been the 43rd President.) We set out to scare Democrats into voting for Senator Sanders. One of our supporters left a comment on our Bernie or Else Facebook page that I shared with our volunteers and tweeted many times, "Follow Bernie's light, or we'll be running from Trump's fire." I can only imagine how we might have changed the outcome if we'd been able to afford to run our ads on television. After the primaries were over, Bernie ended up close enough in the delegate count to put the decision about who to nominate with the establishment and/or corrupted superdelegates. They were the relatively few people we set out to warn of our intention to not vote for Hillary Clinton and push them to unite the Democratic Party by supporting Sanders using the resources we had including our relatively small budget.

The Current

The limited budget we had during the primaries was directly related to my limited time, as I was working full-time. We needed a division of labor that we didn't have. Using the FECfile application isn't rocket science, and the latest member of the RAP committee, Tom Ulcak, is preparing to take over as records keeper and file our reports for us. To every reader who donated to CAP PAC, I want to thank you again for believing in this campaign strategy enough to part with some of your hard-earned money. We sincerely appreciated your financial support.

Chapter 5
Bernie or Bust Caucus Tactics

"We delight in the beauty of the butterfly, but rarely admit the changes it has gone through to achieve that beauty."[117] ~ Maya Angelou

Iowa

The primary season began with the Iowa caucuses. We didn't have nearly the one million pledge-takers I was hoping we'd have by then, but we did have enough people to serve as an army if they were willing to do so. The question was how to deploy our Bernie or Bust "army."

I saw a Sanders campaign produced video about how the Iowa caucuses supposedly work. It explained that caucus attendees would have a chance to speak up after being segmented by candidate preference before people voted for their candidates.

That was an opportunity for Iowa pledge-takers to speak up and announce the Bernie or Bust movement wouldn't be voting in the general election for the Democratic Party nominee unless it was Senator Sanders. Using the BCC feature of AOL, I sent all Iowa pledge-takers an email explaining what we wanted them to do.

Are you going to caucus? How the Bernie or Bust pledge can work in IA

Dear Bernie or Bust pledge-taker,

We are entering Phase II of our strategy: the primary season. (Phase I is ongoing recruitment of more people to take the pledge.) To help Bernie defeat Clinton in IA, we need your help

We are a grassroots organization without the money needed to run a television ad blitz supporting Bernie for President. In Iowa, we're **not** sending out letters to the editor, press releases or doing any media work. Why not? Because in the IA caucuses, you can be much more effective than any of those ideas.

How? If you have attended a caucus previously, you know how they work. If you have not, here is a short video which conveys your opportunity to speak out BEFORE uncommitted voters and supporters of O'Malley decide who they will caucus for. https://youtu.be/W7CDk1NnzU
We're asking Bernie or Bust pledge-takers in caucus states to speak out for just 20-30 seconds or so right after the first count is done, just as you see in the video. What will you say at that point? Watch our 30 second ad we'll be running in media and take your ideas from it. https://youtu.be/tQO-PRV-s0tY

Keep it down to two sentences. You can either personalize it by starting, "I took the Bernie or Bust pledge to ..." or make it an announcement: "Thousands and thousands of voters across the nation have taken the Bernie or Bust pledge to write-in Bernie Sanders in the general election unless he is our party's nominee." At the end, please stress your version of: "Unite behind Bernie or else we risk having the GOP win the election next November." If another pledge-taker beats you to the punch, then right after he/she is done speaking, loudly add, **"I TOOK THE BERNIE OR BUST PLEDGE."**

If your caucus immediately breaks down into just two groups, then there probably is no point; but you can go ahead and make the Bernie or bust announcement anyway if you want to. RAP is interested in finding out roughly what percentage of undecided and O'Malley supporters move into the Bernie camp, so save this email until afterward and let me know please. **Your feedback is very important** as we approach Nevada, a caucus state where we have a better network in place. Please pay attention to and report the numbers or rough percentages of people moving toward Clinton vs Sanders groups in the room after the pledge movement is announced.

If anyone from the media should ask you about the Bernie or Bust pledge, please reply, "no comment." Why? We do *not* want this strategy reported in the media until our planned media blitz later in the month. Our plan is to burn through Hillary's Southern "firewall," and we'll be asking pledge-takers to submit letters to the editor, sending out press releases, coordinating the blitz, etc. We have volunteers in place to be the media there.

Thank you again for taking the pledge. I look forward to reading about the results of your efforts on Tuesday morning. In Iowa, you will convey the "leverage" to help Senator Sanders get the Party nomination for the first time in history. **You will be electioneering *pioneers*.** We're counting on you to apply the theory (leverage) to practice (persuading caucus-goers to side with Bernie Sanders for President). Do not respond to name calling from the Clinton camp. If anyone points out that there are only a few thousand "extremists" or offer some other insult, you can counter that with any part of "we're growing faster all the time. The pledge rate has had increasing momentum. The numbers will increase more as Clinton tries to out-spend Bernie on the TV and radio. By the Convention, we'll be millions of pledged voters providing insurance against corrupt super delegates." Hopefully, the Clinton supporters will be caught off guard. That's our plan: to make this as easy as possible for you to convey

#UniteBehindBernie once, loudly enough and clear, and have an influence on some caucus-goers money can't buy.

After the Iowa caucuses Sanders barely lost, I asked them how many actually spoke up. Only three replied. One reported that chaotic activities made it impossible to convey "it's going to be Bernie or bust." We needed a better plan.

Nevada

We emailed the Nevada pledge-takers before the Nevada caucuses twice, once to give them a heads up on what we were asking them to do and again to provide explicit instructions. Unlike primary and general elections, there is no prohibition against electioneering close to a caucus venue. We decided to take advantage of that opportunity. This is the second message to them:

Using the Bernie or Bust pledge to help Bernie win this Saturday in Nevada

Dear Bernie or Bust pledge-taker,

Attached is the finalized and formatted quarter-page flyer we have for voters going into caucus Saturday. After consultation, we decided against mentioning Clinton's FBI investigations, at least in NV. This is just about the pledge and a contrast between the two candidates. Revolt Against Plutocracy cannot afford to run ads, but we can get the message, **#UniteBehindBernie or lose this November**, into the hands of people lined up to caucus. Here's how:

The flyer:
If you have the capability, please print out the flyer 25 times and cut it up into quarters. If you do not have that capability, print it out once, or have someone print it out for you, and get it copied 24 times. Try to have 100 quarter-sheet flyers printed out by Saturday morning using scissors if need be, otherwise a paper cutter.

Distribution:

Some supporters of Clinton are not going to like the message. To avoid confrontation we recommend arriving before the doors at your precinct open. Wearing a hat, sunglasses and a jacket, go to the front of the line and hand them out to people who are ***not*** identifiable as either a Clinton supporter or a Sanders supporter (by a button, a shirt, etc.). If someone won't take it, keep working toward the back of the line offering them to voters. After you finish handing them out, walk away, around the corner to your car, if you drove, and otherwise out of sight. Remove or change your sunglasses, hat and jacket. If you didn't drive, perhaps use a knapsack or bag to place your hat, glasses and jacket. Go back and get into line to caucus.

Arrival:

Doors may open at 11:00 A.M., so get there at 10:55. If there are not over 100 people standing in line, wait until there are before starting.

The messenger:

What if someone gets out of line to confront you or recognizes you in the caucus and confronts you? Just tell him or her, "I'm just the messenger. Contact the website if you have a problem." Inside the caucus room, you'll be safely divided and standing with Bernie supporters. We do not expect any problems, but if someone should say something, you're "just the messenger."

Thank you. We know it's close in Nevada, and we think this will move just enough of the weak supporters of Clinton to think twice and change (back) over to the Sanders side of the room. This has never been done before, so you will be a pioneer of applied leverage. By waiting until the last minute, the Clinton machine will not know what hit them; and they won't have time to respond before people vote.

Unlike IA, we will not need reports from you unless you had any problem(s) you want to convey to us. We'll know by Saturday evening whether this worked or not.

This is the content of the quarter sheet flyer we asked them to hand out:

Attention

Genuine progressives across the nation are pledging to either write in Bernie Sanders or vote Green in the general election, unless he's the Party nominee. 14% in our party refuse to support another Wall Street-backed Democrat. As much as many of us would like to see a woman in the White House for a change, Secretary Clinton is not a change from the hawkish and pro-corporate government we are all weary of. We can't risk a repeat of 2000 and end up having a Republican appoint the next Supreme Court judges. So, if we want to win in November, we need to unite behind Bernie, an honest politician.

http://citizensagainstplutocracy.org/

For a number of reasons Sanders narrowly lost the Nevada caucus vote. We had to modify the process and get more pledge-takers to engage in this last minute tactic of electioneering. I was concerned that warning them about possibly being confronted for handing out this flyer may have scared some of the pledge-takers enough to blow off our idea to hand out the flyers. Going forward, we modified the caucus state tactic one more time.

Clinton's Dirty Tactics

Before explaining our next modification, there's a story about the Nevada caucuses the media never picked up on. From January until after the DNC in July I would search YouTube for "Bernie or Bust" videos. I found one video by a Bernie caucus precinct captain. Titled "How I became Bernie or Bust," it described a one-time Clinton supporter's experience on the day of the Nevada caucuses. Inspired by Sen. Sanders' historic candidacy, he switched from supporting Clinton to backing Bernie. It was his first experience doing campaign work, and he was asked to become a precinct captain. He arrived at his caucus venue early to get ready and met a helpful Clinton staffer from out of state. To make a long story short, after everyone else—including Sanders' delegates to the first Nevada convention—had departed, the Clinton staffer told him she had "forgotten" to tell the Sanders delegates to fill out forms she handed him. He filled out the forms based on contact information he had taken from the Sanders delegates and kept the pink copies he and the delegates would need for the first state convention. At that convention, he was conversing with other Sanders precinct captains from around the state. He told them about these forms and pulled a handful of the pink copies out of his pocket to show them. All of the captains present had pink copies they had brought with virtually the same story. The Clinton staffers didn't "forget" to hand out the required forms for the Sanders delegates to fill out: it was a systematic effort by them to suppress the delegate count at the first Nevada convention. Unfortunately, the video is missing now and could have been pulled down, perhaps, because the precinct captain has plans to continue his involvement in the Democratic Party. Bernie or Bust can't be highly regarded within Democratic Party ranks after Trump's shocking victory. Leverage is properly understood as a support strategy for the hostile take-over of a major party.

Sanders ended up winning at the first Nevada convention, and the second convention made national news. A rule change was rammed through which made a fair state convention impossible. There was a lot of commotion and Bernie's supporters were yelling and booing. For a minute at one point there was a loud chant of "Bernie or bust."

The Clinton campaign also push-polled Latino voters.[118] Push-polling is a political tactic whereby the caller makes it seem like a poll, but the questions become increasingly incriminating and "pushing" the voter away from the real target of the call, Senator Sanders in this case. Senate minority leader Harry Reid (D-NV) used his influence to have casino workers given time off to go caucus for Clinton.[119] The Democratic Party pulled out all the stops to defeat Bernie Sanders and his grassroots revolution.

Settled Tactic

After Nevada, we modified our caucus tactic a little bit. This is what I sent out to caucus state pledge-takers for the remainder of the caucuses which Sanders won … every time:

If we do not fight back today, we may was well wave the white flag

Bernie or Bust pledge-taker in Maine,

In Nevada, the Clinton machine push-polled voters (a sleazy campaign tactic) and won. We also know of only three people who handed out a version of the attached Bernie or Bust flyers to voters standing in line to caucus *including one precinct captain* who then went inside and did her job there. (This time, we added "not candidate Clinton who is under FBI investigation." Clinton/FBI - 2016 is not a winning ticket.)

In Iowa, almost no one spoke up about the Bernie or Bust pledge as Revolt Against Plutocracy recommended.

Clinton "won" both caucuses. If we, all of us who have taken the Bernie or Bust pledge, do not fight back, **we may as well wave the white flag.**

In CO and KS yesterday, many pledge-takers let caucus-goers know: #UniteBehindBernie or lose in November. How?

Revolt Against Plutocracy does not have the budget to run ads in Maine, so our approach is *grassroots activism* and really easy. Please, just print out, or have someone with a printer print out, the attached flyer this morning. Print out 25 or make 24 copies and cut them up into quarters. Arrive at your precinct Tuesday 15 minutes before the doors open and hand these out starting at the front of the line (**not inside**). Work your way to the back of the line and then get in line and do what you're going to do anyway: go inside and caucus for Bernie.

I understand you did not sign up for this when you took the Bernie or Bust pledge. We planned on asking you for donations to run ads, but our candidate is opposed to that kind of PAC activity. Therefore, we are counting on you to exercise this little act of telling people in line to caucus to #UniteBehindBernie or lose the general election, what we call #leverage. Please, don't let Bernie lose another caucus without a fight, without letting people know it's going to be Bernie as the Democratic Party nominee or President Trump.

Thank you for your help with this effort.

Below is the modified flyer. We wanted to remind caucus-goers Secretary Clinton was under FBI investigation over her emails and private server, something the Sanders campaign was not doing:

> **Attention**
> *Genuine* progressives across the nation are pledging to either write in Bernie Sanders or vote Green in the general election, unless he's the Party nominee. 14% in our party refuse to support another Wall Street-backed Democrat. As much as we would like to see a woman in the White House for a change, Hillary is not a change from the hawkish and pro-corporate government we are all weary of. We can't risk a repeat of 2000 and end up having a Republican appoint the next Supreme Court judges. If we want to win in November, we need to unite behind Bernie, not candidate Clinton who is under FBI investigation.
>
> http://citizensagainstplutocracy.org/

We will never know with certainty how many pledge-takers deployed this tactic. We do know Sanders won the remaining caucuses often by a large number. In Montana, we had very few people who had taken the pledge. I didn't realize that until after sorting the pledge spreadsheets by state in preparation for the Montana caucus mailing, and Clinton did better in Montana than expected. We had a strong supporter of Bernie or Bust based in Montana, but it was too late by then to ask her to make a special effort to recruit Sanders supporters to the pledge movement. By that time, Bernie or Bust was broadly recognized as a movement.

#BustExit2

As the primary season began to wind down, Patrick Walker, the co-founder of Revolt Against Plutocracy, began to make an argument to the committee that we should present the DNC with a list of policy demands when we went to Philadelphia. He sought what was infinitely more important in his mind, actions by Clinton before the election demonstrating that her and Democrats' support for the policies he wanted to demand weren't mere lip service.

Nobody on the committee agreed with this idea. I felt it would dilute the one demand we were going to make, the demand we had been promoting since the very beginning: nominate Senator Sanders or else lose the general election. We didn't trust anything that might come out of Clinton's mouth and more important as I conveyed after Patrick departed the committee the first time, there was no way we were going to send a blast out to our pledge-takers before the general election and encourage them to vote for Hillary because she somehow "proved" her sincerity over a few party platform planks attained by Sanders or demands we might make on her. In the committee's view, that would have been a betrayal of our entire strategy.

Patrick, by contrast, was flabbergasted by what he considered blank, slack-jawed incomprehension of what he deemed to be one of his most brilliant ideas. He reasoned from what he considered an unquestionable premise: that there was not a snowball's chance in hell of swaying the superdelegates, over-whelmingly pledged in Clinton's favor, to flip to Bernie Sanders. Though our pledge numbers had spiked considerably heading into the Democratic Party Convention due to widespread belief by then that Sanders had lost primaries due to voter suppression and election fraud, Patrick judged that they were insufficient to sway superdelegates living in mortal fear of what he termed the "Clinton mafia's" proven political vindictiveness. What's more, he strongly suspected that the Democrats' "political swine" had simply become too addicted to feeding at the corporate and plutocratic trough to care about the ultimate good of the Party. In particular, the 2010 midterm elections had forcibly impressed on Patrick's mind how utterly willing Democrats were to lose to Republicans provided they could quash progressive policies and candidates likely to displease their open-handed donors, no matter how much they appealed to rank-and-file voters.

Thinking we were fools to put all our eggs in the "nominate Bernie" basket, Patrick felt he had a much better way to add credibility and force to our "or else" option of supporting Green Party candidate Jill Stein. He thought we should force Clinton to unmask her insincerity about supporting Sanders' platform policies she added to secure his endorsement by "tests" of sincerity she, under command of her donors, would surely be unwilling to meet before the general election. Releasing the transcripts of her lucrative Wall Street speeches and openly and repeatedly lobbying against the lame duck passage of the Trans-Pacific Partnership are two tests he considered important. Patrick sensed that if Clinton flatly rejected such reasonable proofs of her rightly suspect sincerity in embracing the platform Sanders had helped negotiate, the Bernie or Bust movement would seem much more reasonable to public opinion in urging its supporters to vote for Jill Stein. Democrats' adamant refusal of progressive reform would be obvious to everyone.

Patrick was angry and bitter at what he considered our knee-jerk rejection of his "inspired" proposal. Though he now feels the abrupt manner of his leaving was rash and unfair, he canceled his plans to join Bernie or Bust supporters in Philadelphia, being unwilling to spend that much time and money on what he judged a doomed strategy. Adamant in his judgment of what we were doing, he left the committee in frustration for the last time and has not been invited back.

I knew immediately whom I wanted to recruit to the committee. Niko House was the Bernie Sanders supporter, who was raising the alarm on Facebook about how through a woman named Aisha Dew either the DNC or the Clinton campaign had infiltrated the Sanders campaign in North Carolina, where he had been involved with his campaign. This person undermined local, grassroots activities in support of Sanders. I had interviewed Niko via email about his experience with her for a May 23 *Progressive Examiner* story: "Bernie or Bust pledge-taker explains HRC/DNC infiltration of Sanders campaign."

Privileged Strategy?
One of the common criticisms of Bernie or Bust is it involved white privilege. The implication was blacks and undocumented workers, among others, would be threatened by President Trump, an apparent racist. Michael Arceneaux, writing in the *Guardian* on March 7, was typical. In "Bernie Sanders or bust? That's a stance based on privilege,"[120] he asserted:

> ...like the people who voted for Ralph Nader in 2000 in protest at Al Gore, Bernie-or-nobody voters are making a decision with implications that go far beyond their narrow frame of reference ... Cling to your self-righteousness all you want, but be very clear that only some people can afford this kind of sacrifice ... there are other ways to express your disapproval besides sitting out the vote altogether.

The header image on our website, Twitter account and Facebook pages depicts the act of stuffing a ballot into a box. We never advocated staying home on Election Day. It was Benjamin Dixon, the evening I called into his show on April 20th, who suggested the false claim that "or bust" meant not voting was a form of manipulation of public opinion about our movement.

Furthermore, black and brown workers are more likely to have jobs under Trump than what Clinton would have been allowed to provide. Neoliberal "free-trade" is about, among other agenda items, reducing the cost of corporate-employed labor by moving the factories overseas and/or mechanization. On March 9th I published an *Examiner* column, "Black Democrats are voting like poor Republicans, against their self-interest," which conveyed an understanding of why outsourcing jobs adversely affects blacks more than white Americans. This had been explained by Dr. William Sprigs, chief economist for the AFL-CIO, during a conference call on March 6th to discuss the Trans-Pacific Partnership "free-trade" agreement.

Not only our spokesperson, YahNé Ndgo and Bernie or Bust supporter and podcast host Tim Black, but the pro-Bernie or Bust hosts of Let The Madness Begin, supporters, who helped RAP in Philadelphia, Robert Brown, founder of Bernie or Bust TV on YouTube, and recent RAP committee member Niko House are black Americans. Niko explained why he believed the Bernie or Bust pledge had nothing to do with white privilege in a video monologue on the topic:

> Trump has not been a direct influence on international relations with regards to waging wars, funding weaponry given eventually to terrorist groups, saying war is a business

from a financial standpoint like Hillary Clinton did. There are people who believe a Trump presidency is more dangerous than a Hillary presidency. Trump uses mere rhetoric to play on the emotional appeal of voters because he just likes power and he loves the attention that he gets ... Hillary on the other hand, her policies have reflected a lot of what Trump has said ... Hillary has already waged war on the black community... We don't have to wonder if Hillary Clinton will start a war...

To say that voting Bernie or Bust is a privilege that most of us have is hilarious because most of the people who say that are privileged themselves. Those of us voting Bernie or Bust, we can't afford incremental change ... This isn't a matter of Trump or Clinton winning office. This is a matter of the survival of democracy or the death of it, so to say you're not Bernie or Bust is an inherent privilege because there are those of us who have dealt with race relations our entire life ... If you are not Bernie or Bust, it is very obvious that you are privileged enough to have something to lose because the rest of us do not....[121]

House summarized my perspective when he told the media during our press conference in Philadelphia, "As a revolutionary, we're not scared of anyone or anything."[122]

Bernie or Bust sympathizer Reno Berkeley writes for *Inquistr*. She put together a survey to determine whether Bernie or Busters were privileged Americans or not. Turning Arceneaux's argument on its head, she wrote,[123] "it seems reasonable that voters are against Hillary not out of a sense of privilege, but more out of a sense of duty and maybe even a hint of desperation."

Berkeley's informal survey of Bernie or Busters had 4,559 responses. "At least 52 percent declared they did not consider themselves financially secure," and "nearly 53 percent agreed with the following statement: Bernie or Bust is a group of people who feel that they have nothing (or little) left to lose." Some "privilege." She asked survey takers to respond to criticism that the Bernie or Bust movement is based on racial and economic privilege. One response was interesting:

Their logic is deeply flawed. We are Bernie or Bust BE-CAUSE we are NOT economically privileged, and we cannot afford 4–8 more years of upholding the status quo and protecting the wealthy elite. Hillary supporters are privileged. They can survive and thrive in an economy where large corporations and billionaires buy our politicians and control our government. We can't. And we are ready to stand up to the establishment and push for drastic change. We want our tax dollars to support healthcare and education instead of bank bailouts, wars, and corporate subsidies.

This was essentially Niko's argument. Berkeley conveyed a response from a Clinton supporter who took the survey and "admonished the 'BernieBots' to 'stop with the riots'[124] and fall behind Hillary." This person claimed to not work, but lives in a household with an income of over $200,000. "If anything," Berkeley pointed out, "this showed the economic privilege of some Clinton supporters and not vice versa."

Chapter 6
Bernie or Bust Primary Tactics

"Flexibility is the greatest strength."[125] ~ Steven Redhead

Clinton's Firewall

Senator Sanders was ahead in the polls in the first primary in NH, so we decided to lay low and deploy our platoon of volunteers for the primary in South Carolina and the first Super Tuesday primaries on March 1 where he was behind. We didn't have the money to run ads on television, but we had a plan to burn through Secretary Clinton's southern "firewall."

I had seen a YouTube video of a young man demonstrating how to post Bernie articles on Facebook media pages. It dawned on me I could record a tutorial showing people how to do the same thing using our three ads and my interview with Tim Black.

I noticed a video of Tim Black on Twitter explaining he was Bernie or Bust (he is the host of *Tim Black At Night*.) I reached out to him on Twitter, and he agreed to be interviewed[126] for an *Examiner* piece on black support for Hillary Clinton and the Bernie or Bust strategy. The interview itself was recorded using a Google Hangout and transferred to YouTube. Tim Black is black, and he made the case that Bernie Sanders was the better candidate for black Americans as well as for taking the Bernie or Bust pledge.

I produced a video tutorial showing people how to use browser search to find a list of television stations and newspapers in South Carolina with links to their websites and asked our platoon of volunteers to do the same. Initially I recommended using a copy and paste of the station letters or newspaper name into a Facebook search bar to then copy and paste one of the three campaign ad URLs or the one of my interview with Black as a comment on a post about the Democratic Party primary in that store.

Just before the South Carolina primary, someone sent me a national media listing website, sorted by state, with hot links to TV and newspaper Facebook pages and websites. That was much easier to use for our purposes, so I recorded another tutorial[127] showing our volunteers how to use it instead of searching for media outlets state by state.

I sent another email to our platoon of volunteers:

Fellow acterprenurs,[128]

I've previously shared a website that lists news media state by state. It's far more useful than I realized, so I recorded another tutorial showing how to use it to post on any state's TV and newspaper websites and their Facebook pages starting right from that website without having to copy and paste the call letters or newspaper name into a Facebook search bar.

Nationwide media website listing: http://www.usnpl.com/tv/sctv.php

Updated tutorial showing how to use that website: https://youtu.be/aWnD9e1XnQU

Attached is an updated listing of the ads. Only copy to paste what's indented. I have also added my interview with Tim Black at the bottom. That would be useful to paste as a comment in stories about someone endorsing Hillary.

I think this is much easier to use. If you have any questions, don't hesitate to ask. Please give this effort priority. Bernie has a lot of ground to make up in SC.

For the entire primary season we were waiting for someone in the media to ask Sanders about the Bernie or Bust movement; but, astonishingly, that didn't happen until it was too late to have an impact on Democratic Party voter's consideration. We needed to run ads on television to get the demand across to more of them, but we didn't have the fund-raising potential Sanders' campaign did.

In January, a *Huffington Post* blogger, Amos Elroy, had written a post[129] about the various groups working to help Sanders outside of his campaign. He referred to the Super-Delegate Task Force, Bernie2016.TV, Bernie Sanders Video, Elect Bernie Thinkers and Revolt Against Plutocracy organizers as "acterprenurs."

> Revolt Against Plutocracy are yet another group of grassroots Acterprenurs who are using the hashtag #BernieOrBust to have voters take a pledge, indicating to Democratic Party National Convention delegates that they would not vote with the Democratic party in the general elections if Hillary is selected, but would rather write-in Bernie's name. Their hope is that delegates will be dissuaded of supporting the establishment candidate in place of the one rightfully elected in primaries and caucuses. Somewhat controversially they are also attempting to pressure voters favoring the establishment candidate to switch sides as they would realize a Hillary candidacy would cost the Party seats in the election, if not the presidency.

Throughout the primaries, I would search YouTube for Bernie or Bust. Sometime in April I found Bernie or Bust TV. Robert Brown had found out about the movement at a Sanders rally in LA when someone in the crowd yelled out "Bernie or Bust!" He recorded 60 monologues in support of the movement using Kor Element's song, "Bernie Or Bust,"[130] as the introductory music. His first video on April 16th 2016 started as a rant after the debate in New York City. He saw people discouraged after the New York State Clinton victory. He believed Sanders was robbed by Clinton. Since the election, he continues his channel as BOBTV and calls his show "Freedom in Fire."[131]

Clinton destroyed Sanders in South Carolina, Alabama, Arkansas, Georgia, Tennessee, Texas and Virginia. She also narrowly won in Massachusetts, the state represented by "progressive" Sen. Elizabeth Warren who never did endorse Sanders despite our nearly 24,000 signature petition for her to do so. Although Bernie took Colorado, Vermont, Minnesota and Oklahoma, he lost in every state we targeted with our volunteer-based online advertising tactic.

I have no idea how many people in our platoon of volunteers actually made the effort to post our ads, but what we were doing wasn't working.

Here we were in March, and we still hadn't found someone to serve as our spokesperson. On that first super Tuesday, March 1, I saw messages come into our Facebook page while at work from Fox News and CNN asking someone from our organization to come on and discuss our movement. It wasn't until I got home I that found out why. The *Washington Times* had finally covered our movement. Reporter Kelly Riddell reported, "The movement is called 'Bernie or Bust,' and it means just that: If Sen. Bernard Sanders of Vermont loses the Democratic presidential nomination, a group of his supporters will either write in his name in the general election or consider casting their ballot for a Republican." We never considered or advocated casting ballots for "a Republican," but the coverage was enough to attract the interest of mainstream media. Riddell continued:[132]

> More than 50,000 people already have signed up at the Revolt Against Plutocracy, pledging to vote for the Green Party candidate in the general election or write in Mr. Sanders' name if Mrs. Clinton wins the Democratic nomination. Other groups, such as Grassroots Action for Bernie, are taking to social media, using Facebook and Twitter to try to get the "Bernieorbust" hashtag trending.

There was no link provided to our website, but we got a lot more traffic from search engines than usual over the next 48-hour period.

On Fox Business News

We hadn't found anyone else to be our spokesperson, so I had phone conversations with the staffers from Fox and CNN. Fox wanted me to come on Neil Cavuto's *Coast to Coast* on the Fox Business Network channel. They made the arrangements with the television studio in town at Cornell University. I got dressed in business attire, went to the studio and nervously sat in front of a camera, earpiece ready, waiting for Cavuto to shift from discussion about the Republican primary campaign to the Democratic primaries:[133]

Cavuto: In the meantime though, this is not something that just fractures one party. The Democrats have their own passions to deal with including those who are with Hillary Clinton versus those with Bernie Sanders. [@BernieOrBust] is with a group called Revolt Against Plutocracy. It's a group that is very passionately supportive of Bernie Sanders and makes itself well known in that regard. Now [@BernieOr-Bust], it's very good to have you. You obviously want Bernie Sanders; but right now he's trailing in the polls and it's still early, but if you draw in the superdelegates and all, which I'm sure are a bone of contention to you guys, uhhh, she's half way there. So if she's the nominee, are you saying you wouldn't support her?

@BernieOrBust: That's right Neil. Thanks for having me; appreciate this. We cannot support Hillary for President. She is not a progressive. Every time she makes that claim, she's lying. She's a neoliberal. She's going to support hy-drofracking, and she's every bit as militaristic as John Mc-Cain. And she's going to support these free-trade agreements which are nothing more than Trojan horses for international, corporate rule being imposed on our democratic order. So our position is Bernie or bust. If Bernie doesn't get the nom-ination for the Democratic Party, our 53,000 pledge-takers are going to either write-in Bernie in the general election or vote for the Green Party candidate.

Cavuto: Umm, I know you've heard this before, but that our way or highway, our candidate or no candidate, does sort of sound like sour grapes.

@BernieOrBust: It's not sour grapes. It's a revolution-ary position. First of all, what Senator Sanders is doing, using an establishment to undertake a political revolution, is historically unprecedented in this country. And what we're trying to do, which is to use the leverage of telling Democrats: you have a choice. Either unite behind Bernie Sanders or else you're going to see a Republican win the general election. That's never been done before as a primary campaign tactic on a national scale either. Our intention is to use the synergy of Sanders' really well-run campaign and our grassroots movement to tell Democrats, your choice is to vote for and nominate Bernie Sanders or else you're going to lose the White House. This is unprecedented, and we believe the synergy will work to help Sanders…

Cavuto: But what if your candidate loses fair and square though in the delegate count, even leaving the superdelegates out of it, what then?

@BernieOrBust: So there's two choices. If he's behind in the elected, pledged delegate count, then chips fall where they may and Hillary won fair and square. We're not going to support her. We're not going to vote for her because we don't vote for the lesser of two fascists. We believe her support for these free-trade….

Cavuto: Is Donald Trump the other fascist?

@BernieOrBust: Yes, but he's opposed to the free-trade agreements; so it's really difficult to figure which of those two candidates is, in our view, more fascistic. We're not going to support either of them. Our position is we're either going to write-in Bernie Sanders or we're going to vote for the Green Party candidate.

Cavuto: Alright, we'll see what happens. @BernieOrBust, thank you for explaining what you're up to with Revolt Against Plutocracy; he's the co-founder.

Three minutes and 37 seconds wasn't much time to go into details on why the TPP was fascistic in nature; and I made little mistakes. Instead of "revolutionary position," I should have said "revolutionary commitment."

The Other Corporate Media
I never did get on Carol Costello's morning show on CNN. I don't know if someone on CNN saw my interview with Cavuto and didn't like the harsh

criticism I had for Clinton and/or the TPP; no one explained why they never had me on. They were busy covering Donald Trump though, and for one whole hour, shortly after my "postponed" appearance on CNN Newsroom, they covered a Trump press conference when he was endorsed by Ben Carson.

Despite frequent tweets to MSNBC, Rachel Maddow and Chris Hayes, the phrase "Bernie or bust" was never mentioned on the channel to my knowledge until after the DNC in late July. Maddow then referred to the movement as a "problem."

On March 11, limousine liberal—Bill Maher— addressed our movement on his HBO program, *Real Time*. He explained some of Sanders' supporters have pledged to refuse to vote for Clinton if she is the Democratic Party nominee, calling it the "Bernie or Bust" campaign.[134]

> "On their website, they say they're revolting against the plutocracy. No, actually you'll be helping elect a plutocrat who's revolting."

I had been waiting to use a tidbit of information about Secretary Clinton I had learned on a conservative website, *The Daily Caller*.[135] I wrote and published another column on *Examiner* entitled, "Bill Maher's attack on Bernie or Bust is misleading and not revolutionary." In it I pointed out Clinton had paid herself from her campaign coffers over $250,000 in eight withdrawals. It was well known at the time she had been charging Wall Street banks about that much money for speeches. I tweeted Maher my column, but he never replied and never addressed our movement again.

Redacted Tonight VIP

After reaching out to Lee Camp, the host of Redacted Tonight, on Facebook he interviewed me for his VIP series which aired on March 31. During that interview, I elaborated on Clinton's revolting greed:[136]

> @BernieOrBust: There is no way … genuine progressives and revolutionaries in this country can support the lesser-of-two revolting plutocrats.

Camp: Explain how you came to that analysis....

@BernieOrBust: In the case of Trump, he's doing a very impressive impersonation of Benito Mussolini; and that's pretty revolting. In the case of Secretary Clinton, she's a multimillionaire. The Clintons own five very nice mansions, and that's fine. That's the American dream. Last year, however, she took $250,000 of campaign contributions that ... working class people sent her a dollar a week. She took that money out of her campaign coffers and put it in her bank account. This is ... revolting. It's like reverse Robin Hood. If she actually becomes President, she'll be President Nibor Dooh, which is Robin Hood in reverse.

On April 19 I was invited to call in to the Benjamin Dixon Show[137] to discuss Bernie or Bust for about 23 minutes, and on April 28 I was the guest on Tim Black at Night.[138] Then YahNé showed up on CNN.

2016 RACE — **CLINTON OFFERS OLIVE BRANCH TO SANDERS' VOTERS** — LIVE — CNN

YahNé Ndgo

On a CNN panel discussion of voters supporting different candidates on April 26, just before the Pennsylvania primary, YahNé Ndgo spoke up after one of the facilitators pointed out she is "Bernie or bust" and asked what she'd do if Secretary Clinton is the Democratic Party nominee, said she'd "probably vote for Jill Stein ... I have to cast my vote in a way that I believe in."

The next day she was invited back to *CNN Newsroom* with Carol Costello. She was on with Emily Tish Sussman, a campaign director with the Center for American Progress Action Fund. Showing her bias, Costello told Sussman to "convince YahNé she's wrong." Ndgo destroyed Sussman's argument by explaining toward the end of the segment:

> We don't trust what [Clinton] says, and we don't like what she's done…What I want in a leader is a President who has foresight, who has the ability to know in 1994 that there are issues with the crime bill, not to look back after thousands of lives have been destroyed and say "I made a mistake." I want someone with foresight to say "no, I'm not going to vote for the Iraq war because it's wrong," not somebody who's going to later on say "Oops, that was a mistake." I don't think our country can afford the mistakes that come with hindsight. We want someone with the foresight to make the right decision.

I reached out to YahNé that afternoon on Facebook, but she didn't get back to me. Then I found her on Twitter and made contact. She readily agreed to join the RAP decision-making committee and become our spokesperson. She later told me she had gotten hundreds of messages on Facebook and could not get to them all.

I had also just recruited Greg Haddock from Twitter to be a spokesperson for us. He also joined our committee and did a few interviews for us, but he was based in Germany.

By then, as Costello reminded Ndgo, Sanders was behind in the pledged delegate count. When I was on *Redacted Tonight VIP* with Lee Camp he also reminded me Sanders was behind in the delegate count. I alluded to a new tactic we were going to undertake starting in Wisconsin.

Email Tactic
Starting in Wisconsin, we decided to deploy our Bernie or Bust army online using email. I emailed every pledge-taker in that state and asked them to start building lists of the email addresses of everyone they know in the state. I told

them I would be sending a message for them to forward explaining why the United States needs a political revolution.

Dear Bernie or Bust pledge-taker in Wisconsin,

In Nevada, the Clinton machine push-polled voters (a sleazy campaign tactic) and won. We also know only three people handed out a version of the attached Bernie or bust flyers to voters standing in line to caucus there.

In CO, KS, ME, NE, KS, ID, WA, AK and HI many Bernie or bust pledge-takers let caucus-goers know: #UniteBehindBernie or lose in November. It seems to be helping.

Wisconsin is not a caucus state. Therefore, we recommend **two easy steps** you can take: **1)** use the attached flyer as the basis for a **letter to the editor**. Here's a list of WI's newspapers: http://www.usnpl.com/winews.php; just copy one of the attached flyers, paste it into a letter to the editor, personalize it and submit it for publication. **2)** Use your local/state-wide email contacts (friends, relatives, etc.) and **send them a simple email** as follows:

With the subject line: Why the United States NEEDS a political revolution.

Inside the email: Hello,

Before voting in the upcoming primary, please read this and forward it to your friends and relatives in WI:
http://www.examiner.com/article/viewpoint-explaining-why-the-united-states-needs-a-revolution

I understand you did not sign up for this when you took the Bernie or Bust pledge. We are counting on you to exercise this little act of telling people in Wisconsin to #UniteBehindBernie or lose the general election, what we call leverage. Please, don't let Bernie lose another primary with-

out a fight, without letting Democrats know if they won't follow Bernie's light, then they can run from President Trump's
fire. This has been helping Bernie win caucuses; now we start
fighting back in primary states.

   Thank you for your help with this unprecedented strategy. If you can assist us with the cost of running ads in WI,
please contribute to RAP's CAP PAC.

That *Examiner* piece, "Explaining why the United States needs a revolution,"
was my most widely read column. I sent that email using AOL on March 28th
when Sanders was behind Clinton in the polls. On April 1, I sent them another
email from AOL, again using the BCC feature:

Bernie or Bust pledge-taker in WI,

   Replying to my earlier email to most of you, Patrick wrote:
   Thank you, [@BernieOrBust.] This is a great idea —
something that ... my wife and I can do ... in addition to
[making] contributions.

   FYI, I've drafted our own email with a link to your article. It will be sent to about 300 Wisconsin citizens.

   I have attached that for you to share. Email is an effective
tool we grassroots, political revolutionaries need to better uti-
lize. His attached message can be left attached or copied and
pasted inside an email if you want, but try to think of anyone
and everyone in WI you know to send it to. Consider listservs
you may be on, friends, relatives, etc. Keep the subject as is
because it's important for people you contact to forward this
to other voters in WI they know. The Internet can be an effective tool of populist, progressive political revolution; but
only if we take the necessary but limited time to use it.

   Include in your email, if you want, my interview with
Lee Camp on Redacted Tonight: https://youtu.be
/jvAFLZpBtA0

The contents of the attached email we hoped they would forward to their in-
state contacts was written by a Buster in Wisconsin and read:

Please read these 500 words about the April 5 presidential primary.

Research by Martin Gilens and Benjamin Page proves that "…America's political system has become an oligarchy and plutocracy"—i.e., government by a wealthy few. (See Princeton Study[139]) President Carter, Noam Chomsky, Robert Reich and a host of scholars say the same. The call for a political revolution against plutocracy is widespread and necessary.

Bernie Sanders is the *only candidate* calling for that political revolution. He is the only candidate who is *not* a continuation of the hawkish, pro-corporate system launched in the 70s. He is the *only one* who sees climate change as our most urgent problem. He *alone* stands for the exercise of judgment before the leap to military action in foreign affairs (why Iraqi veteran Rep. Tulsi Gabbard endorsed him). He is the *only one* with an adequate plan to rein in Wall St. He is the *only one* who marched with MLK for civil and economic rights – an effort he has continued for 50 years.

Is Sanders electable? Don't doubt it. The polls say *yes*. [*Real Clear Politics*[140]] analytics say *yes*, because he is winning primaries in "blue" states – those that will elect a Democratic president. Political science says *yes*, because of his high favorability and trust ratings (vs. relative distrust and dislike of Clinton). Sociology says *yes*, because he is the clear alternative to Trump, Cruz, or a brokered candidate, any of whom will deepen the corporatist system. Even muckraking journalism and smear campaigning will say *yes*, because Sanders' history is actually less susceptible to attack than Clinton's (his "socialism" is not much of an issue; even mainstream media says Sanders is an FDR/New Deal Democrat whereas Clinton has a contradictory history of triage and controversy). Campaign financing says *yes*, because his campaign is financed by millions of real persons who are *voters*, not the "corporate persons" of Big Oil, Big Pharma, Big Wall St, *et al.*, which are lavishing money on the other candidates, including Clinton.

Can Sanders govern? Any Democratic president will face Republican opposition in Congress. But Sanders' election will mean a political revolution will have succeeded, with carryover to congressional elections, and that the people and the "bully pulpit" will demand action, as they did in the 30s – 40s and again in the 60s to achieve Social Security, Workers Rights, Civil Rights, Medicare, Medicaid etc. – policies thought to be impossible at those times. The presidents of those times would not recognize Hillary Clinton as a Democrat. As a Centrist she may be able to work more deals with a Republican congress – but there's a large question as to what those deals would give us: continued corporatism, more economic polarization, more militarism, and more environmental damage?

We ask you to think hard about this choice, because it is urgent. Democracy, civil/economic justice, and the planet are all at risk. A vote for Sanders in the April 5 primary will propel his campaign toward the nomination.

Senator Sanders came from behind in that contest and won it by 13.5 points, 48 pledged delegates to Clinton's 38. The superdelegates were behind Clinton 9 to 1. I thought our email tactic helped Sanders take Wisconsin, and I was inspired to continue doing this with the Bernie or Bust pledge-takers to the very last primary in on June 14.

From then on, I emailed pledge-takers state by state twice, once with instructions to build in-state email lists to forward the next message from me and the next the message to actually forward. All the while I was sending out the recruitment reminder to all new pledge-takers:

To secure the nomination, Bernie needs a miracle...
so please fulfill the second part of the pledge you took. It's ***urgent*** now
and ***easy*** to do.

Bernie or Bust pledge-taker,

Thank you for taking the Bernie or Bust pledge. In our effort to support Senator Sanders' political revolution, we must keep in mind that *only* strength in numbers can change the course of history. The pledge was designed to grow exponentially. The second part of your pledge to Bernie (recruiting just two more people to take the pledge) is easy to fulfill.

Just highlight, copy and paste:

> Bernie needs a miracle to win nomination. Will you take the Bernie or bust pledge?
>
> http://wp.me/p6itlU-4f

...into emails and/or social media messages to friends and relatives. Only when only two people reply that "yes," they will take the pledge, will the second part your voter pledge will be completed. 33% of Sanders' supporters will not vote for Hillary, and we need you help to find them for us.

Attached is a flyer you can print out, cut up and hand out to Bernie's supporters offline if you want.

We are working the caucus states with flyers for voters in line to caucus, and we have superdelegates to convince in July. A million pledge-takers may not be enough because Ralph Nader had 2.4 million votes. The Bernie or Bust pledge is the "Nader" problem Democrats can solve by uniting behind Bernie. Establishment liberals like Bill Maher are getting nervous, and that's good. If you Google "Bernie or Bust," you'll see it's exploding at this critical time.

Thank you for your help with this innovative, revolutionary primary campaign strategy.

On April 3rd I began emailing Bernie or Busters in New York:

How the Bernie or bust movement will help Senator Sanders in New York

Hello Bernie or Bust pledge-taker in NY,

In a week or so I'm going to send you an email, as I did to pledge-takers in WI last week, to forward to every Democrat/liberal/progressive you know in NY, but first let me brief you on how we have been helping Bernie win in caucus states. In IA, we asked Bernie or Busters to speak up inside the caucuses to announce the fact that Democrats are pledging to write-in Sanders if he's not the nominee, so we'd better unite behind Bernie or else lose in November. That didn't work, so we changed our approach for caucus states to ask pledge-takers print out a flyer and hand it out to people in line to go to caucus. Below the JFK quote is the contents of the flyer you can modify and submit to your local newspaper. (See #2 below.)

We have not asked Bernie or Bust pledge-takers in primary states to help out, but it's halftime and our candidate needs a come-back from over 200 delegates down to win. In WI, we started our "full-court press." We are suggesting that NY #BernieOrBust pledge-takers prioritize to 1) start gathering email addresses, 2) submit Letters-to-the-Editor and 3) build Bernie or Bust in NY.

1) In *Give Me Liberty*, Naomi Wolf suggest revolutionaries become "democracy commando force multipliers" by building a list of email contacts of people ideologically allied with you. Please start doing that for anyone you know in NY and save them in an email you **do not send out**. Please spend time you are not helping the campaign doing this in preparation for sending the people in your list our Bernie or Bust message after I get back with you next week. If it's only two people, that's better than zero; but try to make your list of email contacts as numerous as you can.

2) Highlight, copy, paste and personalize the flyer (below) to submit to your local newspaper. You don't need to add the Bernie or bust URL, but try to spend just a few minutes getting a LTE submitted to your local newspaper this week. Here is a list of most newspapers in NY: http://www.usnpl.com/nynews.php

3) Help us build our army of Bernie or bust revolutionaries in NY. Attached is a quarter sheet flyer you can print, cut up and hand out to Sandernistas offline, but please reach out to anyone you know in NY, online and offline, and ask him/her to take the Bernie or Bust pledge. Social media is helpful for this undertaking.

Much is being made about NY being "home court" for Clinton and Sanders. It's also home court to the Bernie or Bust revolution. Revolt Against Plutocracy co-founder Patrick Walker and I both live in NY. This is where we shock the Clinton machine with a defeat in her home state! The corporate media pundits, like Charles Blow in the NY Times last week, are baffled by "Bernie or Bust," but be confident. We are the adults in the room.
Bernie or bust pledge-takers are the "adults in the room"
If you get criticized, that article provides plenty of information for you to push back.
Let's "get to work" as Bernie says time and again. It's our time on the primary schedule; help us deliver NY for the revolutionary.

"Bernie or Bust pledge-takers are the 'adults in the room' " was another *Examiner* column I had written making the case only Sanders and the Green Party had an agenda that could adequately address climate change.

Sanders was speaking all across New York, so I sent pledge-takers another message asking if they were going to one of his rallies:

Are you going to a Bernie rally before the primary on the 19th?

Bernie or Bust pledge-taker,

I'm sorry to bother you again. Senator Sanders is holding rallies around the state this week. As I type this message, I'm printing out the attached flyer which I will cut up and hand out tomorrow morning to people in line to see him in Binghamton. I've conveyed already that we busters in NY are going to send out a message to all Democrats next weekend, so it's important to build our movement in NY as much as possible between now and then.

If you can only print out one and hand out four flyers, that's better than none. I'm going to try to hand out 500 flyers between 6:30 (half hour before doors open) and 8:00 when I have to go to work. The more you can print out, cut up and hand out to people in line to see Senator Sanders, the more widespread our #BernieOrBust message will be spread out across the state next weekend.

Do **NOT** hand out the flyers inside the venue. We are not part of the campaign, but "Bernie or Bust" is having an impact around the nation.

The attached flyer is not centered left to right, so you cannot cut the sheet in half lengthwise. Just cut half way between the printing both lengthwise and across. That creates two different sized flyers, but so what?

Thank you for helping with this project.

The morning Senator Sanders spoke in Binghamton, NY, I arrived around 6:45 A.M. with 2,000 of the flyers pictured below and handed them out before clocking in for work at 8:00 A.M. This flyer is one created by of our supporters for us to use:

Bernie or Bust!

Revolt Against Plutocracy

is building a movement of voters pledged to write-in Senator Sanders or vote Green Party unless he's nominated. By taking the pledge, you would be joining an army of democracy commandos who have been demanding Democrats nominate Bernie…or bust,

and **it has been working!**

Busters have been telling Democrats going into caucus to unite behind Bernie. We are going to repeat that tactic in primary states.

bernieorbust.org/

Time is short: take the pledge for democracy today and leave contact information.

I found out months later from a colleague, who went to that rally, the crowd was loudly chanting "Bernie or Bust" before and after his speech. The first known chant of "Bernie or Bust" inside a Sanders rally was on May 17th in Carson, CA. Steve Stokes, positioned to Sanders's left, yelled "BERNIE OR BUST." The crowd yelled its approval followed by many in the crowd chanting this revolutionary demand.[141]

A number of people, who took the Bernie or Bust pledge, wanted me to take them off my list. I asked them to tolerate a couple more messages from me by just taking a few seconds to delete them because I could not at the time figure out how to perform a search on the spreadsheet with thousands of names and addresses to find and delete the line containing their information. To those people, I apologize again. This is a problem I have since solved.

Before the April 19 New York primary, we ran ads in the *New York Post* and in three Gannett papers upstate. I also sent the second email to New York-based pledge-takers to forward to everyone on their lists. Because more pledges were coming in every day, I had to write it with instructions most of the New York pledge-takers had already read. In hindsight, two separate BCC blasts may have been more effective:

This is how #BernieOrBust helps defeat Clinton in the NY primary

Bernie or Bust pledge-taker in NY,

Recently, Senator Sanders wrote:

> Wall Street has contributed more than $21 million to Hillary Clinton's campaign and super PACs, and they are going to do everything they can to stop us in New York.

After the debate this week, *Politicusa* noted, "Clinton has a big delegate lead, and it would take a string of *miracle* upsets for Bernie Sanders to catch up to her." We agree, and this is how we, the #BernieOrBust "army," can help start the "miracle" in NY. Bernie or bust pledge-takers, who have read my previous messages and know what we're doing here, can skip ahead to the Instructions below. For everyone else, a short...

Briefing:
We have to do everything we can to stop the Clinton machine in New York. The Sanders campaign is not asking his supporters to become "democracy commandos." Bernie or Bust volunteers in caucus states have been handing voters lined up to go in and caucus a short message. It seems to be working, so we want you to become "democracy commando force multipliers." It's really simple, essential and it won't take long. If you have not compiled a list of

email contacts, this whole process will take you 10–30 minutes depending upon how many people in NY you can think to forward the message below to. We have thousands of pledge-takers in NY. If every #BernieOrBust pledge-taker sends out the message below, virtually the **same message volunteers have been handing to people in line to caucus**, to just 10 people on average, we'll have over 40,000 messages being forwarded by other people around the state this weekend. This tactic was used effectively by supporters of Governor Bush in 2000, and we don't have a large enough budget to run ads beyond the three Gannett papers upstate and one ad in the *NY Post* on Monday. This is our behind-the-scenes, grassroots plan to help turn what polls indicate will be a defeat coming in NY into a surprise, come-from-behind win for Bernie here. If you remember someone else to send the message to, you'll have it because you're sending the message to yourself. All you have to do is follow these simple…

Instructions:
1. **Forward** this message to yourself.
2. **Replace** the subject line with the one below the Kennedy quote at the bottom of this email.
3. **Highlight** with your mouse and delete everything above "Fellow Democrats" and below Revolt Against Plutocracy.
4. **BCC** every liberal, progressive and Democrat you know in NY. Include politicians, parents, children, everyone but colleagues.
5. **Send**.
6. **Save** this email. If anyone gives you any flack, just let them know Bernie or Busters are the "adults in the room."

http://www.examiner.com/article/bernie-or-bust-pledge-takers-are-the-adults-the-room

That's it. Once completed, you'll be a democracy commando force multiplier helping Revolt Against Plutocracy help Bernie in NY. We don't have enough pledge-takers to become #leverage yet, but we're an army of revolutionaries helping Sanders with this revolution. Thank you for helping Revolt Against Plutocracy help Bernie this way.

In solidarity,
[@BernieOrBust]
Writer, *The Syracuse Examiner*
Co-Founder, Revolt Against Plutocracy

"We, the people, are the boss, and we will get the kind of political leadership, be it good or bad, that we ***demand*** and deserve." ~ John F. Kennedy, Profiles in Courage

Use this as the Subject: **Please forward this important message to New York Democrats**

Fellow Democrats,

Genuine progressives across the nation are pledging to either write in Bernie Sanders or vote Green in the general election, unless he's the Party nominee. 14% in our party refuse to support another Wall Street-backed Democrat, and as many as 33% of Senator Sanders' supporters are telling pollsters they will not vote for Secretary Clinton in the general election. As much as we would like to see a woman in the White House for a change, Hillary is not a change from the hawkish and pro-corporate government we are all weary of. We can't risk a repeat of 2000 and end up having a Republican appoint the next Supreme Court judges. If we want to win in November, we need to unite behind Bernie and not gamble on the hope that candidate Clinton, who is under FBI investigation, doesn't get indicted before November. ***We just can't take that chance.***

The phrase, "democracy commando force multipliers," was a hot link to another column I published in *Examiner*, "Internet essential tool for revolutionaries; how to become a 'force multiplier.'" It described the email tactic we were recommending people make use of. That idea came from Naomi Wolf's book: *Give Me Liberty: A Handbook for American Revolutionaries*.[142] Her book is loaded with good ideas for starting a political movement.

I had been building email lists for years, and after I sent that message out to our pledge-takers in New York, I forwarded the email from "Fellow Democrats" on down to everyone on my personal list of ~2,000 email contacts the Sunday before the Tuesday primary. "Revolt Against Plutocracy" was a hot link to my interview with Lee Camp. Either that was a mistake, or not many people forwarded the message. New York is one of the states in news headlines[143] when it came to the Democratic Party's efforts to make peaceful revolution impossible.

Print Ads

This is a scan of one of the paid ads we ran in the paper:

We threw everything we had into helping Sanders in New York, and he took a large majority of the counties across the state. Clinton took the urban areas of the state to easily defeat him, just as she did in the general election when Trump took most of the counties across the state and lost New York. Voter suppression in the state on primary day included reduced hours for polling stations and large voter purges from Brooklyn where Bernie Sanders was born.[144] That tactic was perceived as another dirty trick from what we came to regard as the Clintoncratic Party machine.[145]

I, nonetheless, continued with this effort, hoping New York was an anomaly. In hindsight, I probably should have given up trying to deploy folks who hadn't signed up for the task and focused on fundraising to run television and radio ads. In Montana, we had very few people who had taken the pledge. I didn't realize that until after sorting the pledge spreadsheets by state in preparation for the Montana primary mailing, and Clinton did better in Montana than expected. We had a strong supporter of Bernie or Bust based in Montana, but it was too late by then to ask her to make a special effort to recruit Sanders supporters to the pledge movement. By that time, Bernie or Bust was broadly recognized as a movement.

We did some fund-raising closer to the Convention, but I was uncomfortable using our list to constantly ask for money. We should have at least tried to raise enough money to get one of our ads on MSNBC before the last Super Tuesday. The idea was to use people power to combat money power, but people had no idea that was what taking a pledge to vote for Bernie or Jill Stein included at the time they took it. The Bernie or Bust "army" was a paper tiger, and this was an ineffective online strategy.

On June 2nd, AOL suddenly and without notification started requiring a comma placed between each and every email address pasted from the spreadsheet the pledges come in on. That was very time consuming and made the final effort for contacting pledge-takers in the last Super Tuesday states difficult. After that, Washington DC was the last primary; and there were not many addresses to add a comma to.

After YahNé joined our team, we sent her to the West Coast to advocate for Bernie or Bust in Oregon and California. Immediately upon landing in Oregon she went to a Bernie office, where she met volunteers working for the campaign. She informed them of her presence, canvassed and phone banked for them, learning a bit more about the community in the process. Before heading to the West Coast, she designed flyers and had them printed out in

Oregon where she picked them up after she landed. She used the remainder of her time distributing the flyers and informing community members and campaign volunteers of the Bernie or Bust campaign. She also gave several media interviews and met with community members to discuss their support and continued promotion of the Bernie or Bust campaign.

YahNé flew back to Philly briefly, and then flew to California where she spent three weeks. During that time she traveled from San Diego to San Francisco distributing the flyers, meeting with community members to discuss their promotion of the Bernie or Bust campaign, promoting the campaign herself by meeting with media, co-organizing events, and speaking at events. Spending most of her time in the Los Angeles area, she went into a variety of neighborhoods that usually do not get much attention from campaigns, including lower-income black, Asian, and Latino communities. She spent time in public parks and at busy intersections passing out flyers, inviting people to conversation, and communicating through various official and street media makers.

In addition to Tim Black, we had another ally in the media who endorsed first the write-in strategy and shifted his to support for Jill Stein as the "or bust" option of choice. We asked H. A. Goodman, "the full-throated avatar of the Bernie-Or-Bust movement,"[146] to speak at our rally, but he had commitments elsewhere that day. He published stories in support of our strategy in *Salon*[147] and the *Huffington Post*.[148]

The Alternative Media

If you search Bernie or Bust in your browser, and click on the News tab, you'll find a lot of coverage of the movement, pro and con, in the alternative media. *Slate*,[149] *Salon*,[150] *The Atlantic*,[151] *Bustle*,[152] *Huffington Post*,[153] *Fusion*,[154] *Rolling Stone*,[155] *Mic*,[156] *Observer*,[157] *In These Times*,[158] *Inquisitr*,[159] *Think Progress*,[160] *Attn:*,[161] and the *Daily Beast*.[162] The list goes on and on. With a rare exception or two, the authors never reached out to ask us questions or for an interview. This became a source of frustration as our intentions were frequently misrepresented.

Professor Peter Gaffney, writing in *Salon*, offers an example. He asserted "Bernie or Bust will save us: The foul stench of 'lesser evilism' has made our politics useless"[163] to make an argument about political advertising and the influence the founder of modern propaganda, Edward Bernays, had on Clinton's campaign.

It is another thing entirely when advertising *is* your platform. This is political realism: the doctrine that power can and should beget more power. Political realists do not deal in constituents, they deal in consumers. And putting one in charge of fixing America's crisis of trust, incrementally or otherwise, is like putting the petroleum industry in charge of clean energy. Unfortunately for Democrats, this is also where Clinton utterly fails to distinguish herself from a candidate like Trump.

What "really is" the Bernie or Bust movement according to Gaffney? "Not the ideological purity of dreamers, or the bad sportsmanship of losers, but a struggle to do something responsible with our faith in politics now that we've found it again." Actually, it was the "ideological purity of dreamers" combined with a hard-headed demand by revolutionaries for a political revolution we call leverage. We drew a line in the sand we were not going to cross to support another neoliberal regardless of the consequences. "Faith in politics" was, if anything, lost when WikiLeaks published the emails from the DNC in late July.

I reached out to Gaffney, while writing this story, and asked him if he considered contacting us for our view on what this movement was about. He replied, "I should have quoted you. With better journalistic instincts I surely would have." That could be said about virtually every other "journalist" and columnist who wrote about the movement.

One more column about the movement warrants a direct response. Writing in the *NY Times*, columnist Charles Blow published "'Bernie or bust' Is Bonkers."[164] He referenced and transcribed part of Susan Sarandon's interview with Chris Hayes on MSNBC in late March. Blow asserted Sarandon's "comments smacked of petulance and privilege."

Be absolutely clear: While there are meaningful differences between Clinton and Sanders, either would be a far better choice for president than any of the remaining Republican contenders, especially the demagogic real estate developer. Assisting or allowing his ascendance by electoral abstinence in order to force a "revolution" is heretical.

This position is dangerous, shortsighted and self-immolating.

Our website, Facebook page and Twitter account have a header image that depicts the act of voting.

We were and remain unalterably opposed to "electoral abstinence," but he's right about the deployment of leverage: it is heretical to liberals who were willing to support neoliberals like Secretary Clinton. Liberals like Blow could not begin to understand how dangerous Clinton is, an argument I elaborate on in the next chapter and again in Chapter 10. The "privilege" is his, as Niko House explained in the last chapter. I wonder if Blow would have considered the abolitionists petulant. Like us, they were making a demand: free the slaves. Our demand, Bernie or Bust, was even more urgent. Senator Sanders was the only major party candidate who was willing to take measures needed to preserve the climate. He was the only major party candidate we trusted. Blow went on to point out, "Elections are … sometimes between common sense and catastrophe." Our view then and now remains the same; Clinton vs. Trump was a choice between two different catastrophes. It requires some uncommon sense and a good comprehension of the so-called "free-trade agreements" coming down the fast track to understand that. Blow, like virtually every other public opponent of Bernie or Bust, never replied to tweets addressed to him challenging his analysis.

Sanders On Bernie or Bust

The movement we started finally received coverage on mainstream television after YahNé mentioned it on CNN in April just before the last Super Tuesday. We kept media personalities abreast of our pledge count via Twitter. The last time was around May 13th after I covered the 100,000 pledge threshold on

Examiner. The only corporate news media channel to treat the movement as a story was CNN. They finally covered the movement once Sanders essentially had no chance of winning a majority of pledged delegates on June 3 first as a news story, interviewing activists in Philadelphia preparing for the DNC, and then again on the 5th in the form of an interview question to Sanders we had been dreading.[165] Jake Tapper asked Sanders if Bernie or Bust was "a palatable position."

"The idea that I can snap my fingers and have millions of supporters just march in line, that is not what our effort is about ... It is Secretary Clinton's job to explain to these people why she should get their support."

By then, we had gathered too many damning articles about her on our HRCC page to somehow forget we knew how unacceptably dangerous her neoliberal political economic philosophy and her neo-conservative foreign policy were for us to even consider voting for her. Bernie or Bust was a line drawn across the political terrain: we were going to vote progressive on Nov. 8 one way or another. This movement to do so was and can be used as leverage against establishment candidates running as Democrats. Libertarians could do the same in the Republican Party. The former is a commitment to revolution, and the latter is a commitment to climate counter-revolution.

We knew Bernie Sanders was never going to become "Bernie or Bust" from the beginning. The original idea was to foist him into the general election regardless of his wishes. He was never critical of the movement either, and that's all we ever wanted from him.

The mainstream media made damn sure to keep Bernie or Bust below the radar for the voters. Print media would mention us, but they were either critical or supportive of our strategy. I was interviewed several times, twice by the *Wall St. Journal*, twice by Reuters New Service and once by *Vox*, but nothing I said to the journalists made it to publication. The American media did not want our strategy to get conveyed to the public. Tapper presented viewers of his interview with this interpretation of Bernie or Bust: "These are people who say if you're not the nominee, that's it. They're out of the process...." No, we're out of the Democratic Party. We believed Tapper was misrepresenting Bernie or Bust intentionally to manipulate public opinion about the movement and/or describing a revolutionary demand through the values and perspective of the establishment's values. Were we "palatable?"

Hardcore Harel B

While the media did their best to keep the Bernie or Bust pledge movement below the public's perception and understanding, our supporters continued to promote the pledge. We wanted to go into Philadelphia showing we had momentum. To help us with that, Harel B spent just over $550 running ads on Twitter promoting the pledge for us. This volunteer, who had been involved with online activism since the 1990s and who ended up becoming an ongoing collaborator/friend of RAP, felt it was a truly make-or-break moment. This "make-or-break moment" was for Harel whether the corporate Democratic Party would do the right thing to win in November and nominate Bernie. After a string of many grassroots "moments" of millions of us trying to get the word out in person and online via email, mailing lists, social media and even paid advertising, that didn't happen. To track the success of HB's efforts, I wrote one last Bernie or Bust narrative published on July 10 which ended up with 1,344 views:

> **Hillary Clinton** is not going to be indicted for her multiple violations of federal statutes and careless handling of classified information. That means it's up to the superdelegates, and the only way they will change from voting for Clinton at the Convention this month to voting for Senator Sanders is if they become convinced nominating Hillary will cause the Party to lose in November. It is up to Sanders' supporters to do that convincing.
>
> **Bernie or Bust is a pledge** to either write in Sanders on the ballot in November or vote for the Green Party candidate. However, no one will accompany you into the voting booth, so at the end of the day, you can take the pledge to scare the superdelegates and vote however you feel you need to. We recommend the Green Party because Secretary Clinton is more dangerous and Nixonian than Donald Trump.
>
> **One million Sanders' supporters** taking the Bernie or Bust pledge will serve two purposes: 1) it will send a message to

the superdelegates to either nominate Bernie or lose in November and 2) it will send a message to Senator Sanders. He will know he has such strong support from people he may strongly consider running as a third–party candidate himself[166] in order to defeat Trump. Admittedly, this will become possible only if the Stop Trump effort of Republicans ends up putting an establishment candidate up against him.

If Clinton and Trump are your options, what do you have to lose? Please take the pledge, so we can apply the leverage of Bernie or Bust at our press conference on July 25th and again at our rally on July 26th in Philly. Only you can send the message to the superdelegates and Sanders: we will not support Hillary Clinton for President in November. Anyone can take this pledge because privacy is guaranteed.

Bernie endorsed Hillary? That does not mean the superdelegates have to vote for Clinton, especially when the progressive base can be shown rejecting her. Several possibilities are in play. 1) A combination of scandal, legal problems and health problems might cause HRC to either quit or be seen as "even more of a liability than we thought" for superdelegates. 2) The DNC might then try to have someone like Biden replace her, in which case our pledge movement will convey to Sanders he has a lot of support to run as a Green Party candidate[167] if enough of his supporters take it. 3) New fraud/corruption by DNC or the Clinton campaign in the electoral process is exposed, leading to new poll(s) showing Trump ahead of HRC. In that case, even if 1) does not happen, getting a LARGE number of pledges to not vote for Hillary could very well convince Sanders to run as a Green *despite* having previously endorsed Hillary. One million pledges (along w/other factors) could make him feel not only morally justified but also having enough popular support to do so.

To make this work, you need to become the media. Our poll indicates 59% of Bernie's supporters will not vote for Hillary in November (second paragraph, last sentence),[168] and we cannot afford the tens of thousands of dollars it would cost to find them. If millions of his supporters are unwilling to support Hilary, they can't be hard to find online. Use Twitter or Facebook messaging and even old–fashioned email to find more people to take this pledge. It's urgent, so please give this your highest priority in the next few days. Please find as many of those people as you can; it is the only hope for a political revolution to capture the White House this year.

Because of WikiLeaked emails, many voters came to find out how unpalatable the collusion between mainstream media personalities and the Clinton campaign turned out to be. The establishment media had to cover Sanders' campaign because he was drawing huge crowds and moving up in the polls nationwide. They made just as sure his grassroots, revolutionary support was not televised. They did not want voters to find out their choice for the next president was, by popular demand, Bernie Sanders or bust. They were provided the information. The corporate media is responsible for President-elect Donald Trump in more ways than one. They helped make peaceful revolution impossible, but they had a secondary role compared to the DNC and especially the superdelegates' votes at the Democratic National Convention in Philadelphia.

Chapter 7
Philadelphia: Our Last Stand, Sanders' Last Hope

"Desperate affairs require desperate measures."[169]
~Horatio Nelson

Go Green 6/19

With apparent defeats for Sanders in California and New Jersey on the last super Tuesday, June 7, we began to prepare for the first wave of what would come to be known as #DemExit. After consulting with Black Men for Bernie, YahNé suggested we organize an effort we called #GoGreen619.

June 19 is Juneteenth, the anniversary of the day emancipation was announced and the last American slaves were liberated in Texas in 1865.[170] We were going to help lead a progressive liberation from the shackles of the Democratic Party. That was five days after the final primary in DC, and I sent a blast out to our pledge-takers encouraging them to switch to the Green Party that day, a Sunday, if they could do so online and that week if they could not. This idea at this point was to send the Democratic Party elites a message: without Sanders leading your party, there was no reason to remain a Democrat.

Sanders had won enough of the pledged delegates that the superdelegates could vote at the Democratic Party Convention to nominate him, but they would have to be persuaded. We hoped a movement of Democrats changing their party affiliation would send a message to the superdelegates: either nominate Sanders or face defeat at the polls in November. We would take that message to Philadelphia and do our level best to make sure the superdelegates got the message: Bernie or Bust!

Letter To The Superdelegates

In July it dawned on me we needed to make sure the superdelegates knew exactly what was in store for the Party if they nominated Secretary Clinton. I reached out to someone who had been organizing a snail mail effort to ask the superdelegates to nominate Sanders and obtained a spreadsheet of almost all their snail mail addresses. I crafted a letter to them and started asking people to help out by printing the letter and mailing it to a share of superdelegates, preferably in their own state. The following are the contents of our letter[171] to the superdelegates, which was intended, like the flyers for Democrats going in to caucus, as a warning:

Why Donald Trump will defeat Secretary Clinton in November:

- **The Bernie or Bust movement is** not like "Party Unity My Ass." They consider Secretary Clinton more dangerous in the short run (a mistake-prone neo-con in foreign policy) and the long run (supporting the "free-trade agreements" coming down the fast-track) than Donald Trump. They make up **approximately 50% of Senator Sanders' supporters** and will not follow Bernie's lead to get behind a candidate they do not trust, like or believe.

- Senator Sanders' **delegates are planning to walk out of the convention** the moment if and when Secretary Clinton is nominated. Imagine the front page headlines around the nation the next day if that happens.

- Although Secretary Clinton will not be indicted, Trump and his super PACs will make a lot of noise about her [being] *"extremely careless in their handling of very sensitive, highly classified information"* and the lies she told about her use of private servers over the last year.

- Revolt Against Plutocracy is the organization that launched the Bernie or Bust movement. On their Facebook page and tweets, they claim if Secretary Clinton is the Party nominee, they will change the candidate designation to Jill Stein, remove the self-imposed donation limit, and raise enough money to **run ads in October in swing states to attack Secretary Clinton** from the left. Their donor base comprises over 120,000 of Senator Sanders' most ardent, anti-Clinton political revolutionaries; and that number will only grow as Green Party members and other interested parties discover their PAC.

We had another FEC report due on July 15, and this time there were a lot of donations to enter. I had to hand off the coordination of the letter-writing project. Charlie Hobbs accepted the task of doing that, and I sent out another blast to our Bernie or Bust "army" asking for volunteers to assist with this effort. Hundreds of them contacted Charlie, and we had the task completed about a week before the DNC was to begin on July 25. However, we could not be sure they even opened their mail.

YahNé lives in Philadelphia and served as coordinator for our plans to hold a press conference outside of City Hall on the 25th, the first day of the Convention, and a Bernie or Bust rally across from City Hall on the 26th. That was the day the delegates would vote to either win in November behind Senator Sanders, the most popular member of Congress in the nation, or lose in November behind one of the least liked and most distrusted politicians in American history.

We wanted to make sure the superdelegates got our message. Senator Sanders had endorsed Secretary Clinton on July 12,[172] essentially dropping his willingness to have a contested convention. Before he got up on that stage to join with her in New Hampshire, he dropped the metaphorical torch of revolution. Bernie or Bust was there, picked it up, and took it to Philadelphia, where we would hand it off to Green Party candidate for President Jill Stein if the superdelegates voted as expected.

Billboard, A Warning

We got the idea of running a billboard somewhere the superdelegates would see it. I contacted Keystone Outdoor Advertising. They had space on an electronic billboard off Route 95 between the airport and downtown Philadelphia

NOMINATE SANDERS
— OR —
LOSE IN NOVEMBER

PAID FOR BY CITIZENS AGAINST PLUTOCRACY PAC

I sent the blast asking for donations the same day Bernie endorsed Clinton. While we received enough money to pay for the billboard, I also got a lot of feedback from Busters expressing anger, frustration and a sense of betrayal toward Sanders. One Buster wrote back, "He should have not done that! I'm furious! He's a sellout. Sorry he's dragging you with him." Another wrote, "It's over. Bernie's endorsement caused me to loose (sic) all respect for him. You should focus your energy on Jill Stein, the woman who deserves to be the first woman president." A third replied, "Every movement needs a leader, and our leader has deserted us." You get the idea, but keep in mind we still had a lot of support for our last-ditch effort: "I will be in Philly all week and able to help do any volunteering you might need to progress the movement forward," one pledge-taker replied. Another wrote, "He is the only public figure I have believed in and had respect for MANY years!" and Jim was succinct: "[@BernieOrBust], you da mon!!!"

Rally Campaign Signs

We made arrangements to have 1,000 Bernie or Bust campaign signs made to hand out for our rally. We were contacted on our Facebook page by a representative of a print shop near Philly in New Jersey. We contracted to have them print the signs, and once again my wife volunteered to create the sign. She created the broken font used for "BUST," and after deciding it was to be white on a blue background, we submitted the design to the printers. The stage manager for our Bernie or Bust rally, Michelle Manos, kindly picked them up on July 22 to avoid my getting stuck in traffic going over and back Monday morning, potentially missing the press conference.

After I got the rental car parked on Sunday, July 24, I went to City Hall where various demonstrations were taking place. I found the plaza where our rally was to be held and spent the rest of the day handing out quarter-sheet flyers promoting our rally on the 26th.

Rally to demand Sanders nomination
Tuesday, July 26, noon – 3:00 P.M.
Thomas Paine Plaza
1401 JFK Blvd.
Across from City Hall
Bernieorbust2016.org
Join us to hear why Hillary Clinton is
more dangerous than Donald Trump.

Sunday Evening

YahNé had organized a Sunday evening event in Germantown with musical guests, celebrities and a showing of Josh Fox's most recent documentary, *How to Let Go of The World And Love All the Things Climate Can't Change.* The first person I met there was the unofficial surrogate for the Bernie or Bust movement, Susan Sarandon. I introduced myself and thanked her for her support. She had been on MSNBC's *All In with Chris Hayes* explaining why some of Sanders' supporters would not be voting for Secretary Clinton. The slogan "Bernie or bust" was never mentioned during the interview or on MSNBC during the entire primary season.

After meeting YahNé in the flesh, I continued to hand out the flyers and got help from someone who was camping at FDR Park. Later on Kor Element took a bunch to hand out because my voice was starting to get strained by so much talking throughout the day.

Press Conference

YahNé had decided to hold the press conference just outside of the west entrance of City Hall. Move to Amend field organizer David Cobb wanted to speak to us before the press conference, but YahNé and Niko showed up just before the presser began. As we were positioning ourselves and the media gathered in front of us the morning of July 25, an official from the city told us we had to get on city property. This meant we had to cram into the west passageway into the City Hall building. Cobb was instrumental directing our supporters holding our Bernie or Bust signs behind us to keep a path for people walking in and out of the west entrance we were compelled to squeeze into.

YahNé discussed the problems the Democrats were facing with voter registration:[173]

> You saw what happened when Hillary was endorsed by Bernie Sanders, right? Immediately the Green Party got 1000% increase in fundraising. Immediately people began to leave the Democratic Party because we don't love the Democratic Party...But this is what people need to understand...There are going to be millions of people who are going to immediately remove themselves from the Demo-

cratic Party. DemExit is not a threat. DemExit is actually going to happen…

The other thing you need to understand is that there are so many people, people who walked from Washington DC to Philadelphia. There are people who jumped into cars and cabs and trains and came all the way … There are people here from all over the place … people have thrown their entire lives into this election … I know people who are living in their cars … Those people are not going to do all of this work and then turn around and walk into that voting booth and secretly vote for Hillary Clinton. This is not the PUMA movement. We are absolutely Bernie or bust, and when we say we will never vote for Hillary, we will never ever, ever, ever, ever, ever, ever, ever, ever, EVER vote for Hillary Clinton.

Niko House discussed his experience working for the Sanders campaign in North Carolina:[174]

I was one of the ones in the beginning who broke the story about Hillary Clinton and the DNC infiltrating the Bernie Sanders campaign. We have found out from Wik- iLeaks that was true. We conspiracy theorists are looking mighty sane right now. People [ask] me all the time, "why can't I let Hillary Clinton win? Aren't you scared of Trump?"… Do I need to be scared of the person who, unfor- tunately, won the majority of the Republican votes through a legitimate election? He won by breaking records. However, on the other side of the fence, Hillary won by voter suppres- sion … Simple logic will tell you, if you run a candidate who won by suppressing votes vs a candidate who won by break- ing voting records, who do you think is going to win in an national, general election?

We're now left with a choice because the voter situation isn't limited to Hillary or Donald Trump … It affects our congressional seats, our House seats … our Senate seats. It affects every single facet of the electoral process because she won through voter suppression and election fraud. Bernie or Bust … is about the preservation of our democracy. Bernie's name just happens to be the catalyst because of what he represents to this generation … It is a symbol that we all unite [around], but that symbol is democracy. That is why we're Bernie or Bust. It has nothing to do with the fact that we don't like Hillary. We just love our democracy more….

When I spoke to the media, I talked about the letter our volunteers had mailed to the superdelegates and showed them a black and white photo of our billboard. Both of these were included in the press kits we handed out to the media present. I stressed one point I was hoping would get through to the superdelegates in town: "Bernie or Bust is not Bernie or bluff." If they nominate Hillary Clinton at this convention, the Democrats would lose the general election.

Cobb spoke to the committee members present after the rally about sending a "Please Join Move to Amend" email blast to our pledge-takers. Then I ran into rapper Maurice Randle, aka The Ultimate Rage. I had invited The Ultimate Rage to perform his song "Bernie or Bust" at our rally, and he came in with his posse from Chicago. We had lunch together and made our way to FDR Park—next to the Wells Fargo Center where the DNC was taking place—to hand out more promotional flyers for Tuesday's rally.

Bernie or Bust Rally

Green Party candidate for President Dr. Stein was invited to speak at our rally. Other speakers were to include Tim Black, Lee Camp, Debbie Lusignan (the Sane Progressive[175] on YouTube), Gary Frazier (candidate for City Council in Camden, NJ), and Niko House, and I were to speak at the rally. YahNé also spoke and performed her song, "Feel the Bern"[176] a capella. The Ultimate Rage[177] and Kor Element[178] both performed their songs, "Bernie or Bust." The schedule of speakers and performers immediately went awry when the opening act, The Ultimate Rage from Chicago, got stuck in traffic. We metaphorically tore up the schedule and forged ahead.

The single largest media audience for the demand, "Bernie or bust," occurred the night before inside of the Convention when former Sanders supporter then backing Secretary Clinton, "comedian" Sarah Silverman stated from the DNC podium, "Can I just say to the Bernie or Bust people, you're being ridiculous."[179] I didn't know until I got home Thursday, Silverman's mention generated a near-record amount of traffic to our website via browser searches and hundreds of new pledges.

One of the first people to speak at the rally was Tim Black who addressed Silverman's claim:[180]

> I watched a little clip of a little lady saying some things about Bernie or Bust. See that? Sarah Silverman has never been funny, and what she said wasn't funny. I have a reality check for Sarah Silverman. When she said Bernie or Bust people are being ridiculous. She is a phony, brother. You know what's ridiculous ladies and gentlemen? It's ridiculous that a Bernie or Bust supporter or Bernie voter would ever, ever vote Hillary.
>
> [...]
>
> Let's talk about Trump. People say, "Tim Black, what about Trump? Maybe you want to go Trump." They say, "You scared of him? You must support him if you're talking against Hillary." First of all, let's get something clear. Hillary is much more dangerous than Donald Trump. Hillary Clinton's control has power. We've learned that, right? You've learned that during the selection bit. The DNC and the Democratic Party and Hillary Clinton are able to manipulate the media. You guys know that? You say what you want to say about how dangerous Trump is, but you know what? He can't tell the media what to print.

Gary Frazier speaks in a style reminiscent of Malcolm X that cannot be conveyed in writing, but his ideas and words merit inclusion here:[181]

> I know many of you saw the first day of the DNC. Today, not even an hour ago, I just left CNN, where I was ridiculed, for calling out the First Lady…You see, you can't play on the

emotions of the race anymore because we are unified …You recalled a room, where former slaves built what you live in; that is a race card played.

We understand that this movement is bigger than a Bernie Sanders. We understood that going into this revolution. When we said "Bernie or Bust," we meant "Bernie or Bust." The Democrats for far too long have walked all over the blighted and the minority communities all across this country. They are to be held accountable for what they have done …You cannot expose us to the corruption of this political system and then ask us to get in line like sheep to go along with this same corrupted system.

What we must understand, what has brought us all together, is the unification energy that we have to see change in America, an America that speaks to the majority of its people … I see folks, who have given up their jobs, lost their homes and traveled all over this country for Bernie Sanders. I don't see that for Hillary Clinton. What I see out here are folks who understand that the buck is up. We understand we will no longer be divided. They must understand they must yield to the people. And if they do not, as the Green Party candidate that I am, we will cause a massive deregistration across this nation…

Because *Redacted Tonight* host, comedian Lee Camp, had me on his VIP series,[182] we wanted him to speak at the rally. He did not disappoint:[183] He used salty language in his speech.

How you doing, Bernie or Bust? We going to make our voices heard? Fuck ya. Feels good …This is amazing. This is what matters, not what happens in that convention center. This is people standing up.

People tell you you're too political, right? You've lost some Facebook friends, right? Too political is the way to be, alright? Be too political. All my life I've been told I'm too political. Oh Lee, you wear your politics on your sleeve, all on the outside ... I've been told I'm too political to perform on college campuses, I'm too political for most television networks, at every children's birthday I've performed at. They filled out the complaint form. We didn't like that the clown put the balloon animals inside cages and said they were factory farm balloon animals. Well fuck you; I don't care. I came here to educate these kids.

Whenever somebody tells you you're too political, tell them this. Silence is a political stance. It is a full-throated endorsement of the status quo. It is saying shut up, stop talking and get behind everything, these wars, the decimation of the middle class, of the poor people ... get behind all of that. That is what people tell you, you're too political. They are voicing that without saying it out loud ...

Bernie Sanders said all of this. We're in the middle of something very serious, and they tell us we don't have enough money to do anything, right? We don't have enough money to fix our schools. We don't have enough money to fix our infrastructure. We don't have enough money to educate, house and feed everyone. Oh but we have enough money for the largest surveillance infrastructure that has ever existed in the history of mankind. Yeah, we don't have enough money; but we have a thousand military bases around the world. Meanwhile our economy is filled with debt. Our people filled with Kentucky Fried Chicken. The chicken is filled with hormones; the hormone's filled with mercury. And we don't know what the fuck mercury is filled with because we defunded NASA.

We're in a country that put a man on the moon; we can do this shit. We can; we can fix this shit. We're in the middle of something very serious. This is dark vs light. This is evil vs good. This is Mel Gibson now vs 1993 Mel Gibson. This is a drop down, drag out, bloody fucking war for the soul of our culture, for cultural hegemony. This is something very serious, and a lot us are too dumb, medicated blissfully une-ducated to realize it. They've anesthetized us with shiny shit and zombified us with televised reality bullshit. They have done that to us, but the truth is we're like a fishbowl. We're like fish in a fishbowl. Just give us a little bit of food and a plastic treasure chest or a chest of plastic treasures, and we will never even question this, all of our thoughts and all of our soul takes place inside of a two foot bowl.

Alright? We are bigger than this. We have so much fuck-ing potential if we just think outside of this two party para-digm they force us into. It's bullshit, alright? This unfettered, unregulated capitalist domination of the mental sphere, the natural here and now, it's an extraction, it's a decimation. It's a defecation of anything and everything that matters to the average human being.

The question now is really just is whether we'll take our differences and put them aside for three seconds in order to tell the assholian than thou titans of dickery at the top to go fuck themselves...We can do this, and it's all on us now. It's a privilege to be fighting and marching along with all of you guys, alright? Just one more time I want to say KEEP FIGHTING!

Rally Speech

I was the last speaker at the Bernie or Bust rally, addressing the crowd right after Jill Stein. YahNé introduced me, and just as I got to the mic to begin speaking, Kor Element said: "You can do louder than that. He has organized this. He is Bernie or Bust. HE IS BERNIE OR BUST!"[184] I commenced:

Thank you. You have it backward. I applaud you. If you weren't here, we wouldn't be here. If you didn't go out and find more people to take the Bernie or Bust pledge, there would be no movement. You built this. Many of you con-tributed to our PAC and made this possible. We have a bill-board running between the airport and downtown that states:

NOMINATE SANDERS OR LOSE IN NOVEMBER. You paid for that. You made this possible. I applaud you. Thank you [clapping my hands] so much for making this happen.

If there's media here ... pan this plaza because this is what revolution looks like ... and this [taking a folded piece of paper out of my back pocket] is what sets it free. This is a letter our volunteers in the Bernie or Bust ... movement printed out, signed, stuffed into an envelope addressed to the superdelegates. They all have this letter. This letter tells them Bernie or Bust is not Party Unity My Ass. That was a hissy fit. This [holding the letter up] is a revolutionary commitment.

It also tells them, it's not just that we're not going to vote for Hillary. We're coming after her. We have a PAC that we have limited donations to $1,000 per person out of respect for Senator Sanders; but, if he does not come out of this [convention] as the nominee, the gloves come off. We're telling them this. We're going to be attacking her in swing states. Bernie or Bust is a 50 state strategy, so we will be building support using the super PAC for candidate B, or bust. And we're taking off the gloves, and they know this.

This letter is our get-out-of-the-two-party prison free card. If they go ahead and nominate Hillary anyway, and then Donald Trump gets elected; they can't blame us now. They know what our plans are ... If they go ahead and nominate her anyway and Trump gets elected, that's on them. This is our letter of liberation. You are now free to go about the country and vote your conscience.

If you read the media or watch what they're saying, you would think that "Bernie or bust" means if he's not the nominee, we're just going to stay home in November. This is manipulation; they want people to think we're lazy or apathetic or we don't care. That's not true. It's the opposite. We are revolutionaries. We are going to vote. We're not going to vote for Hillary Clinton, but we are going to vote.

The media would have you believe, and this comes from Comedy Central, thank you very much, that we are Bernie or Trump. We are Bernie or Jill at this point. Bernie or Green...

The media will also have us think that this is a millennial movement. We don't have a lot of demographic information other than what's on our Facebook page. Only 20% of the people who like our Facebook page are under the age of 35, which means we are mostly Gen Xers and baby boomers. This is because we remember the first Clinton administration.

Bill Clinton gave us NAFTA, which screwed millions of people out of their jobs. Bill Clinton gave us the crime bill which put hundreds of thousands of brown and black [people] in prison. Bill Clinton gave us welfare reform which threw hundreds of thousands of poor women and children into extreme poverty. And Bill Clinton gave us Wall Street deregulation which [caused] the Great Recession of 2008. And all this happened with the full-throated support of Hillary Clinton. She is not our friend. If there was a theme song for Bernie or Bust, it would have to be we "Won't Get Fooled Again."

A lot of the people who support Bernie Sanders are telling pollsters that they're going to vote for Governor Johnson, the Libertarian. Johnson and Hillary Clinton and Donald Trump are all FRACKERS! They're all equal when it comes to protecting [coastal] cities in the future from going under ocean water. They're all going to destroy civilization as we know it. They're all coming from the same [mindset]; let's destroy the Earth and make energy plentiful. We don't need to. Everything Jill Stein talked about in terms of alternative energy is off the shelf technology. It's available. We can do it. We just need the [political] will.

I need to describe Bernie or busting responsibly because we know the superdelegates may do the wrong thing. Because of the superdelegates, we may end up with Donald Trump because we are definitely not with Hillary. To do this responsibly, it's very important. I can't tell you who to vote for; it's up to you. This is our suggestion as the founders of the Bernie or bust movement.

In the Senate, vote Blue no matter who because that's how we stop Donald Trump if the superdelegates are too stupid to win this election behind Bernie Sanders. In the House we take out our revenge. Are you angry; are you pissed off? Every member of the House that endorsed Hillary Clinton goes. Out. We clean out the dirt bags in the House who endorsed Hillary Clinton ... That means the House turns [more] red, and that's how we stop Hillary Clinton if she's elected. That's a possibility because we know the system is so rigged that she stole the primary systems; and if these people who wrote this software in these voting machines did it once, they can do it again. This whole thing is rigged.

Some of the Hillbots are going to say, "You're going to help a bigot get elected to the White House." You direct them, you direct those people to hillaryantisemitism dot com because we will not vote for the lesser of two bigots.

Senator Sanders is an extraordinary leader. He wants to form another progressive organization to function inside the Democratic Party. Let's review the history. With Jesse Jackson we got the Rainbow Push. What have they done for you lately? Jerry Brown: We the People. Dennis Kucinich: Progressive Democrats of America. Howard Dean: Democracy for America. And Obama: Organizing for America. What have they done for us lately? All these progressive organizations within the Democratic Party, and we still got the fast track [bill] to corporate hell passed last year. There was not a progressive organization in this country that supported fast track. There was not a union that supported fast track, but guess who did. Hillary Clinton.

That's the line Bernie Sanders should have [drawn] during that debate. What makes you the decider of who's progressive and who's not? [Clinton wanted to know]. That fast track vote was the distinction between those who are on the payroll of the corporations and those who will still represent the people, left and right.

[I forgot to circle back at this point and add: The Democratic Party has become a hospice where progressive organizations go to die ever since the Carter and the Clintons turned it into a party of Wall Street's agenda.]

A lot people say we should vote for the lesser of two evils. We don't even buy that whole concept…Think about it. Supporters of Trump think Hillary's evil, and Hillary's supporters think Trump's evil. It doesn't make any sense. Evil is a concept that's relevant [only] to your perspective. From our view, they're both dangerous, revolting plutocrats.

Donald Trump is way more revolting; Hillary Clinton is way more dangerous in two ways. First, she is the hawk's hawk. She is John McCain in a pantsuit. Why are the Democrats putting forward a Republican like that? If that's not bad enough, FBI Director Comey said she's extremely careless with classified information. What could go wrong with that? And how many times does a candidate for the White House have to say, "I made a mistake. I made a mistake?" What could go wrong with President Oops-War Clinton? It's clear Donald Trump wants to get blood on his hands, but Hillary Clinton is already covered head to toe with the blood of innocent women and children from Iraq and Libya.

The second reason, this is important because I'm … addressing Thom Hartmann and other progressives who are arguing, "Don't make this a 50-state [strategy], you know, go ahead and hold your nose. Vote for the lesser [of two evils], and this is Chomsky, I'm addressing Noam Chomsky, who 99.9% of the time I agree with. There's no one more in the United States I respect than Chomsky, but on this issue he's wrong. We have to draw a line sometime, or else the Democrats will keep moving closer and closer to the Republican Party. 2016, we draw the line: Bernie or Bust is a 50-state strategy, and here's why she's more dangerous than Trump.

They're going to [ask], "What about his Supreme Court nominees?" They're going to be bad, but those judges are going to die off. And those decisions will eventually get overturned because this country is not regressive. In fits and spurts we are progressive. Otherwise we'd still have slavery and child labor.

Hillary, on the other hand, supports the TPP. She says she's against it. Before, she was for it. If she's against it, ask yourself what it's doing in the Party platform. We know Sanders is against it. He's been against them for years, and we know he tells the truth. Hillary Clinton claims she's against it, but she's been for these for years. And we know she lies.

This Trans-Pacific Partnership is a Trojan horse for the imposition of corporate-crafted rules and regulations that happened inside of secret negotiations. These are going to be imposed on our legislators.

[Audience member: "Corporations are not people."]

It's worse than that. It's worse than corporate personhood. They're literally overtaking our system of lawmaking. They are imposing their rules, their regulations on our representatives in government. This is a corporate coup. What they're attempting is a corporate takeover. If this thing goes through and President Clinton [implements] this thing … democratic self-government will be replaced by corporate self-government.

And it gets worse. On top of the fact that it's corporate self-rule, it's *Citizens United* on crack. *Citizens United* gave corporations [the freedom] to basically buy the democracy. The difference is the rights being asserted in the TPP have no legal sanction. They didn't even go before the Court.

They're just getting them asserted to bump up against our rights.

And these corporate rules and these corporate rights are going to be enforced by private tribunal systems that function like a legal, corporate version of a criminal protection racket. Think about it. You know how these [crime] syndicates work. They tell a business owner, "Your company is going to burn down this Saturday if you don't make payments to us, and we'll protect you." That's a criminal protection racket.

In [investor state dispute settlements], Obama stopped the Keystone XL pipeline. Good. Excellent. Good move. The company that was going to build it, Trans-Canada, is now suing us for $15B. They're suing us. When they sue the government, they're suing us … under the tribunal system of NAFTA. Thank you Bill Clinton; we really appreciate that. If they win that case, we're going to have to pay them to protect our water systems that would be under the pipeline. It's a criminal protection racket legalized in these so-called "free-trade agreements."

Even that's not what makes Hillary Clinton more dangerous than Donald Trump. There's no exit from the TPP. There's no way out of the TPP. Unlike Trump's Court decisions, there's no way out. It's permanent. We're done; it's over unless somebody runs for President on the platform of pulling out, which would be an American Brexit.

I don't have time to describe neoliberalism today because it's too complicated, so I'm going to recommend one pamphlet, online. Search One Party Planet and read it. It's free; it's 60 pages. It gives us a common understanding of what our problem is, who the enemy is, what neoliberalism is; and it puts us on the same basis for opposing their attempt to destroy the planet.

The Democrats, within a couple of hours, are going to have a choice. Either we're going to all be united against Trump and elect Bernie Sanders, or we're going to end up with President Trump. It's up to them. They have to decide.

It's appropriate today we're meeting here in Tom Paine Plaza. Paine said, "We have it in our power to begin the world over again." We have it in our power to begin the world over again. We're going to do so with the Green Party, and we're going to defeat Hillary, defeat Trump. We're going to make Jill Stein the next President of the United States if the superdelegates screw up.

I have a question for the superdelegates: what's it going to be, President Sanders or President Trump? It's up to them. In other words, putting it the same way [we]'ve been putting it for [13] months now, it's going to be Bernie or Bust.

I completely forgot to make the case against casting a write-in vote, an act we perceived by then to be a mere protest vote and a wasted opportunity to build opposition to the two major parties of corporate control. Also, my understanding of election fraud has improved since the Convention. Election integrity will be discussed in Chap. 11.

Delegate Walkout

Later that evening, the superdelegates nominated Secretary Clinton. We watched the ritualized state-by-state delegate count on a large screen in FDR Park. I left the park dejected but not surprised. After getting in the rental car, I logged into the company laptop I'd brought with me and found a story about Sanders' delegates occupying the media tent. Exhausted from a day in the near 100-degree sun, I left the park believing there was nothing more to be done in Philadelphia. I was wrong.

After I arrived at the apartment, where I was staying in Philly, I logged into the computer again and checked my Twitter account. That's where I saw a video by Josh Fox (*Gasland* director) showing hundreds of empty convention seats resulting from a walkout by Sanders' delegates. I was thrilled.

Since the last week of June, I had been quietly urging selected Sanders delegates to walk out of the Convention the moment Secretary Clinton was nominated. I was not aware until after the convention Occupy Wall Street and Movement4Bernie were also reaching out to his delegates to do the same. I didn't announce it would happen during my speech, although it was part of our letter to the superdelegates, because I had no idea they would in fact walk out at that moment.

I fell asleep around midnight, but my eyes popped open again around 3:30. The walkout, I thought, was more than a protest. It sent a message to the Party establishment they were not in control. I postponed my plan to depart that morning and sent YahNé a message: Let's get into the media tent and hold a press conference to let the Democrats know they had better change their minds or else they will lose the general election.

While I was waiting for the Black Men for Bernie rally to begin, the local NBC affiliate interviewed me about previous day's nomination of Secretary Clinton. The answer to one question is something I had forgotten to say during my speech:[185]

> NBC cameraman: Bernie is supporting the candidate you don't want [unintelligible]. What do you say to that?
>
> @BernieOrBust: We're not followers. Bernie or Bust was never a campaign strategy. Right? He was never Bernie or Bust. We're Bernie or Bust; this is a grassroots effort. This isn't up to Bernie. We're not followers; we're not sheep. We are leaders, and we're leading a political revolution. We're not political revolutionaries because of Bernie Sanders; we're Bernie or Bust because we're political revolutionaries.

I had called YahNé early, and she made acquiring credentials part of her day. We arranged to meet at the NE corner of FDR Park around 6:00 to go inside the Center and make our way to the media tent. Bruce Carter, organizer of the Blacks for Bernie and their rally, let me speak to his assembled crowd for a couple of minutes. I told the people there YahNé and I were trying to get into the media tent and I needed delegate credentials to get into the Wells Fargo Center. About a minute after I made that announcement, someone came up to me and offered me his credentials. I thanked him profusely and called YahNé to let her know I was good to go.

Then I texted a documentary filmmaker who had come up to me during the Bernie or Bust rally and told me I should have someone like him with me. He got back to me later that day, and I told him of our plans to hold a press conference in the media tent. I thought I could get him credentials to get inside because another delegate had expressed a willingness to leave the Convention and loan me her credentials to use for a couple of hours. The documentary filmmaker started to make his way to FDR Park, so we could go inside together. Unfortunately, the delegate texted me she could not break away. I called the filmmaker, who was almost to the park by then, and apologized; we could not get him in with us.

After I caught up with YahNé in the media tent, she and I went around to all of the media booths and tables announcing to no fewer than 80 publications we'd be holding a press conference to discuss last night's walk out and Bernie or bust plans going forward.[186] In hindsight, we should have made every effort to hold the presser that afternoon, before the evening news. Virtually all of the media was focused on the Convention hall, which explains why a Bernie or Bust press conference—in part addressing what the previous night's walkout meant whether the establishment knew it or not— was covered by maybe six news media organizations. We were going to help defeat Clinton in support of the Green Party candidate, Dr. Jill Stein. YahNé told the assembled media:[187]

> They're calling for unity, but the reality is the Democratic Party has not done anything to move us towards unity. They have done nothing to appeal to Bernie Sanders supporters … that is what the walkout yesterday represents. All the [Sanders] delegates are not "Bernie or Bust." But the Bernie delegates walked out because their voices haven't been heard … As soon as Bernie endorsed Hillary, her numbers dropped, and people immediately began to exit the party. The Democratic Party has been excluding the individuals who they need in order to win this election. And they're going to lose.

I didn't mince words. *Philadelphia* magazine reported[188] on our letter to the superdelegates and I added:

> They chose to believe "Bernie or Bust" was "Bernie or Bluff." What the superdelegates did yesterday was elect Don-

ald Trump to the White House. Their job as superdelegates is not to rubber stamp the results of the primaries …Their job is supposed to be to choose the candidate that has the best shot at defeating the Republican. Instead, they chose the candidate we are going to help defeat.

The same publication accurately reported neither of us wanted Trump as the next President.

Democrats will lose elections without the progressive wing of the Party base. The Clintonian, neoliberal/corporatist wing of the party probably would have been better than a Cruz presidency had he come from behind during the primaries to secure the Republican Party nomination. Keeping Clinton away from becoming Commander-In-Chief mattered more than even fighting climate change. Even if she had avoided a hot war with Russia, another cold war and attendant nuclear arms race would have accelerated under her presidency.

Chapter 8
From Bernie or Bust to Jill or Bust

"Endless war is going to be continued, whether it's Trump or Clinton."[189] ~Chris Hedges

Jill Not Hill?

When I got home on Thursday, July 28th, I immediately set about transforming our website from Bernie or Bust to one that would be supporting Jill Stein in the general election. In Philly "Jill not Hill" was virtually a constant chant after the DNC nominated Secretary Clinton.

I wanted to make the choice Americans faced as stark as possible, and in discussions with committee members on wiggio "Jill Not Hill" was rejected as too vague. Initially I made the homepage of the website and our Twitter account name Jill or Trump. It wasn't long before negative feedback came into my email account. After another few hours of back and forth on wiggio, I suggested Jill or Bust, which was accepted by all.

I spent the 29th rewriting Bernie or Bust narratives into Jill or Bust narratives and deleting posts that were no longer useful. By Saturday the pledge narratives were either deleted or converted to "Jill or Bust." I also acquired the URLs jillorbust.com, jillorbust.org and jillorbust.info. The first two point to our website, and the latter to our Revolt Against Plutocracy Facebook page.

Once the website was recrafted to support Jill Stein, I tweeted to Clinton supporter and feminist pioneer Gloria Steinem. "We'll see your woman in the White House and raise you one revolutionary, @DrJillStein." She never replied.

YahNé Goes Green

YahNé was invited to speak at the Green Party convention a week later. She was then asked to become a Stein surrogate, which meant she had to depart from the RAP committee. That was to avoid direct or indirect coordination between the Stein campaign and CAP PAC, a violation of campaign finance law.

Before she departed RAP, she suggested we build another website called Who Is Jill Stein? I requested authorization from the committee for the funds required to create such a website, and YahNé put us in touch with Darryl Arrington with Invincive Labs. He took less than a week to build a site loaded with videos of Dr. Stein being interviewed and a one minute introductory video entitled "Who is Jill Stein?" [190]

I requested another page on the website called "The Other Three Candidates"[191] to describe Trump, Clinton and Gov. Johnson, the Libertarian candidate. For Trump, I embedded a monologue by Keith Olbermann listing 176 reasons why Donald Trump shouldn't be elected President. I also embedded a video of myself explaining the 72 reasons why Secretary Clinton shouldn't be elected. I used a video of Gov. Johnson explaining at a press conference there's no reason for the government to take action on climate change because the sun would eventually grow in size and fry the Earth anyway. Once we had the website set up, any time someone on social media criticized Stein, I would reply:

> Which of these three stooges will you be supporting?
> http://www.whoisjillstein.com/the-other-three/

Another task we paid YahNé to complete before departing was to craft and narrate two campaign ads in support of Dr. Stein, which she did. She tried to put us in touch with someone who could synchronize the audio to video and still pictures, but that woman never got back to me as I indicated in Chapter 4. I reached out to the producer of our three primary ads, but he claimed he was tied up for the next three months. Without a large bankroll to pay someone to do this for us, it was not going to get done. We would not be able to run attack ads on television against Trump and Clinton on Jill Stein's behalf.

On social media we continued to promote the pledge, now to vote for Jill Stein in the general election. Like Revolt Against Plutocracy, a sizable majority of Bernie's Facebook groups switched over to support Jill Stein and the Green Party. Regardless of our movement's claims, there was a lot of #NeverHillary sentiment on Facebook. They weren't necessarily Bernie or bust; they just made that switch on their own.

Sandernista Tug Of War

RAP wanted to turn as many of Sanders' supporters away from being herded like sheep into Clinton's neoliberal fold, so on August 7th I published a post on our website[192] we asked our volunteers to share on social media.

10 reasons why no Sanders supporter should vote for Hillary Clinton

"We're not a movement where I can snap my fingers and say to you or anyone what you should do because you won't listen to me. You *shouldn't.*" [emphasis added] ~Senator Sanders

Most of Bernie's supporters are telling pollsters they are going to vote for Secretary Clinton in November, but there are many reasons why they may want to reconsider that position.

1. The Clintoncratic machine stole the primary election from Bernie.[193] Would you hire a burglar to watch your apartment while on vacation?
2. The TPP is the name of the first knife Clinton will plunge into the backs of her working and middle class supporters. Secretary Clinton is more dangerous to democratic self-government in the long run than Donald Trump would be.
3. Clinton is a neo–conservative war–monger.[194] She's Sen. McCain in a pantsuit. FBI Director Comey stated she's "extremely careless" with classified information, and she's prone to making "mistakes." You want

President Oops–War Clinton? She is terrifying with her talk of war in the Middle East. She will represent the establishment including the corporate actors within the military-industrial complex.

4. The superdelegates were warned Trump would win if they went ahead and nominated Clinton. They chose to divide the Party instead of uniting it behind Senator Sanders. They chose President Trump over President Sanders![195]

5. The Clintons are neoliberals, a pernicious form of corporate fascism (see 9th characteristic[196]). Neoliberalism is destroying our planet.[197]

6. Hillary is a bigot[198] and a covert racist.[199] You want to choose the lesser-of-two bigots, whichever one that is?

7. Party platforms are campaign documents, not governing documents. Hillary will toss the Democratic Party platform into the round file the day after the election and advance Wall Street's agenda. That's why the Wall St. bankers are paving her path to the White House with $100.00 bills, just as they did Bill Clinton before her.

8. The Clintons have a long, suspicious wake of dead bodies in their paths to power. Coincidences?[200]

9. Hillary Clinton is proud of her "conservative roots"[201] and a former supporter of segregationist Senator Barry Goldwater.

10. Clinton,[202] Trump and Libertarian Gov. Johnson all support hydrofracking of gas and oil, an extreme extraction process that

is accelerating climate change, at a time when we're already veering toward a tipping point of no return. If you want to have coastal cities around the globe under water by the next century and desert Earth sometime after that, any of those three candidates will suffice.

There is no tactical, no "less-than," reason and certainly no moral obligation to support Hillary Clinton because she is the greater of two, dangerous plutocrats.[203] The so-called "free-trade agreements" and "globalization" Clinton is running to support, are becoming a dangerous corporatization of our very system of government. "Agreements" coming from Executive Branch's "trade representative" appointee are the ninth characteristic of fascism on steroids. The TPP will not "protect" corporate power; these "trade agreements" will be corporate power grabs. Hillary Clinton is with the transnational, corporate interests intending to handcuff our representatives' power to regulate corporate behavior. The TPP would be a historically unprecedented, major leap into corporate fascism. The Clintons are not on our side. The first Clinton administration makes that clear. Noam Chomsky is wrong about who is the "lesser-evil" in this two-party contest.

Hillary Clinton does not deserve the vote of one Berniecrat. While we want a woman in the White House, we desperately need a political revolution to abolish oligarchy. The Green Party candidate, Dr. Jill Stein, is a two-for. She is the only progressive running for the White House showing up in the polls. The Green Party platform is much closer to Sanders' than any other party platform. Voting for a third party candidate will not get Trump elected because the Clintoncratic machine rigged the primary elections, and they will do the same in November. RAP intends to help build opposition to the destructive policies of neoliberals like the Clintons, and 2016 is a safe year to do so because Trump appears to be a plant trying to lose.[204] We can build an independent, revolutionary movement to rise from the ashes of a corrupt, rigged election system that cannot survive close scrutiny. There's nothing to lose, and "only" survival of our civilization to gain by voting Green in November. Please help Revolt Against Plutocracy* help Jill Stein by:

taking our #JillOrBust pledge[205] to vote for Stein in November,

quickly find just two more angry Berniecrats and anti-corruption activists to take that pledge. It's not a petition; it's a short-term commitment to build a revolutionary movement,

and donate, if you can, to our now-unleashed PAC.[206] RAP's CAP PAC intends to run ads against #CorporateClinton in support of Jill Stein in October and November as announced to the superdelegates before the DNC. Running for the White House without a super PAC in this era of peak corruption is like stepping into the boxing ring against Mohammad Ali in his prime with one hand tied behind your back. The revolution has a super PAC. RAP's PAC is a public interest committee. There are not many wealthy radicals, so CAP PAC is expected to function as a grassroots PAC supporting the best of the acceptable candidates still running for President, Dr. Stein.

Thank you. "Jill or Bust" means just that. Building a large movement behind our support for Dr. Stein will make our demand clear: elect Stein to the White House or else we'll end up with President Trump. The media will have you believe Trump is too dangerous, but he's running to Hillary's left on foreign policy and claims to be against globalization. We can be reached on Facebook for an interview, but the corporate media doesn't want to hear why Hillary is more dangerous than The Donald.

Only with enough voters support can a revolutionary movement make a difference. Let's get to work. Three months to let the voters know about #JillOrBust, the same leverage the Democrats ignored. Bernie or Bust. Or bust means casting a revolutionary vote, not a protest vote.[207] It could be a close election if Donald Trump wasn't taking a sound bite-by-bite fall to make sure Hillary wins. Clinton is corrupted by money; Trump is one of the corrupters as he bragged during the Republican primary debates. He donated money and got something in return. They are two sides of the plutocratic system RAP is opposing.[208]

Specifically pointing to the first reason listed, I frequently made the point in social media that asking a Sanders supporter to vote for Clinton is akin to hiring a burglar to house-sit for you when you're away on vacation. Regarding the eighth bullet point, I understand there to be no substantiated connection between the Clintons and their many dead opponents; but I made that campaign argument based on the reasoning of Occam's Razor. The most likely explanation for all of the dead people in the wake of the Clintons' climb to power is the simplest, i.e., a professional hit man or two working on their behalf. If that's less likely than over four dozen dead coincidences, then I don't understand the phrase "simplest explanation."

Getting Stein on the Ballot

The next task we undertook was to help Jill Stein get on the ballot in the remaining states where that was not yet the case. The following is the first post-DNC blast I sent to our pledge-takers:

> *We are not political revolutionaries because of Bernie Sanders.*
> *We were Bernie or Bust because we're political revolutionaries.*

Bernie or Bust pledge-taker,

We warned the superdelegates our movement was not "Bernie or bluff" in snail mails and again during our press conference on July 25th, but they chose a candidate we cannot and will not support for a wide range of reasons. Not least among those reasons is the election fraud which, along with a long list of sleazy but legal operations to undermine Sanders state by state, means voting for Hillary Clinton is like asking a known burglar to home-sit for you when you're on vacation!

Bernie or Bust did not work, but we're still working on the revolution we need. #JillOrBust is general election leverage. Even though it's possible the outcome is predetermined by rigged voting ... we aim to scare the hell out of liberals and 1% feminists by demanding Dr. Stein or else ... President Trump! At the Bernie or Bust rally in Philly, I argued Secretary Clinton is more dangerous than Donald Trump. There is no tactical, no "less–than," reason and certainly no moral obligation to support Hillary.

Be angry and please stay angry because then we will get even. After that, we'll win. The Green Party candidate for President urgently needs our help getting on the ballot in the following states.

CT: deadline Aug 10, need 5,000 signatures, contact [the CT Green Party state coordinator]...
MT: deadline Aug 17, need 5,000 signatures, contact [the MT Green Party state coordinator]...
AL: deadline Aug 18, need 5,000 signatures, contact [the AL Green Party state coordinator]...
NH: deadline Aug 10, need 3,000 signatures, contact [the NH Green Party state coordinator]...
MN: deadline Aug 23, need 2,000 signatures, contact [the MN Green Party state coordinator]...
DE: needs to have 650 new voters register as members of the Green Party. Easy. "Are you registered to vote?"
ID: deadline Aug 24, need 1,000 signatures, contact [the ID Green Party state coordinator]...

WY: deadline Aug 30, need 3300 signatures, contact [the WY Green Party state coordinator]…

VA: deadline Aug 26, need 5,000 signatures, contact [the VA Green Party state coordinator]…

ND: deadline Sept 5, need 4,000 signatures, contact [the ND Green Party state coordinator]…

KY: deadline Sept 9, need 5,000 signatures, contact [the KY Green Party state coordinator]…

If you do not live in one of those states, please help us find a couple of angry Berniecrats and ask them to take the new #JillOrBust pledge. Use your mouse to highlight, copy:

> Revolutionaries don't give up. Join the #JillOrBust movement and show corrupt Clintoncrats we're not afraid. http://Jillor-Bust.org

…and paste that into social media messages, posts and tweets.

We have a lot less time before the general election than we had before the primaries when we launched Bernie or Bust in June of 2015, but we are much further ahead. Our Revolt Against Plutocracy is an American movement for political revolution. That is not going to come from the three hydrofrackers: Clinton, Trump or Gov. Johnson. #SteinOrBust #JillNotHill #GreenIn2016 #SheepNoMore #WeAreNotAfraid

Thank you for your efforts, for building this movement and for your ongoing efforts to deploy online and office tactics to shock the establishment this November. This isn't something we want to do; it something we have to do to save our civilization from the ravages of neoliberal economics.

In solidarity,
@BernieOrBust
Co-Founder, Revolt Against Plutocracy

When people would click "Reply," the emails always came to my AOL inbox. There was some pushback, with some people calling me a traitor for abandoning the write-in Sanders strategy. Samples of my replies to them:

One pledge-taker was typical: "I wanted Bernie, and failing that, I will write in his name." I replied to her,

> Please listen to the monologue version
> https://youtu.be/_tjRVMf5Wk0
> ...of my Philly speech: https://www.periscope.tv/w /1ypJdPoDgMQJW
> We're not mere protesters; we're revolutionaries.

In solidarity,
@Bernie or bust

Before the DNC, we had started a petition to Senator Sanders asking him to hold talks with Jill Stein to consider running on the Green Party ticket. Another wrote: "Tell Bernie to run." I replied to him,

> We did; he won't. https://www.change.org/p/bernie-sanders-senator-sanders-speak-with-dr-stein-about-a-sanders-stein-green-ticket
> He said all along he would not; it's on us now to support the last revolutionary left standing: Jill Stein. #HillaryMade-MeGreen

In solidarity,
@Bernie or bust

Another woman wrote me:

Maybe you could explain to me, how voting for Stein would help. Surely as an unknown she would not win, so tell me how will voting for her help or make a difference.

Now that Sanders is backing Hillary, he cannot do anything and I don't trust her and Bernie shouldn't either. I believe that her acknowledging working with Bernie is just another ploy to get his votes.

Unless you can help me understand with more clarity how getting behind Stein will begin the world over again, I'm voting for Trump only to prevent Hillary from winning.

I replied to her:

A vote for Stein is a vote against Hillary, and one that is not a vote for a proto-fascist, Trump. This whole thing was rigged and will continue to be rigged. It doesn't matter who we vote for, so let's build an opposition movement/party for after the system is smashed.

I agree, Hillary is worse than Trump, but he's a racist and a buffoon. Please listen to my monologue: https://youtu.be/_tjRVMf5Wk0

or Philly speech: https://www.periscope.tv/w/1ypJd-PoDgMQJW

In solidarity,
@Bernie or bust

Before continuing with another set of replies, I want to address something this woman wrote explicitly that Secretary Clinton could not be trusted and implicitly, in agreement with my argument in Philly, that she is more dangerous than Trump. That claim is likely the most controversial part of this story, so I want to buttress it one more time since we made this argument throughout the general election period. It was an argument that was also made by Green Party candidate Dr. Jill Stein.[209]

Clinton's "Opposition" to the TPP

The Trans-Pacific Partnership trade agreement would have fundamentally transformed the United States' legal order into a system of imposed, corporate-crafted regulations. Clinton once called it the "gold standard" of "free-trade agreements" and came out against it to better compete with Senator Sanders and garner support from the unions. We did not believe her, and two of her supporters buttressed our distrust of her supposed "opposition" to it.

Gov. Terry McAuliffe, a longtime good friend of Secretary Clinton was asked on the day she was nominated during the DNC if she would support the trade deal she "opposed," and he replied,[210] "Yes. Listen, she was in support of it. There were specific things in it she wants fixed." The Governor's spokesman later clarified "McAuliffe … has no expectation Secretary Clinton would change her position on the legislation, and she has never told him anything to that effect." McAuliffe's slip wasn't the only one.

Because of WikiLeaks we also found out Rep. Eddie Bernice Johnson (D, TX) had privately told a group of her supporters, "that she speaks with HRC 2–3 times a week and that she was told by the Secretary that the only reason she opposes TPP is to get 'labor off her back' and that once she is elected President she will reverse position," according to Clinton Labor Outreach Director Nikki Budzinski.[211] Budzinski had a surrogate reach out to Johnson's Chief of Staff to "clarify the inaccuracy of what she said…." Whether or not Secretary Clinton would have implemented the TPP as President or not is to some extent moot. She was the establishment's candidate, and they want corporate globalization to advance.

I believed then and now that Clinton's "opposition" to the TPP was a false populism she learned from candidate Obama in 2008. Paul Street explains:[212]

> Obama's top economic adviser, the neoliberal University of Chicago economist Austan Goolsbee would tell Canada's U.S. ambassador to disregard Obama's criticisms[213] of the corporatist North American Free Trade Agreement (NAFTA). The criticisms were just campaign oratory geared toward winning working-class votes in the Midwest Rustbelt. Obama, Goolsbee explained, was just saying the populist-sounding

kind of stuff Democratic presidential candidates had to mouth to get nominated and elected. Obama's anti-NAFTA language was not to be taken seriously, the economist said.

One more exchange with a pledge-taker. A woman replied to me:

> I understand your desire to leap into action. I am not saying what you believe in is wrong. I am saying it is not yet time to decide. I have heard your speech and diligently listen to all others trying to make a success for a third party. The only one who could bring that off by November is Bernie with a united following. You are dividing members of the new Political Revolutionary movement which always spells defeat.
>
> Always an outside chance that Trump could drop out and Hillary could be brought down.
>
> Sadly the Green party does not have a broad enough base of support –YET. And you don't have time before November to build one. It took Bernie 15 months. And he did win the votes. They were simply stolen.

I replied simply, "The Democratic Party is a hospice where progressive groups go to die." That is a line I neglected to state during my Philly speech, and I still believe that although we wish Sanders luck remaking the Democratic Party into the progressive party of FDR (minus the internment camps).

Two Other Revolutionary Candidates

Another blast I sent to the Busters was in support of a member of the Green Party for U.S. Senate and of Nancy Pelosi's progressive opponent. I was interviewing progressive candidates for Congress as a *Progressive Examiner* reporter:

> Fellow revolutionaries,
>
> There is a push to replace members of Congress with Berniecrats and other progressive revolutionaries. Revolt Against Plutocracy fully supports this effort.

In my Philly speech at the Bernie or Bust rally on July 26th, I argued for "busting" *responsibly*. In the Senate, vote Blue no matter who to counter the possible consequences of the superdelegates choosing to lose behind Hillary. I forget to add, "with one exception: Green Party candidate for U.S. Senate, Margaret Flowers." She is probably the most qualified Green Party candidate for U.S. Senate in American history.

Please support Flowers against her Democratic Party rival, corporate darling Chris Van Hollen. Open Secrets reports his funding is coming from K Street lobbyists, including people who primarily give to Republicans. Donate to her campaign here:

https://flowersforsenate.nationbuilder.com/donate

In the House, I argued we need to clean house of the dirt-bags who endorsed Hillary Clinton. I interviewed Nancy Pelosi's challenger Preston Picus, a Bernie-Independent. He's smart, revolutionary and unabashedly progressive. You can listen to my interview with him here: https://youtu.be/ts61keqBBmY

However much you have available to donate to candidates this week, please divide it between Flowers and Picus. Support Picus' candidacy by donating here:

https://picus2016.nationbuilder.com/donate

Near the end of my speech in Thomas Paine Plaza, I quoted Paine: "We have it in our power to begin the world over again." If we do not displace the neoliberals and their corporatist agenda, the world as we know it will end all too soon. Hydrofrackers Clinton, Trump and Johnson will support policies that will see coastal cities under water in the next century.

Donating to candidates won't take much time. We must also work hard to convince ALL of the Berniecrats you know of Jill Stein is the only candidate worth supporting. Nay–sayers like Michael Moore and Noam Chomsky are locked inside the two-party prison, but the letter many of you printed out, signed, stuffed into envelopes and sent to the superdelegates was our get-out-of-the-two-party-prison free card. The superdelegates, not revolutionaries, will be responsible for Clinton losing in November. Friends don't let friends support #CorporateClinton, a dangerous and revolting plutocrat. Let's work to get Stein up to 15% in the polls, so she can participate in the debates.

Thank you for supporting these two revolutionary candidates. We can start the world over again; indeed, we must.

In solidarity,
@BernieOrBust

Promoting Who Is Jill Stein?

After the Who Is Jill Stein? website was completed, I sent out another blast:

Fellow revolutionary,

I wrote in the last blast we were working on a new website. Today, we launched it: Who Is Jill Stein? http://www.whoisjillstein.com/

I assume *you* know who she is; this is designed for us to share, as I have been on Facebook and Twitter today. Whenever you post it or tweet it, encourage people to share it. The **Home page** has a slew of videos that will be updated periodically. At the very bottom is Dr. Stein on Democracy Now addressing issues raised in the debate between the two corporate candidates this week. (Apparently, Gov. Johnson backed out of participating in that debate.)

The **About Us** tab simply links to our Facebook page. The **Jill TV** tab has two of her tweeted videos using Periscope on the left. They may or may not work for you. On the right are videos from Dr. Stein's Facebook feed.

The **Other Three Candidates** tab is provided for contrast. It features videos listing reasons why Trump and Clinton should not be elected. Gov. Johnson's video shows him talking about climate change, and it's followed by a written list of reasons Johnson is on the extreme, far right. Following them are a couple paragraphs addressing the "spoiler" argument.

The **Support** tab is still under development, but essentially it's an elaboration on the second paragraph of this blast. Share, share and share the website far and wide.

We built Bernie or Bust on a minimum budget using volunteers to spread the word about the pledge on social media. Do not underestimate what 100,000 of us can do if we put the time and effort into getting the word out. You can share the home page, the Other Three Candidates page, any page you think appropriate.

Do you use **Disqus**? You can embed the URL into a comment as follows:

> Do you really know <a href="http://www.whoisjillstein.com/"> who Jill Stein is</a>?

That will show up in a comment as:

> Do you really know <u>who Jill Stein is</u>?

You can put the URL of any page between the quote marks and your anchor word or phrase—any word or phrase you want—between > and <. I save emails with this coding to copy, paste and modify as needed rather than memorizing it.

Can we really turn the tide against corporatism and plutocracy in this election? There's only one way to find out: time and effort for the next six weeks. As Bernie said time and again, let's get to work.

In solidarity,
@BernieOrBust

Lesser Evil 2016

On October 10 I sent out yet another blast:

Fellow revolutionaries,

We have one month left to change the course of this election. While Sanders is shilling for Hillary, a militaristic and dangerous neoliberal, we're still supporting a revolutionary—Green Party candidate Jill Stein. We have two tools you can use (share, post, etc.) to help her rise in the polls against the two most unpopular major party candidates in American history.

One of our allies has created a website about Secretary Clinton:

http://www.lesserevil2016.com/index.shtml

You can share that or any of the several pages listed anytime you see stories, posts, tweets or comments favorable to Hillary Clinton.

We understand many people could not get our new website, Who is Jill Stein?, to load. One of the pages, The Other Three Candidates, has damning information about Trump, Clinton and Gov. Johnson. You can use that to counter arguments for any of those three candidates. It also makes the case to vote for the greater good at the bottom. http://www.whoisjillstein.com/the-other-three/

Finally, we hope you will contribute directly to Jill Stein's campaign. The donate button is top–right on her website. http://www.jill2016.com/

It would be helpful if she could raise the kind of money Sanders did during the primary. Please donate what you can today. We can also help in ways money can't buy. Please make part of your online time for the next 28 days promoting Jill on social media and in comments on news websites.

If anyone asserts you are making it possible for Trump to win the election, remind them it was the superdelegates who made that decision at the DNC. They were warned:

http://citizensagainstplutocracy.org/2016/07/28/dem-superdelegates-guilty-of-dereliction-of-duty/

Before the leaked speeches of Secretary Clinton were published by WikiLeaks last Friday, I was certain she would, if elected, implement the TPP. In last night's debate, she essentially admitted to having a "public" policy position and a "private" policy position on difficult issues. While I just about never agree with Trump, I believe he was right during the first debate when I asserted Clinton would implement the TPP. As I argued in Philly at the Bernie or bust rally, this so-called "free-trade agreement" makes her more dangerous than Trump, not that having him in the White House would be safe.

Senator Sanders wants to make sure Trump is defeated which is great. Our mission is to make sure Clinton is defeated. While the idea of President Stein may seem a pipe dream, I refuse to give up, to lose without fighting. I hope you'll join us in our effort to make what we need (revolution) into what we have (President-Elect Stein).

Keep in mind, those who made Sanders' political revolution impossible are members of President Kennedy's party. Given how dangerous and reactionary Secretary Clinton is, we owe the Democrats nothing. We owe it to our great grandchildren to do what we can to save the climate from the three climate change-accelerating frackers Clinton, Trump and Johnson.

In solidarity,
@BernieOrBust

The lesserevil2016.com website was produced by Harel B. Harel is a progressive who's been active online since the '90s.[214] The website is loaded with information about Secretary Clinton. In Harel's view, Clinton was worse than Trump on civil and minority rights, woman's rights, the treatment of Muslims, as a threat to world peace, as a bigot and with regard to who has "done more harm to immigrants." Harel had also produced the hillaryantisemitism.com website I referenced in my Philly speech. One of the pages of that website presents three witnesses claiming Hillary Clinton made use of the N-word, not just during the 1970s and '80s but as late as 1996 as First Lady.[215]

> Larry Patterson, a former state trooper who was assigned to protect Bill and Hillary Clinton when Mr. Clinton was governor of Arkansas, said: "I heard the first lady, Hillary Clinton, and Bill Clinton both use anti-Semitic and racial slurs. The words—this is the verbiage they used—either Jew bastard or Jew boy or Jew MF [motherfucker].
>
> "Four, five, six times. I do not remember the exact amount of times that she used this kind of verbiage, but she certainly used it on a number of occasions. When she would be upset with some of the black leaders in the state or detractors of the governor she would use the N word."

Those websites remain active as testaments to our view Hillary Clinton was not the "progressive" she repeatedly claimed she was. She wasn't even a liberal; Secretary Clinton stood for a corrupt, un–American neoliberal status quo—the conservative of the 2016 election! Harel, Patrick and I are not asserting that Hillary Clinton was worse than Trump on every issue, far from it. Her proposal for a minimum wage of $12/hour is more than what Trump will offer. Her support for "debt-free" college is better than what Trump will propose, and her Supreme Court nominees would not have been as far-right as those selected by the 45th President.

This earnest volunteer also had bumper stickers made up and sent me one.

THE WOLF IN SHEEPS CLOTHING IS ALWAYS MORE DANGEROUS THAN THE WOLF

The lesson to be drawn from this sticker was font size. It's too small to read from the distance of a driver sitting at a stop light behind one's vehicle.

Last Campaign Blast

On November 6 I sent out the last blast to the pledge-takers:

Hello,

Please read and **forward** this vital election message either individually to everyone you know and/or to every email address you have using BCC. Before sending, delete everything you see above "Hello." If you want to share this message on social media, it is available here.[216]

Four Candidates, One Safe Choice:

Secretary Hillary Clinton (D) wants to impose a no-fly zone over war-torn Syria. General Dunford, Chairman of the Joint Chiefs of Staff, told a Senate panel[217] "for us to control all the airspace in Syria would require us to go to war with Syria and Russia." She made a grave mistake voting for the Iraq war. Proving she didn't learn from that mistake, she made the deciding argument of support for the destabilization of Libya in the Obama administration; and she will pick a fight with nuclear-armed Russia if elected. While there are many reasons why she should not become the next president, a Syrian no-fly zone would pose an existential threat to the United States and the entire world if that conflict should escalate to an exchange of nuclear weapons with Russia. She is arguably the greater of two proverbial "evils." Voting for Secretary Clinton out of fear of Donald Trump is like jumping off the top of a burning sky-scraper.

Donald Trump (R) is the fire to escape from. He wants to nominate Supreme Court judges like Antonin Scalia, a supporter of the democracy-destroying *Citizens United* decision. His Court picks would set the nation back decades if the Senate were to confirm them. While less dangerous than starting a war with Russia, he is an unqualified, revolting, sexist pig who would also accelerate climate change even faster than Clinton with unregulated and pervasive hydrofracking. There are at least 176 reasons why he should not become the next president.[218]

Governor Gary Johnson (L) supports the anti-democratic Trans-Pacific Partnership, a brazen corporate power grab.[219] He opposes a minimum wage, net neutrality and any government actions to address climate change. He also supports hydrofracking, a methane-releasing oil and gas drilling technology that will accelerate climate change and lead to coastal cities around the world submerged in ocean water by next century if not sooner.

Jill Stein (G) is the metaphorical parachute voters can use to safely jump off the burning sky-scraper. She wants to:

- Eliminate all student debt
- Stabilize the economy with regulations on Wall Street banks
- Provide universal health care with Medicare for All
- Reform campaign finance
- Halt the flow of weapons into the Middle East
- Mobilize the economy for a green revolution and transform the energy sector to sustainable energy sources to slow climate change
- Stop unnecessary police violence against citizens

Do not believe the deceitful anti-Stein propaganda[220] coming from the establishment media and entertainment personalities. Many U.S. Presidents may have had prior governing and legislative experience, including President Obama; that experience has usually defined their adaptability to seriously weaken their rhetorical policy stances when confronted with the systemic, establishment, corporate power within government. Stein's lack of experience is a positive quality for a candidate seeking to rid government of corruption. We need more intelligent, high–level office-holders who have and share her "inexperience."

If enough people reject the three dangerous candidates, Dr. Stein would win the election; but if her support should fall short of the plurality needed to secure the 270 electoral college votes and win the election, Donald Trump could get elected. The most effective voting strategy citizens can use to block his Court nominees and his regressive agenda would be to make sure the next U.S. Senate is Blue/Green. If you live in MD, vote for Dr. Margaret Flowers. Otherwise, vote Blue if the contest between Democrat and the Republican is close. For example, in NY, polls indicate Senator Schumer will easily win his bid for re-election. That is a safe state to vote for the Green Party candidate for Senate.

Conclusion:
In this election voters will either take this country back from the corporate interests running it, or else war with Russia or eventually climate change will doom the human race. Not since the moral requirement to abolish slavery has the need to elect a third party candidate been so urgent. Vote your fears of warmongers Clinton, Trump and fracking Johnson by voting your conscience. Vote as if your life depends on it because it does. To stop the wars and reverse climate change, vote Green in 2016.

One of the Busters pointed out I shouldn't have listed Clinton first because it might establish an immediate, psychological connection between her and "one safe choice." I have no idea how many of our pledge-takers forwarded this blast to people around the country, but in the end, Stein/Baraka received 1.457 million votes, just barely over 1% of the total in the general election. That wasn't enough to attain the crucial 5% a party needs to become an official minor party in the U.S., but it was enough in Wisconsin, Michigan and Pennsylvania to deny the presidency to Secretary Clinton. Those accusing Stein of being a "spoiler" don't understand how dangerous corporate globalization specifically and neoliberalism in general are to American standards of living and our very system of government. More on that in Chapter 10.

Chapter 9
#OpDeny270

Write-in Redux

An early supporter of Bernie or bust and one of our best volunteers, left a Facebook comment for me on Oct. 10th.

> People are pushing several different write-in Bernie campaigns... which are FUTILE and take votes from Jill.
>
> EJUSA [Election Justice, USA] has a mole, in my opinion, sliding in the Bernie write-in on their national call... I am really ticked... this will blow their reputation.
>
> My point... Bernie write-in campaigns are hurting Jill... and need to be shut down.

She composed a series of memes, some of them blaming this new write-in effort on David Brock's Correct the Record, a Clinton super PAC; but this was not the case. On Oct. 12th, she messaged me again:

> I have been researching this whole #DemEm270 [sic] and the people pushing it... I am putting together a google doc of my findings... We are putting together a conf. call on it...I'd like to record you for it....reiterating the Bernie or Bust intention...
>
> Look at this crap... this gal is a libertarian in NV who was supposed to be a Berner: "How Bernie Sanders Could Become President With Only 130,000 Votes."

I dialed into her conference call number one day, while driving down the road; and we recorded a conversation with me explaining why we decided against the write-in strategy. The conference call service she uses has a record capability she was able to use in playback mode for a national conference call on Oct. 29th. A Q & A session followed my recorded message.

First, the article on that since deleted Embols dot com post[221] she sent me had a comment worth transcribing:

> One MASSIVE assumption in this that makes the possibility totally unrealistic. What if the EC vote ends up being 275 for Clinton and 258 for Trump? $hillary still wins, even with Bernie's 3 EC votes.
>
> The most meaningful solution for the revolution is to make sure an appropriate third party gets official acknowledgment the next time around. The appropriate party is of course the Green party. The MSM is propagandizing Jill Stein's popularity down by claiming she has only single digit support. That's horse shit, just like what they did to Bernie while he was running.
>
> We need to dump this CTR ruse and focus on what we can actually do to get our government back from the oligarchs. Writing in Bernie is not it; it will literally be throwing away our votes.
>
> For perspective, I was a #BernieorBust pledged delegate to the utterly corrupt DNC convention. Bernie was my hero.

I also thought Stein had more than the 1% support the pollsters were claiming at the time. The author of this comment also believed this strategy derived from David Brock's Correct the Record (CTR) PAC, but it did not. That was a widespread criticism of this movement, but it was based on paranoia more than anything else.

Dawn Papple
That deleted Embols post, a copy and paste job from the Michael Spark's blog,[222] began:

After reading Dawn Papple's excellent article in The Inquisitr a few days ago, about how it was theoretically possible for Bernie Sanders to still become President, I shared the article with some friends and found that they were confused at how this scenario could occur, so I decided to write my own article and hopefully answer everyone's questions, as well as recruit a few hundred people to help make this into a reality.

Papple, apparently, started something that a good number of Sanders' supporters ran with. In "Could Just Thousands in Wyoming or Vermont Hold the Key to a Surprise Bernie Sanders Presidency?"[223] she asked, "is there any chance that Sanders could end up in the White House because just thousands of people write him in?" and claimed, "it could happen in theory."

The theory was based upon the Twelfth Amendment and a whole lot of wishful thinking. Papple referenced "the National Archives," but her theory was based entirely on the Constitution's Twelfth Amendment:

> The Electors shall meet in their respective states, and vote by ballot for President and Vice-President, one of whom, at least, shall not be an inhabitant of the same state with themselves; they shall name in their ballots the person voted for as President, and in distinct ballots the person voted for as Vice-President, and they shall make distinct lists of all persons voted for as President, and all persons voted for as Vice-President and of the number of votes for each, which lists they shall sign and certify, and transmit sealed to the seat of the government of the United States, directed to the President of the Senate.
>
> The President of the Senate shall, in the presence of the Senate and House of Representatives, open all the certificates and the votes shall then be counted.
>
> The person having the greatest number of votes for President, shall be the President, if such number be a majority of the whole number of Electors appointed; and if no person have such majority, then from the persons having the

highest numbers not exceeding three on the list of those voted for as President, the House of Representatives shall choose immediately, by ballot, the President. But in choosing the President, the votes shall be taken by states, the representation from each state having one vote; a quorum for this purpose shall consist of a member or members from two-thirds of the states, and a majority of all the states shall be necessary to a choice. And if the House of Representatives shall not choose a President whenever the right of choice shall devolve upon them, before the fourth day of March next following, then the Vice-President shall act as President, as in the case of the death or other constitutional disability of the President.

The person having the greatest number of votes as Vice-President, shall be the Vice-President, if such number be a majority of the whole number of Electors appointed, and if no person have a majority, then from the two highest numbers on the list, the Senate shall choose the Vice-President; a quorum for the purpose shall consist of two-thirds of the whole number of Senators, and a majority of the whole number shall be necessary to a choice. But no person constitutionally ineligible to the office of President shall be eligible to that of Vice-President of the United States.

Attempting to be thought-provoking more than movement building, Papple wanted the voters in Wyoming and Vermont to write-in Sanders, where he would not have to be registered as a candidate; and throw the election to the next House of Representatives. "If Berniecrats won even one or two states by writing in 'Bernie Sanders,' and Trump and Clinton both fell even one electoral vote below the majority, the House of Representatives would have to choose [among] Hillary Clinton, Donald Trump, and Bernie Sanders."[224] The choice of Sanders' home state, Vermont, was obvious enough, but why Wyoming?

The liberals of Wyoming might still feel like they have a bone to pick with the DNC after they resoundingly chose

Sanders,[225] but thanks to the superdelegate system, Hillary ended up with more of their delegates. Plus, Wyoming isn't a huge Trump-supporting state. In the caucus, Trump only took 7.2 percent[226] of the Republican vote.

Handing the entirety of the state's electoral votes to Bernie Sanders instead of to one of the two candidates that they did not choose could feel very satisfying to voters in Wyoming.

Also, Berniecrats could work until the very last moments to win over the people of Wyoming, because the state offers Election Day registration. Wyoming is overwhelmingly Republican, but as of September, there were only **219,320 registered voters**. Berners are just thousands of votes away from turning that Red state Bernie Blue.

Turning Wyoming "Bernie blue" was a tall order, but if the next House of Representatives would perhaps select Sanders as the next President, it would have been worth dividing the left between support for Sanders in Vermont and Wyoming and for Jill Stein everywhere else. The problem was there was no way the next, now current, House of Representatives would elect Senator Sanders to the White House.

The Embols article focused solely on writing in Sanders in Vermont.[227]

Doesn't Bernie Have to Register As a Write-In Candidate For His Win to Be Counted?

Nope. Most states require this, but Vermont, New Jersey, Alabama, New Hampshire, Oregon, Wyoming, Delaware and Iowa do not require the candidate to register in order to win a write-in campaign.

So Why Not Organize a Write-In Campaign For All of The Above States?

It's not necessary. Bernie only needs to win one state in order to get into The House of Representatives lottery. Vermont is the easiest state to do this in ...

Run Away Write-In Train

Papple's article in *Inquistr* was sparked by a letter to the editor in the *Baltimore Sun* by Rowland E. King,[228] who was trying to get a libertarian candidate as the third option for the House of Representatives to consider, but Governor Johnson's supporters didn't make an effort to pursue that strategy. A woman named Meg was pushing #DenyEm270 since soon after the DNC in July. Her effort didn't pick up steam; but Michael Spark's Embols article, which was sparked by Papple's *Inquistr* column, did ignite another write-in movement.

Unfortunately, many of the activists, who got involved with the effort to deny Clinton and Trump 270 Electoral College votes, did not stop with Wyoming and Vermont. They created a now-deleted Facebook group, #Op-Deny270, and expanded the strategy to the states of Washington, Oregon, New Hampshire, Rhode Island, Iowa, New Jersey, Pennsylvania and Alabama: 10 states in all. Sanders supporters in California also took the initiative to get Bernie on the ballot as a write-in candidate against his will. Not only would their scheme make it virtually impossible for Dr. Stein to reach the important 5% threshold needed to make the Green Party an official and funded minor party, but it could completely backfire on them and help elect Secretary Clinton.

My Opposition

I recorded a video monologue entitled "Write in Bernie Sanders and you'll elect Hillary Clinton"[229] to explain this:

> Revolt Against Plutocracy the organization [that was] behind the Bernie or bust pledge movement which stated, nominate Bernie Sanders or we're going to go ahead and write him in anyway. Last year we discovered that was not such a good idea for a variety of reasons. It is a protest vote; it is not an act of revolution. Unfortunately, there is a movement called OpDeny270 which is attempting to write in Bernie Sanders in 10 states [to] get him electors that will vote for him in the electoral college and send this decision to the…next House of Representatives.
>
> However, on their website, they have some misleading information. They claim "This is not taking away any votes

from Jill Stein. Everyone, who will switch to Stein, already has. Nobody else is going to switch to Stein." False. Her numbers are continuing to build. The problem isn't whether more people are going to Stein or not; the problem is Bernie Sanders' supporters, who have gone to Stein, might be hoodwinked by this con job that they are undertaking to send this to the House of Representatives as if next year's House is going to elect Bernie Sanders.

It won't. It's dividing the left; it's undermining the Green Party's chances of becoming a…formal minor party. That means they need to get 5% of the national vote. So if you do this in Vermont, which is the only state Bernie Sanders says ya, go ahead and write in my name because I'm sure Hillary Clinton is going to win, they're going to [subtract] from the number of votes the Greens need to have easy access to the ballot and government funding in 2020. It's counter-revolutionary.

Their hopes, their false hopes, are based upon this going to the…next House of Representatives. I emailed the organizer of this effort, and he fired back, it's the next House. We're going to have Berniecrats elected. There are, according to the website berniecrats.net, 63 Berniecrats running, including incumbents, people who endorsed Bernie during the primaries. That's six incumbent Democrats. The rest are Berniecrats running in the Democratic Party, a few independents, three write-in candidates and four Green Party candidates on that page. That's 63 Berniecrats supporting him in the next House of Representatives if every one of them gets elected.

Remember, according to the Twelfth Amendment, which is what they keep pointing to, each state will serve as a delegation. There will be 50 votes cast for the next president if this goes to the House of Representatives. The state with the largest number of Berniecrats is California. That's six out of 55 members of the next House, if they all get elected in California, six of them out of 55 will be Berniecrats, would vote for Bernie. That's not going to carry the state. California will be carried by Representatives in the House who support Hillary Clinton.

If this isn't a strategy to help beat Donald Trump and mostly to undermine the Green Party [and] prevent them from becoming a minor party, if this isn't a strategy by the establishment to do this, it is at least misguided and misinforming. Again, from their website on their Q & A page, "if the House liked Hillary so much, why do they keep trying to prosecute her for everything?" First of all, they're not trying to prosecute her for everything, and second, they're talking about Republicans.

63 Berniecrats in the Congress are not going to elect Bernie Sanders as the next President. Republicans are not going to elect a revolutionary socialist to the White House. Again, on their website, "The entire Republican Party hates Trump." That's not true either. Something like two dozen Republican members of the House oppose Trump. The rest of them support Trump including my congressman, Tom Reed.

They're providing misinformation on their website in order to con people and take votes away from Jill, to write in Bernie which will accomplish nothing even if they do send this to the House. The only person this will help elect in the House is Hillary Clinton. If the Republicans hold onto the House, which is what most prognosticators believe will happen, they might get Donald Trump elected. If there is enough opposition to Trump from the Berniecrats and the Democrats and the Republicans who oppose Trump, they're not going to elect Bernie Sanders. They're going to elect Hillary Clinton. This is the concern.

This is a con job providing those of us who were strong supporters of Bernie Sanders a false hope that, hey, he might get elected in the House…Don't fall for this. Do not write in Bernie Sanders. The people, divided, will always be defeated, and that's what they're trying to do whether they're willingly doing it as part of the establishment, and that's who they really are, or they're well-meaning Berniecrats [who] are misguided. They are going to help elect Hillary Clinton to the White House. Don't fall for this gimmick.

Vote for Jill Stein. Let's build the Green Party. Let's get an opposition party built in this country, and let's take over. Revolutions take [power]. They don't fall for con jobs.

I spent my days sharing both my video monologue and a link to a Facebook page[230] our volunteer had set up to promote the conference call scheduled for October 29th on Facebook and Twitter. She then shared the latter along with the recording of our conversation she had made and saved online.[231] According to Jonathan Easley and Ben Kamisar writing in The Hill, with the House remaining in Republican control, it "would almost certainly certify Trump's victory."[232]

While Sanders considered any third party or write-in vote a "protest vote,"[233] we differentiated between the two. Voting for a revolutionary in the general election was a revolutionary act. Casting a write-in vote for anyone, who is not a candidate, is a protest vote.

Mende Smith Fires Back

Our volunteer and I were not the only people in the country alarmed about this. Mende Smith was a Sanders delegate at the DNC and, like those of us in the Bernie or bust movement, had shifted her support to Jill Stein. On Oct. 28th, she recorded a Facebook live stream[234] addressing OpDeny270:

> I feel extremely motivated after seeing a friend's post about being…an elector for Bernie Sanders…I'm going to use…Ballotpedia to explain this so that we all understand once and for all why Jill Stein is the choice, not Bernie Sanders…
>
> Thirty four states require candidates to register for write-ins and nine states don't allow them. Although the con-

cept of a write-in candidate sounds like you can write in whomever you feel like and have your vote count, it actually does not work that way…Most states require that a candidate registers to be a write-in candidate before your vote for him or her will count.

We needed to know that before launching a vote pledge movement, but we didn't research our idea. Whether #BernieOrGreen2016 from the very beginning would have made a difference in the general election or not can only be guessed about, a road not taken. We will never know the full impact of the write-in voters because the candidate himself needs to be in on that strategy for the effort to be counted in most states.

Mende continued:

> I love Bernie Sanders…I would love more than anything for him to be President of our United States, but it is not going to happen. It is ridiculous to take votes away from the Green Party and Dr. Jill Stein when we have worked so hard since Bernie's endorsement of Hillary Clinton and his step down of talking about any running at all…and even gone as far as to say he's not going to accept the nomination…Why are the people, who listened to every word that Bernie ever said…and now going off their heads and going, "Oh, but maybe that's not what he really meant?" It is what he really meant.
>
> Only seven states allow write-ins without registration… with no requirements. PA, NJ, VT, RI, NH, IA and OR. What's missing from that list? Could it be CA people? It's missing because…it's not an option…
>
> You're not giving old grandpa Bernie a pat on the back. You're slapping Dr. Jill Stein and the Green Party members in the face…Let's knock it off; let's wake up. Let's stay [awake] and don't just throw away a vote for Bernie Sanders. He doesn't want it…It is ridiculous for you guys to keep going on…about this.

They told us in Norwalk they remake the ballots, which means Hillary Clinton is going to get every single one of those votes in all but those few states.

Mende wasn't accurate about California's rules. The California Secretary of State's website states, "California Elections Code only specifies that 55 registered voters/electors can pledge themselves to a write-in candidate. State law does not specify that the candidate must consent to being certified as a qualified write-in candidate."[235]

On October 23rd, I sent another blast out to our pledge-takers

Fellow revolutionaries,

Those of you, who have been reading my communications, already know why the Bernie or bust organizers dropped the write-in Sanders strategy for a variety of reasons I cover in my latest video. Today, I want to 1) address the Op-Deny270 movement that is gaining some traction and 2) ask you to prepare for the next message which will help make Jill Stein the next president. Don't laugh, "it works."

1) Rather than go into detail here on the reasons why writing-in Bernie Sanders' name is a bad idea, why we dropped that strategy in favor of supporting the Green Party candidate and how Operation Deny 270 electoral college votes will in fact elect either Hillary Clinton or Donald Trump, I encourage you to view my video monologue explaining all of that here:

https://youtu.be/e-DOxmMF7HQ

Please share that video whenever you see someone online encouraging Bernie supporters to write-in Sanders' name in 10 states. It is a misguided strategy that will undermine the revolutionary movement we're helping build.

2) I have been asking you all to build mailing lists of essentially everyone you know. Naomi Wolf recommended doing this as an organizing tool in her book *Give Me Liberty: A Handbook for American Revolutionaries*. I recently read an

article on Forbes[236] of all places that reinforced this idea. "In fact, a lot of Bernie Sanders' amazing campaign success among young people has been through email. 'No one talks about email. It's not a sexy tool, but *it works*.' "[Emphasis added.]

My next message to you will be in November, and we'd like you to forward it to everyone on your email list(s) you're hopefully building. No doubt, some people will reply to you arguing that voting for Jill Stein in large numbers will get Donald Trump elected. Dr. Stein and I agree: Hillary Clinton is more dangerous than Donald Trump.[237] As Billy Taylor, a DNC protest organizer, told CNN,[238] "we're just not going to automatically vote for the demon because you're saying the devil may be there." Hillary Clinton and Donald Trump are dangerous, unacceptable candidates. #JillOrBust

The subject line of the next email to forward to everyone on your local, state and national email lists will likely be, "An important message to voters." If you have an idea that might work more effectively, reply and make your suggestion. The idea is to get people to read the message.

In solidarity
@BernieOrBust

#OpDeny270 Known Results:

In Vermont, where Senator Sanders offered limited support[239] for write-in votes, he received 18,183 write-in votes, more than Dr. Stein and Governor Johnson combined. As predicted by Sanders, Secretary Clinton easily won the state by 36 points.[240]

In California, where Sandernistas registered as electors and formalized Bernie as a write-in candidate, he received 79,341 votes,[241] amounting to 0.6% of the votes cast in that state.

In Rhode Island, there were more write-in votes (9,409) than votes cast for Jill Stein (6,188). In Iowa, write-in votes amounted to only 1.1% of the total; and the state won't even count them unless they reach 5% of the total. In Oregon, the write-in votes are counted only if the total number of them exceed the number of votes cast for the candidate who won. Clinton received over 930,000 votes there.[242]

While it's unlikely Jill Stein would have reached the 5% threshold needed to obtain minor party status if all of the write-in votes Sanders received had gone to her instead, this was clearly an effort that was not going to bear any fruit. Unfortunately, for some of Sanders' supporters, Bernie had become a cult figure. No argument could convince his cult followers to focus on revolution and abandon a scheme with no chance of success.

On November 8th one of the first states where the results came in was Vermont. Clinton garnered over 60% of the vote with over 178,000 votes. That should be the end of #OpDeny270 since most effort was directed to Vermont, and if Bernie can't take his own state, clearly he would not secure any Electoral College votes in this election.

I went to the now-deleted Deny 270 Facebook group[243] and reached out to the administrators and implored them to call off the strategy to give Stein a chance to maximize her vote count:

> @BernieOrBust: VT went to HRC. Please call off the fool's errand, unless this is just a scheme to help Trump. If not, the strategy will divide the left for nothing.
>
> Administrator A: omg r u nuts Trump won. Even a Rock is better than Hitlary... Don't write me PM again as it is harassing to my PUBLIC opinion.

Her current Facebook avatar is an upside down American flag, a sign of distress, and so is mine as of February 2017.

> @BernieOrBust: VT went to HRC. Please call off the fool's errand, unless this is just a scheme to help Trump. If not, the strategy will divide the left for nothing.
>
> Administrator B: Jill is at 1.95 % there is a fools errand, and they have only counted 40 k votes so far. YOU ARE A MAJOR ASSHOLE,,,,AND DON'T EVER CONTACT ME AGAIN

Strike two. I tried another administrator:

> @BernieOrBust: VT went to HRC. Please call off the
> fool's errand, unless this is just a scheme to help Trump. If
> not, the strategy will divide the left for nothing.
>
> Administrator C: If instead of being an idiot, you chose
> to work with us instead of against us, not only would you have
> reached your 5%, but you would have exceeded it, and we
> would have won Vermont and Washington, while McMullin
> would have taken Utah and Johnson New Mexico. But, un-
> fortunately, you and 90% of the rest of the Jill supporters are
> too stupid to realize it.

How working to divert more votes to Sanders, who was not a candidate, would
have helped Jill Stein or McMullin or Gov. Johnson is not clear. I followed
up:

> @BernieOrBust: I wagered $1,000.00 Bernie would not
> take any state all across Facebook Monday. No one took me
> up on that bet because everyone who saw that post is smarter
> than you are.
>
> Administrator C: I would have placed the exact same bet.
> But not because he didn't have a chance to win Vermont or
> Washington, but because I knew we didn't make enough
> calls. We convinced about 47% of those who we called to
> write in Bernie. Most already wanted to, but we're (sic) too
> afraid. Or didn't know it was possible.

He knew Bernie wasn't going to win one state, but he persisted with the write-
in scheme even after Clinton had won in Vermont.

He also accused me of lying because of a mistake I made. "You and your
lies took more votes away from Jill than anything that we have ever done. You,
Sir, are nothing but a liar who has spent the last month spreading misinformation." It was not until the #Deny270 movement was gaining momentum
that I finally called the California Secretary of State's office in October to find
out what happens to the ballots in California that have a write-in vote. I was

told they would be set aside and counted because 55 of Sanders' supporters registered as electors. In California, the people can make an unwilling citizen a write-in candidate. In theory that could be a road to progressive victory, but the role of big and corporate money in politics makes it nearly impossible for small donation progressive to outspend those candidates. The cost and dominance of political advertising on television will require good data and innovations for progressives to secure a seat in the House of Representatives. It will still cost a lot of money getting enough progressives elected to the next Congress for an independent outsider to secure enough votes to take over the Executive Branch of government in a three-way contest.

A Mistake Is Not a Lie

My "lie" was repeating what we had been told on Facebook three times in my first, now deleted video monologue[244] recorded to explain why 63 Berniecrats in the general election were not going to make Sanders the next President. The establishment does not want a revolution, political or otherwise, and there are more neoliberals in Congress than revolutionaries even if all 63 had won their races.

To correct the record, down-ballot votes in California are registered immediately, electronically; and the write-in votes are counted later. Lesson for Administrator C and everyone else who does not know the difference: Mistakes are not lies. Mistakes are corrected. Lesson for revolutionary organizers: get the facts from the source before making decisions. Bad, inaccurate information led to a major RAP committee decision when we didn't have all of the relevant information.

California has enough Electoral College votes to get a one-state candidate for president before the next House in a three-way contest. That could be handy someday and perhaps what Sanders' electors and their supporters were hoping for. Sanders California elector Lauren Steiner explained in LA Progressive:[245]

> If you don't like Jill or the Green Party, or if you don't think third parties have a chance in our rigged system, or if you simply want to vote for the man who you supported all year in the primaries and stick it to the DNC, you can write in Bernie, and your vote will be counted.

Our position, since going Green in January, has been if you don't like the Green Party, vote for the socialist on the ballot. Just cast a progressive, revolutionary vote. There are a lot of ways of sticking it to the DNC, but writing in Sanders and having him win in California would not have changed the outcome in 2016. It was also not possible as a consequence of starting very late and having little for an advertising budget. It was a mere protest vote when it was clear getting the Green Party to 5% of the total vote count was more important for the revolutionary movement tactically. The best tactic American progressives can make is to register with the Green or other opposition party. #DemExit can contribute to leverage during the primaries. About 14 million Americans have departed the Democratic Party since the election,[246] but they are not joining to build an opposition party. The Green Party must have an image problem, and they are the largest progressive party in the United States. No opposition candidate needs to be competitive in three or four-way contests to serve as leverage to Democrats voting in primaries. Having a Green or a new, independent, progressive party candidate on the ballot makes the threat to reject the neoliberal "centrist" Democrat in the general election possible to carry out.

Avoiding Pointless Divisions

We need to legalize democratic order, and that's going to require revolutionary tactics and strategies. Leverage can be one tactic. The Twelfth Amendment can be another. Ideally, the various factions of a political movement (libertarian or progressive) should communicate their strategies across organizations. Agree or disagree, at least have a conference call or some communication device to discuss the most effective and best practice ways to get from oligarchy to revolution. As Steiner put it, "Let's hope that the various movements on the left can unite. Maybe the first step would be to attend Occupy Inauguration, where organizers want to 'build a united movement and political party for the 99%, to put people and the planet over profits.'"[247] Next time progressives need to unite before the general election, so we have a fighting chance of attending the inauguration of our preferred candidate, not protesting the consequences of pointless, highly unrealistic divisions.

We need to build institutions of both political and civil opposition to both the Trump emergency and the neoliberals' corporate globalization. The period between elections, when people are in the streets and active either again (baby boomers) or for the first time, is an opportunity to make the case against Trump and the establishment for an agenda of ecological survival, peace, human rights and economic cooperation supporting all three. Community groups could form in support of a common set of principles. The economic system is in crisis and will either wipe humans out or revolutionaries can come together and save America from the duel threat of fascism and neoliberal capitalism. The stakes have never been so high; we have to figure out how to take power from the 1%. The next chapter explains why and the last two chapters suggests how.

Chapter 10
The Blame Game

"Those who make peaceful revolution impossible will make violent revolution inevitable."[248] ~JFK

Two Poisonous Pills

Because the Democratic National Committee's collusion with the Clinton campaign and likely election fraud[249] during the primary season, we were offered two poisonous pills by the major parties in the general election. The blue pill would have meant cold or hot war with Russia, acceleration of climate change and a renewed nuclear arms race along with democracy destroying, so-called "free-trade agreements." The red pill will mean cold or hot war with China, a renewed nuclear arms race, ironically with Russia since they have far more nukes than China, and rapid acceleration of climate change.

The Green pill was the only sane one to take, but 94.3% of American voters are locked inside the two-party, mental prison the establishment uses[250] to maintain the current neoliberal, economic order. Even though Dr. Stein received just barely over 1% of the popular vote, the Green Party could be perceived as having caused Trump to win. That's how close the vote counts in Michigan, Wisconsin & Pennsylvania were between Clinton and Trump, but blaming citizens for voting their conscience does not make sense.

Secretary Clinton blamed her loss to Donald Trump in the general election on FBI Director Comey's letter to Congress notifying them the investigation into her emails was being reopened and then on Russian President Vladimir Putin with claims of Russian hacking of DNC and Clinton campaign manager Podesta's email accounts. However, she started dropping in the polls before Comey sent his letter to Congress on Oct. 28th.[251] Clinton told her fat-cat financial supporters, who collectively poured about $1 billion into her campaign effort:[252]

> This is not just an attack on me and my campaign, although that may have added fuel to it. This is an attack against our country. We are well beyond normal political concerns here. This is about the integrity of our democracy and the security of our nation.

Oh, the irony. Revolt Against Plutocracy is opposed to foreign and domestic interference in campaigns via hacking, sabotage, etc. The Trans-Pacific Partnership was well beyond normal political concerns; it was an unprecedented threat to self-government, to American sovereignty, national self-determination and to American jobs. For people who share her neoliberal political philosophy, un-democratic, corporate-crafted "free-trade agreements" designed to grab the power to regulate transnational corporations from people's representatives are the norm. Clinton did not oppose the TPP for nearly enough reasons, if she honestly opposed it at all.

The Superdelegates Chose Trump

It must be clear by now to the most casual reader we blame the superdelegates for nominating Secretary Clinton, a deeply flawed and scandal-ridden candidate. Michael Hudson, writing in *CounterPunch*,[253] suggests what we suspect, they chose Trump over Sanders. He argues the party machine of Edward Bernais, an American it's fair to describe as the grandfather of media manipulation of social and political values as propaganda, and the Clintoncrats' made up, made for TV reality, was defeated by Trump and his jobs-through-trade-agreements promised future.

> Perhaps some leading Democrats preferred to lose with their Wall Street candidate Hillary than win with a reformer who would have edged them out of their right-wing positions. But the main problem was hubris. Hillary's coterie

thought they could make their own reality. They believed that hundreds of millions of dollars of TV and other advertising could sway voters. But eight years of Obama's rescue of Wall Street instead of the economy was enough for most voters to see how deceptive his promises had been. And they distrusted Hillary's pretended embrace of Bernie's opposition to TPP.

Trump's victory was a populist revolt against neoliberal "free-trade agreements." Even if Clinton really did oppose the TPP, we could not trust her based on her record of dishonesty on NAFTA.[254] There was so much at risk in this election—so many included issues associated with the "fundamental transformation" and "new world order" (VP Joe Biden's phrase[255]) the nearly 6,000 page TPP would impose as a next step of corporate globalization—Clinton's defeat was nothing less than dodging a bullet. Trump's low wage and high tariff agenda is safe by comparison even though he's clearly more dangerous than Clinton on other issues such as Supreme Court nominees, health care insurance and cabinet picks.

Blaming Bernie or Bust

There are a couple of people I've seen online blaming our movement for Trump's victory on November 8th, a blogger[256] and someone who wrote a letter to the editor.[257] Some people leaving comments on Revolt Against Plutocracy's now-deleted[258] Bernie or Else Facebook page also blame our movement. We would be thrilled to claim responsibility for contributing to Clinton's defeat if the state-by-state voting totals supported the claim.

In order for #CorporateClinton to have won the general election, she would have had to take Pennsylvania, Wisconsin and Michigan. Two of the three would not have been enough.

Before reviewing the vote counts in Florida, Pennsylvania, Wisconsin and Michigan, it is worth answering Sec. Clinton's general election, campaign season question, "Why aren't I fifty points ahead, you might ask?"[259] As I'll elaborate below, she was not defeated by Trump because of the Bernie or Bust movement; she was defeated by Hillary Clinton, the candidate who was:

- The establishment candidate of a broken, neoliberal status quo,
- Dishonest,[260]
- Distrusted,[261]
- Prone to making mistakes,[262]
- A reckless and "bloodthirsty"[263] warmonger.

Trump rode to victory on the strength of rural voters, who turned out in astonishing numbers. Likewise, Sanders was highly popular among many of these same voters during the primary; doubtless a number of his supporters ultimately opted for Trump. A survey conducted just before the general election indicated he could have defeated Trump by a sizable margin.[264] Revolt Against Plutocracy stands firm on why the Democrats lost. The superdelegates chose to divide the Party against Trump—evident by the Convention delegate walk-out and the extent to which "Bernie or Bust" was in the news by then—when they could have united the Party behind Senator Sanders. It was their job to pick the candidate with the best shot of unifying the Party to win the general election, but they used their position to protect the neoliberal establishment's control of the Executive Branch of government instead. Michael Hudson isn't the only person who suspects they could afford to ignore our warning letters, press conference and billboard message because they would rather risk having Trump in control of the Executive Branch of government than a democratic socialist. Perhaps they believed Trump could not possibly win a general election because of his many faults even though it was coming into focus how he has a Teflon surface. How could Trump win in states Obama had taken? Trump's victory is a blow, not to female candidates, but to neoliberalism. Dismissing the other excuses for Clinton's defeat, author Naomi Kline essentially make this same claim and points out:[265]

> Under neoliberal policies of deregulation, privatisation, austerity and corporate trade, their living standards have declined precipitously. [A hell of a lot of people] have lost jobs. They have lost pensions. They have lost much of the safety net that used to make these losses less frightening. They see a future for their kids even worse than their precarious present.
>
> [...]

Elite neoliberalism has nothing to offer that pain, because neoliberalism unleashed the Davos class. People such as Hillary and Bill Clinton are the toast of the Davos party. In truth, they threw the party.

Bernie or Bust's Impact on Election

Charlie Hobbs and I examined the vote counts in four swing states in which Trump narrowly defeated Clinton: Florida, Pennsylvania, Wisconsin and Michigan. All the Bernie or Bust movement could be honestly and logically held responsible for were the Sanders write-in vote totals and the increase in vote count attained by Jill Stein compared to 2012 when she ran against President Obama. If, for example, Stein received 1,000 votes in a given state in 2012 and 2,500 votes in 2016, the most we could be held responsible for would be the difference, 1,500 votes since anyone who voted Green in 2012 would probably have voted for the same candidate again in 2016 regardless of whom the Bernie or Bust movement motivated revolutionaries to vote for.

In Florida Trump defeated Clinton by 112,975 votes.[266] Stein received 64,399 votes in 2016, a 55,466 vote increase from 2012. While RAP would like to take credit for that entire increase, I have no doubt much of Stein's improvement in Florida in 2016 was due to the unwillingness by progressives to vote for a DINO (Democrat In Name Only) like Hillary Clinton regardless of our Bernie or Bust strategy. Even if we were completely responsible for the 55,466 vote increase in 2016, Sanders would still have needed 57,445 write-in votes by people, who would have otherwise voted for Secretary Clinton, for Bernie or Bust to have caused her to lose in that state. Unfortunately, Florida did not tabulate their write-in votes because he was not a registered candidate; so we'll never know. This does confirm our realization from late in 2015, however: a national write-in strategy for a candidate unwilling to register as such was a stupid idea. If it's used again, leverage will be expressed: "Candidate X or Party Y in 2020." As leverage a write-in strategy could in theory have general election ramifications, but it needs to focus on specific states that count write-in votes without candidate registration.

Michigan is another state where they will not count the write-in votes cast for Sanders. In Michigan alone, which sealed Clinton's loss after Trump defeated her by an 11,612 vote margin; a jaw-dropping 87,810 voters cast a ballot but left the presidential field blank.[267] Stein garnered 21,204 votes in that state four years ago and 50,700 votes in 2016. The difference of 28,803 was far greater than the narrow margin of Trump's victory over Clinton in that state. Assuming only half of the 28,803 increase was a consequence of Bernie or Bust instead of the #NeverHillary movement or other anti-Clinton considerations, it could be argued our movement cost Clinton the state of Michigan.

In Wisconsin Trump received, before the recount in that state, 1,409,467 votes, and Clinton received 1,382,210 votes for a margin of victory of 27,257 votes. Jill Stein received 30,980 votes in 2016.[268] Subtract from that the 7,665 votes she received in 2012.[269] If our movement was wholly responsible for the increase of 23,315 Green Party votes, it would still require 3,942 write-in votes for Sanders for Bernie or Bust to be perceived as responsible for Trump winning there. Like Florida, Reid Magney, Public Information Officer for the Wisconsin Government Accountability Board informed us, "Senator Sanders was not a registered write in candidate so there will be no count of votes cast for him." Even if we were responsible for Trump winning in Wisconsin, which is not likely, the state has only 10 electoral votes. Trump defeated Clinton 306 electoral votes to 232 electoral votes. Our movement would have had to affect the outcome in a larger state to rationally and honestly claim credit (or accept blame) for helping defeat Secretary Clinton.

That leaves Pennsylvania where the recount was halted again, this time by a federal judge.[270] Vote count separation between Trump and Clinton in Pennsylvania was 44,292 votes.[271] Stein received 49,941 votes, an increase of 28,600 over 2012 (the "or bust" effect). That means, for #BernieOrBust to have caused Pennsylvania to go to Trump, Sanders needed 15,692 write-in votes. According to the PA DOS elections office, the total number of write-in votes for Sanders was 6,060. (The Pennsylvania Department of State provided Charlie this information in an email based on a "right to know" request). This means while people can try to blame the Green Party voters for Trump (or give them credit for helping defeat Clinton), Bernie or Bust cannot take credit for Clinton's general election defeat. Pennsylvania voters supported Trump over Clinton because they accurately perceived her as a candidate of the "free-trade" with the resulting outsourcing of jobs. Clinton was the candidate of an unacceptable status quo for a majority of voters in states devastated by the neoliberal, globalization agenda.

The Bernie or Bust Wikipedia page[272] was merged back into the Sanders campaign page around the time of Trump's inauguration. Wikipedia had announced they were contemplating the merge after re-establishing it as a separate page right after Trump's Electoral College victory. Had RAP been able to claim some responsibility for the defeat of Clinton, I would have argued on the "Talk" tab to keep the page up as a historical marker.

"Bust," i.e., leverage, never worked as intended. It did not get Sanders the nomination, and it did not help Dr. Stein reach 5% in the results to obtain formal minor party status with the FEC. We can't claim victory or credit on any level. If the voters we influenced online were "busting" responsibly as we recommended in Philadelphia and again in email blasts to our pledge-takers, the U.S. Senate would be majority Blue/Green. In Philadelphia I forgot to mention the one exception to Blue-no-matter-who for Senate, Dr. Margaret Flowers (G). She wasn't elected either.

Neither the Russians,[273] WikiLeaks, the FBI nor Bernie or Bust caused Secretary Clinton the election; she did. Why was there an FBI investigation in the first place? Her "progressive" defender at *Mother Jones* Magazine[274] doesn't acknowledge Secretary Clinton decided to have her own email server, another one of her "mistakes" she admitted making.[275] Her campaign's own polling people found one turning point was right after she called half of Trump's supporters a "basket of deplorables."[276] I was initially shocked when I heard her offend voters, and she has only herself to blame for that blunder. The Democratic Party superdelegates could have blocked her and saved the election, but they chose instead to make peaceful revolution impossible.

Why Clinton Lost

So why did Clinton lose the election? According to Juan Cole writing in *Truthdig*,[277]

> It was because in some key states like Minnesota, Wisconsin and Michigan, she suffered from a lack of enthusiasm on the part of Democrats. In those states, it is true that perhaps 14% of the white working class defected to Trump.[278] But **another 21%** just stayed home. As Konstantin Kilibarda and Daria Roithmayr argue at Slate, the idea that Trump

flipped the white working class is incorrect. It was Sec. Clinton's inability to get them to come to the voting booth for her that was decisive.

In addition to the Clinton campaign's failed[279] "action" plan, Sean King, columnist from *The Daily News* pointed out that:[280]

> …while progressives were fighting against police brutality, against the Dakota Access Pipeline, against TPP, against fracking and for a $15 minimum wage, Clinton was consistently on the wrong side of each of those issues. That's what cost her the election. Each of those issues are fueled by an energized base of supporters who knew full well that they did not have a true friend and ally in her or the Democratic Party establishment.

One of Clinton's supporters, Max Weiss, published an article of blame for her defeat in The Huffington Post called "Things I Blame For Hillary Clinton's Loss, Ranked."[281] He claimed they were:

1. **MISOGYNY,**
2. **BERNIE SANDERS,**
3. **FAKE NEWS,**
4. **JAMES COMEY,**
5. **RUSSIA/WIKILEAKS,**
6. **THE MAINSTREAM MEDIA,**
7. **JILL STEIN** and Susan Sarandon for endorsing Stein,
8. **THE CLOSE TO 100 MILLION WHO DIDN'T VOTE**
9. **VOTER SUPPRESSION**
10. **HILLARY'S MESSAGE**
11. **HILLARY'S CAMPAIGN**
12. **HILLARY'S SUPPORTERS** including himself

What did he not blame? **"HILLARY HERSELF."** I posted his column on our Facebook page and asked for comments to explain "why Secretary Clinton could not defeat Donald Trump?" With rare exceptions, I have not brought in the voices of our movement into this story; and I want to. Before I do, Max was correct about "voter suppression," and I'll address that in the next chapter. Only one person insisted on citing his comment by name; every other comment will not be identified except as a gender clarification. All comments are transcribed as posted.

- It's obvious to anyone with a brain that Hillary Clinton was the reason for her loss, who she is and how she ran her campaign. She could have overcome her negatives, but she constantly compounded them. The only reason it was close was because she was up against such a monster of a candidate, but she still couldn't defeat someone less favorable then herself.

- I blame the super delegates for not doing their jobs. They picked a candidate …who couldn't rally up a high school gym full of people.

- She cheated to get the nomination the DNC cheated for her - she lost because she was horrible - she lost to trump - that says volumes.

- Interesting that the article doesn't address voter suppression during the primaries as well as marginalized groups. Fact is she couldn't win unless she cheated to get to the general election in the first place. Perhaps a mirror is the first best and last place she should look. And then apologize to America for what she's done. Unbelievable.

- Fracking, TPP, Debbie Wasserman Schultz, Donna Brazile, platitudes, Tim Kaine, not quite $15 minimum wage, platitudes, the entire Bill Clinton presidency, superpredators, baskets of deplorables, not… campaigning in the State of Wisconsin, arrogance, platitudes, Koch brothers endorsement, Iraq, most amateur server setup ever, elitism, The Hamptons grass roots movement, everyone thinking she's lying when her lips move, platitudes…

- Debbie added to that list: I think you got all of them, except maybe poking Putin and a possible war with a nuclear power.

- I blame…1. Intelligent people who saw through the lies. 2. Fed up people who were tired of the lies. 3. The loss of credibility of those who started the lies. 4. The loss of credibility of those who spread the lies. 5. The blatant inaction of those whose job it was to expose the lies. 6. Did I mention the lies?

- She didn't stand for anything, just she was a woman running for president and thought she was entitled.

- Hillary was the worst candidate in the history of electoral politics. She knew it, her campaign knew it, the media knew it, the Republicans knew it, the DNC knew it, EVERYBODY knew it, including the American people who rejected her once again. And it is funny how they said misogyny, but then mention Stein. Like somehow all of these people hated women so much, they didn't vote for a woman so they could vote for a woman.

- The main reason she lost: People are desperate for change. Obama rode a wave of young voters and enthusiasm to two terms only to disappoint all of those who placed their HOPE in him. (Not all his fault, I get it) HRC represented more of the same....More breaks for the rich and less for the working people of this country. More taking care of donors and not the majority. So, even though he is the most vile of all Presidential candidates, she lost this election by the rules everyone understood. And now, the establishment Democrats want to say it was the Russian and James Comey that lost the election so that they don't need to change the party that favors the elite class. Bern it down!

- What a load of Tripe. Clinton and the DNC are to blame for her loss. Her brain-dead supporters attacked the youthful supporters of Sanders on social media and were condescending assholes towards anyone who voiced legitimate concerns about Clinton or her obvious weaknesses against Trump and the Republicans in general. Hell, one of her PAC's hired a bunch of paid trolls to attack Bernie and his supporters on social media. Millennials aren't stupid. They saw all that bullshit and it insulted their intelligence. And Misogyny? Clinton supporters and her campaign labeled anyone who was critical of Hillary "sexist" or "misogynist". That was the go-to deflection for Clinton supporters any time I or anyone else was winning a debate with them on social media. It was pathetic and reminded me of how many Republicans act when they are losing an argument. Clinton's gender was never a concern for most of us. If it was a concern, it was only so for conservative males who wouldn't be supporting her anyhow. If this is how Democrats really feel then I'm glad I left the party after their ludicrous behavior during the primaries. I was hoping they and the left wing press would realize Neoliberal establishment shills were not the people progressive are going to support going forward, but it's obvious they have learned nothing. It looks like it's time for a true progressive party. A new party that's true to progressive ideals and willing to fight for those ideals instead of capitulating to the whims of big money donors and special interests, free from the baggage and historical failures of the Neoliberals.

- This person has to be out of his mind and totally out of touch with reality. If [people] with any intelligence can't see that $Hillary defeated herself, they are idiot[s]. Whether it was Russian, Bernie, or Genghis Khan from the grave, the hacks only revealed the truth. How anyone could accept her for POTUS is beyond me. Am I a Bernie supporter? You bet your ass. I can only hope that all Americans aren't as stupid as this guy. And as far as being a misogynistic person, if Jill Stein had been on my ballot, I would have voted for her. I'm not opposed to a woman president, I just can't accept $Hillary.

- Hillary is to blame. Hillary's ARROGANCE is to blame. All she had to do was do SOMETHING progressive; maybe speak out about DAPL in favor of the natives and water protectors. She lost because SHE left the party behind in search of gaining conservatives. SHE is 100% at fault. There's NOTHING that changes the fact that she could have won if she leaned at all to the left. Hillary: "I'm left leaning because I'm pro-choice." And? What else, Clinton? What do you bring to the table?

- Hillary Clinton didn't lose Pennsylvania, Michigan, Wisconsin and most importantly Florida because a small percentage of voters switched from her to Trump in those states. She lost those states because millions of Sanders voters nationally, and hundreds of thousands of Democrats and independent progressives in those key states decided not to vote for her because they were disgusted by both her and the Democratic Party.

- This article mostly misses the boat. The author, obviously a DNC shill, doesn't even list the OBVIOUS number one culprit: the DNC!

They ran an uninspiring candidate, they ran a breathtakingly STU-PID campaign (NO press conferences, SERIOUSLY?), and they expected a bunch of overworked, underpaid, disappointed and demoralized Democrats to make up the enthusiasm gap? Are they even conscious???

- Christina wrote, I blame Hillary Clinton. This is bullshit that she doesn't get she began to lose the people the minute she rigged the primaries against Bernie. She's a shit candidate. She's corrupt. She's a liar. I have zero respect for her. The SOS and Senate positions she held were a joke because this bitch is GOP all the way. She didn't do squat in the 30 years she was in politics. Nothing. No bills passed in the Senate. All bs. She's a war monger, a corporatist, militarist. You name it. She is her own worst horror show.

- Rick Todisco, who wanted to be identified, added: Straight up Kkkillary goddamned kkklinton is a criminal, she has committed treason and deserves to hang by the neck, no firing squad or electricity or drug but a short rope for full effect. She has the blood of millions on her filthy hands including American soldiers and an ambassador, she deserves, no sympathy, empathy or even a kind word, only a stiff hemp rope.

You get the idea. I asked Rick who he voted for because his tone was so bitter, antagonistic and hateful. "Jill, the only person worth voting for," he replied. Some "misogynist!" Andrew Levine noted,[282] "Had Hillary been a less awful candidate, even her version of neoliberalism, liberal imperialism, warmongering and Russia-baiting might actually have prevailed over Trump's showy, too-good-to-be-true promises to marks desperate enough to believe anything." The superdelegates chose a truly hated and uninspiring candidate over a beloved and inspiring candidate.

Blaming Jill Stein does not mathematically make sense,[283] but even if it did we would give the Green Party *credit* for helping defeat Wall Street's golden child. Weiss' criticism, however, was absurd. Stein, he argued, is a "publicity-seeking, bourgeois woman [who] gave disenchanted Bernie or Busters a place for their protest vote…" Anyone running for public office not seeking publicity is doing a very bad job as a campaigner. As for his accusation she's "bourgeois," he might consider her net wealth compared to Secretary Clinton's. Hillary made more money in an hour talking to Wall Street banks than Stein and 99% of the rest of the nation's income earners make over the course of an entire year. More important, a vote against the candidates of the neoliberal establishment and nationalistic fascism is not a "protest vote." It's an act of revolution, a necessity Weiss seems completely oblivious about, cast in order to undermine neoliberal tyranny of so-called "free-trade," privatization, extreme extractions of resources, etc.

Dave Lindorff believes Clinton lost the general election because of her treatment of Sanders' supporters. In *CounterPunch*,[284] he wrote:

> Her repeating lying about Sanders during the campaign, and her gratuitous dissing of Sanders and his supporters even after it was becoming clearer that she would win the primary because of the corrupt support she had lined up from the party's unelected so-called "superdelegates," and her decision in the fall, after winning the nomination, to ignore the 13 million Sanders voters from the primary and instead to pursue the support of what she hoped were disenchanted Republican voters upset that Donald Trump had won the Republican nomination, all doomed her in the general election.

In other words, we didn't need to deploy Bernie or Bust to stop this particular neoliberal candidate; Clinton and the DNC pretty much turned off Sanders' supporters without our help. The superdelegates chose to ignore the considerable #NeverHillary movement, which could have overlapped with many of those in the Bernie or Bust movement, who took our pledge; and her long list of negatives that rival those of Donald Trump. Clinton was the lessor of two liars, but that's not an inspirational reason to get to the polls.

Clinton Better Than Trump? Foreign Policy:
In Philadelphia, I expressed my differences with Chomsky regarding Clinton's dangerous characteristics. After the election he asked, "How did Trump and Clinton compare?" and added, "I think they're very different. I didn't like Clinton at all, but her positions are much better than Trump's on every issue I can think of."[285]

While Trump is also dangerous in his own, special ways, to be sure, at least his presidency promised a détente with Russia. That could save the country a lot of money spent on weapons we cannot use again, except in retaliation for a first strike against the U.S. Hillary Clinton planned to go to war against nuclear-armed Russia over Syria. Voters concerned about avoiding a nuclear war noted that.

Asked by Sen. Roger Wicker (R-Mississippi) about what it would take for the United States to impose a no-fly zone over Syria, and *"control the airspace"* before a Senate panel in September of 2016, the Chairman of the Joint Chiefs of Staff, General Dunford (not Trump and not Putin) explained, *"Right now… for us to control all of the airspace in Syria would require us to go to war against Syria and Russia."* A sufficient exchange of nuclear weapons with Russia would probably lead to the end of human life due to sun blockage which would result in what's called a nuclear winter that lasts for years thereby decimating plant life.[286] The bombs and radiation would kill many people before the rest of them finally run out of plant and animal food to eat. Détente with Russia offers peace of mind about imminent nuclear holocaust a Clinton administration would not have permitted. Her proposed no-fly zone over Syria was reckless and dangerous on the face of it.

Chris Wallace, moderator of the third and final debate between Clinton and Trump, asked Clinton if she'd have U.S. pilots shoot down Russian jets over Syria; and she dodged the question below.[287] Greg and YahNé understated their case against Secretary Clinton during the primaries: Trump is specifically worse than Hillary Clinton,[288] but he seems much better on relations with Russia. While he is certain to make mistakes with world affairs, Secretary Clinton had a history of making mistakes and a pro-war inclination.

> **Wallace**: …if you impose a no-fly zone and a Russian plane violates that, does President Clinton shoot that plane down?

> **Clinton**: First of all, I think a no-fly zone could save lives and could hasten the end of the conflict. I'm well aware of the really legitimate concerns you have expressed from both the president and the general. This would not be done just on the first day. This would take a lot of negotiation, and it would

also take making it clear to the Russians and the Syrians that our purpose here was to provide safe Zones on the ground.

We've had millions of people leave Syria. And those millions of people inside Syria who have been dislocated. So I think we could strike a deal and make it very clear to the Russians and the Syrians that this was something that we believe was in the best interests of the people on the ground in Syria. It would help our fight against ISIS.

Trump is far more likely to strike a deal with the Russians and Assad than the belligerent "make it very clear to the Russians" Clinton would have. Trump having access to the nuclear codes is arguably no more frightening than having Clinton as Commander-In-Chief. Trump is scary and an unknown in foreign policy; Clinton is a proven belligerent. Trump didn't seem to expect to win the election, and when he was on the steepest section of the very steep learning curve all new Presidents go through in order to function once he won; he went on a victory tour. He should have been studying. Trump may be warm toward Putin and initially belligerent with the Chinese because he's a racist; we just don't know what to expect in the next four years other than his wanting American energy independence and American businesses to stay in or return to the United States. Trump is making the United States even more corporate friendly than it already is, just as Clinton would have by advancing corporate globalization.

Trump's "energy independence" will accelerate climate change; a threat to national security Sanders was correct to argue is our most serious concern. What's coming is historically unprecedented and inherently includes the whole planet. Hydrofracking Hillary was not much better on the issue. Before getting to that, though, allow one more point about who is to blame for the 45th President.

A story in Politico demonstrated the Clinton campaign was also poorly run and had an ineffective plan:[289]

Clinton's loss could be attributed to any number of factors... but...in-state battleground operatives worry that a lesson being missed is a simple one: Get the basics of campaigning right.

The superdelegates chose a terrible campaign organization lead by an untrustworthy candidate when a populist, they could have nominated, was filling stadiums just like Trump was. If I were a Democrat, I'd demand the resignation of every superdelegate who voted for Hillary Clinton. The Democrats need to keep losing elections until they unite behind real progressives. Neoliberals are conservatives who support abortion and LBGTQ rights, and their support of Wall Street's agenda, i.e., corporate globalization, makes them a threat to the American system of democratic self-government. The TPP was not a free-trade agreement for two reasons: there was no language preventing the manipulation of currency by governments and the few chapters that do lower tariffs in the agreement serve as a Trojan horse for the corporate takeover of the system of government established by the Framers. The advance of corporate rights has been underway for well over a hundred years, but in the aftermath of the Citizens United decision, the corporate interests have completely taken power in 2014. Obama has been a neoliberal all along, but the TPP and other so-called "free-trade" agreements still under negotiation should make it clear even to his supporters. Now we know to follow the money. Obama's campaigns were largely funded by Wall Street bankers, and they do not donate to presidential candidates out of kindness or compassion. They have a dangerous, anti-democratic agenda.

Corporations should not be party to international regulation-writing efforts, and it's Congress, according to the Constitution, that should be home for the U.S. Trade Representative. That office should have congressional committees to oversee the rules being negotiated with other nations. Once finalized, an agreement should either go before the Senate for ratification as a treaty or in both houses for 2/3 support and sent to the states for ratification, depending upon the extent and type of corporate rules and regulations contained in it.

Harmonization of international rules and regulations among trading nations is the goal of transnational corporations. Doing so using the rules crafted by the corporations themselves in secret negotiations would have led to a fundamental transformation that should but probably will not remain a stain on Obama's legacy. Trump's supporters may have saved the nation from this dangerous turn toward corporate self-government, or the new President is going to negotiate bilateral versions of trade (free or taxed) agreements similar to the TPP. I can't tell if he's sincere about his opposition to globalization or a con-man at this point.

On nuclear security, Trump tweeted[290] on Dec. 22nd:

> The United States must greatly strengthen and expand its nuclear capability until such time as the world comes to its senses regarding nukes

So much for détente with Russia. Since the United States is the only nation to ever use a nuclear bomb as a weapon of war, what does the "world" need to do to come to its senses? Disarm? I tweeted Trump a reminder the planned upgrade to our nuclear weapons stockpile was Obama's plan. Independent columnist, Caitlin Johnstone, argued[291] what I've been saying since at least the DNC when she wrote, "I think it's a pretty safe bet that we won't be in any more danger of nuclear annihilation than we were under Obama, if that helps, and we're certainly a lot safer than we would have been under the lady who was trying to start a war with Russia."

Threats to Democracy

The legacy media's flagship, the *NY Times*, published a column on December 16th by Steven Levitsky and Daniel Ziblatt entitled "Is Donald Trump a Threat to Democracy?"[292] Referencing the research of Juan J. Linz, they pose a "litmus test" of "democracy's demise" based on their research. The tests are "failure to reject violence unambiguously, a readiness to curtail rivals' civil liberties, and the denial of the legitimacy of elected governments."

They are correct to point out Trump encouraged violence among his followers, but his promise to prosecute Clinton was a campaign tactic he had already dropped when they published their essay. Clinton supporters were on record sending people into Trump's rallies to start trouble. Trump conned many Hillary haters for their vote. There are a good number of Sanders supporters who are not happy he made that post-election decision. Those who voted for him for that reason got conned by a deceitful campaigner who insulted his way into the White House. It's a remarkable feat by the type of candidate the Framers considered a major reason the Electoral College was put into place to block from Executive Branch power.

Levitsky and Ziblatt are also right to point out Trump threatens legal action against unfriendly media, but his suggestion "that he might not accept the election results" was repeated by the Green Party candidate who walked her talk on the matter, not to challenge the results, but to find out why people were disenfranchised in Detroit, Michigan, and examine other red flags coming from the electronic voting machines many Berners believe are rigged to support one candidate over another. The Green Party recounts in Pennsylvania and Michigan were stopped by legal challenges, so the people can't even find out if their voting system is legitimate. When it comes to the 2016 election, Trump was the least of our concerns about "legitimacy" of the government. The $3.5 million cost for the recount in Wisconsin is a threat to democracy.

President-elect Trump withdrew from the Trans-Pacific Partnership.[293] He stated he's going to negotiate "bilateral," two-state agreements, but there's no certainty his agreements will be any less corporate-crafted or corporate-oriented than the TPP was. He seems to be opposed to the establishment's globalization agenda. That is a vital issue on which Trump's nationalism is much better than Clinton's corporate globalization. Unfortunately, Trump is choosing Clinton's "corrupt establishment" to advise him on domestic economic policy.[294] Again, we don't know what to expect on trade policy. Was his nationalism sincere or not? If Vice-President Pence doesn't take over first, we'll find out. Continued U.S. involvement in the massive Trade in Services Agreement is not a good sign.

During the general election season I kept stressing on social media the TPP is the name of the first knife Clinton would plunge into the backs of Bernie Sanders and every working class American who supported her. The WikiLeaked Podesta emails confirmed this suspicion in two ways. A published speech to a Wall Street bank conveyed Secretary Clinton has two positions for contentious issues, a public (dishonest) position and a private (actual) position.[295] In another leaked email, her speechwriter, Dan Schwerin, wrote,[296] "This is indeed a hard balance to strike, since we don't want to invite mockery for being too enthusiastically opposed to a deal she once championed, or over-claiming how bad it is, since it's a very close call on the merits." He crafted revealing language for Secretary Clinton to use: "I still believe a strong and fair trans-Pacific trade agreement is both possible and necessary, so I will build on the Obama administration's valuable work and negotiate a deal that meets our tests and delivers for everyday Americans."

I stand by my Philadelphia speech claims: Secretary Clinton would have implemented the TPP either modified through renegotiation or as-is with a "promise" to renegotiate certain chapters. Her "opposition" was premised, supposedly, in large part on helping American workers. However, discussing net job growth or decline under the TPP is analogous to complaining to the baker for reducing the number of walnuts in a brownie recipe that was laced with arsenic. Sanders, Clinton and debate moderators discussed trade policy in this shallow manner. Clinton had no apparent problem with corporate self-regulation, no problem with corporations asserting rights with no judicial sanction and no problem with private tribunals that function an awful lot like legal versions of criminal protection (of profits) rackets. She was the greater of two dangerous threats to democracy for President. No doubt, Trump's time in office will set the country back decades; but the direction in global, economic affairs coming from the power elite, the "establishment" in Sanders' word, is a betrayal of the Framers' vision. Neoliberal globalization via so-called "free-trade agreements" would have foisted the nation into some kind of corporate dystopia, and it still may.

If the TPP had passed in Congress and been implemented, it would not matter who we vote for when it comes to regulating behavior of foreign-based transnational corporations operating in the United States. Republican, Democrat, Libertarian or Green, their hands would have been tied by the rules and regulations contained in the "trade agreement." It would also render the Tenth Amendment moot on issues of corporate behavior. It would do what Obama promised five days before the general election in 2008: fundamentally transform the United States. Democratic self-government would have been transformed into corporate self-government. Obama and Clinton, neoliberals in general, are a greater threat to democracy than anything Trump has stated or implied to date. The corporate power grabs in the next stage of corporate globalization (the TPP, Trans-Atlantic Trade and Investment Partnership and TiSA trade agreements), unlike political power grabs of the past, are unprecedented and not recognized or reported by the legacy, neoliberal media as the clear and present danger to our very system of government that it is.

Neoliberal globalization is an attempt to corporatize everything. Life is a profit opportunity. As I said on Tim Black at Night,[297] Secretary Clinton is a corporate tool; Donald Trump is a corporation. Her agenda was to be a continuation of the status quo, to carry on Obama's legacy. She was the status quo conservative in the contest. Addressing Levitsky's and Ziblatt's concerns, Paul Street's observation[298] is one we agree with:

> It is absurd for American liberals to claim that Trumpism threatens to crush our "great democracy." What "great democracy"? It is well established that the United States' political order is a corporate and financial plutocracy – an oligarchy of and for Wealthy Few. You don't have to be a supposedly wild-eyed radical Leftist radical like me to know this. Just ask the establishment liberal political scientists Martin Gilens (Princeton) and Benjamin Page (Northwestern).

The F Word

The essay in Chapter 1, "Standing on the Edge of the Next American Revolution," argues "the United States is sliding toward fascism." During the primaries, I wrote an *Examiner* piece entitled "Who is more fascistic: Donald Trump or Hillary Clinton?" I used the 14 characteristics of fascism[299] to compare not only Clinton and Trump but Obama and Senator Sanders as well. *Examiner* is gone, but the 14 characteristics quoted below remain available as a checklist of what to look out for with Trump in power.

Two points about going through this exercise: people will disagree with my assessments, and readers are encouraged to take out a pencil and mark their own "score" in the margins or on a sheet of paper. Don't guess about what someone may do in power; use what you know to be true to assess the politician on these 14 characteristics. This is an interactive exercise for you, the reader, to compare your assessments with ours. Assessments will vary. Where we offer no explanation for our assessment, it's because we see the situation as undeniable and intuitively obvious to the most casual observer. Get out your pencil and resist the temptation to embrace your own biases over what can be applied by fact-based, disciplined objectivity.

One, "Powerful and Continuing Nationalism: Fascist regimes tend to make constant use of patriotic mottos, slogans, symbols, songs, and other paraphernalia. Flags are seen everywhere, as are flag symbols on clothing and in public displays."

> Trump, check. Clinton, no. Obama, half check. Sanders, no. To be fair to Obama, nationalism is inherent in the office of the presidency. Nationalism really is Trump's orientation. Corporate-oriented internationalism with the United States as the enforcer is Clinton's neoliberal ideology. (More on that later on.)

Two, "Disdain for the Recognition of Human Rights: Because of fear of enemies and the need for security, the people in fascist regimes are persuaded that human rights can be ignored in certain cases because of 'need.' The people tend to look the other way or even approve of torture, summary executions, assassinations, long incarcerations of prisoners, etc."

> Trump, half-check. Clinton, half-check. Obama, half-check. Sanders, no. If Trump turns that half check into a full "check" when it comes to dealing with non-violent Americans, then people will know he's a genuine, hard-core fascist. On the day after the Inauguration, he tweeted, "Peaceful protests are a hallmark of our democracy. Even if I don't always agree, I recognize the rights of people to express their views."[300] Actions will speak more loudly than tweets, so we'll see. Where Trump wants to stop the immigration of Muslims, Clinton and Obama were killing them in the Middle East as Trump will continue to as well. While it's tempting, we're not ready to increase Trump's score to full check for his war against the media. If he continuously blocks all legacy media but the conservative media corporations that support him from obtaining information, he would deserve a full check.

Three, "Identification of Enemies/Scapegoats as a Unifying Cause: The people are rallied into a unifying patriotic frenzy over the need to eliminate a perceived common threat or foe: racial, ethnic or religious minorities; liberals; communists; socialists, terrorists, etc."

> Trump, check. Clinton, check. Obama, half-check. Sanders, no. Trump started out expressing the need to eliminate undocumented workers. Clinton scapegoated Trump's supporters, and Obama invoked our terrorist enemies enough to deserve a half-check.

Four, "Supremacy of the Military: Even when there are widespread domestic problems, the military is given a disproportionate amount of government funding, and the domestic agenda is neglected. Soldiers and military service are glamorized."

> Trump, check. Clinton, check. Obama, check. Sanders, half-check. Trump began his campaign critical of military over-extensions, entangling alliances and cutting the Pentagon's budget. Now he's talking about increasing it. Obama has increased the military budget, and Clinton planned to do the same. Senator Sanders has never stood up to the Washington Consensus on militarism and votes to support it, including terrorizing drone strikes on foreigners overseas.

Five, "Rampant Sexism: The governments of fascist nations tend to be almost exclusively male-dominated. Under fascist regimes, traditional gender roles are made more rigid. Opposition to abortion is high, as is homophobia and anti-gay legislation and national policy."

> Trump, check. Clinton, no. Obama, no. Sanders, no. To those who will point to the fact that Kellyanne Conway was Trump's campaign manager and serves as his Counselor: the Access Hollywood tape of Trump bragging he grabs women by the pussy was the locker room talk of a sexist man. He uses women to hide his sexism.

Six, "Controlled Mass Media: Sometimes the media is directly controlled by the government, but in other cases, the media is indirectly controlled by government regulation, or sympathetic media spokespeople and executives. Censorship, especially in war time, is very common."

> Trump, half check. Clinton, check. Obama, half-check. Sanders, no. Trump is calling out the media as dishonest for correcting his misstatement of "facts" and possibly moving them to a larger space on the White House complex. Trump will earn full check if he bans all legacy media from access to the White House press briefing. Clinton's campaign flat-out told the press what to print. Obama deserves half check for his war on whistle blowers, but he shouldn't get dinged for, like Trump's tweets, going around the media using new online sources and applications to communicate directly to the public.

Seven, "Obsession with National Security: Fear is used as a motivational tool by the government over the masses."

> Trump, check. Clinton, check. Obama, check. Sanders, no. Again, this is the constitutional role of any President.

Eight, "Religion and Government are Intertwined: Governments in fascist nations tend to use the most common religion in the nation as a tool to manipulate public opinion. Religious rhetoric and terminology is common from government leaders, even when the major tenets of the religion are diametrically opposed to the government's policies or actions."

> Trump, half-check. Clinton, no. Obama, no. Sanders, no. Trump is quite willing to use appeals to the religious right as a vehicle to power.

Nine, "Corporate Power is Protected: The industrial and business aristocracy of a fascist nation often are the ones who put the government leaders into power, creating a mutually beneficial business/government relationship and power elite."

Trump, check. Clinton, double check. Obama, double check. Sanders, no. We have no doubt Trump will protect corporate power; his cabinet appointments reinforce that certainty. He may end up worthy of a double check as direct corporate control of the ship of state has frightening possibilities for destruction. The double checks come from the neoliberal globalization agenda described earlier in this chapter. The imposition of corporate power via "free-trade agreements," which would significantly abolish democratic self-government, is the ninth characteristic of fascism on steroids!

Ten, "Labor Power is Suppressed: Because the organizing power of labor is the only real threat to a fascist government, labor unions are either eliminated entirely, or are severely suppressed ."

Trump, check. Clinton, half-check. Obama, half-check. Sanders, no. Trump supports anti-union, right-to-work laws.[301] Neoliberals have to be secret enemies of labor unions which require concerted efforts of concealment.

Eleven, "Disdain for Intellectuals and the Arts: Fascist nations tend to promote and tolerate open hostility to higher education, and academia. It is not uncommon for professors and other academics to be censored or even arrested. Free expression in the arts is openly attacked, and governments often refuse to fund the arts.

Trump, no. Clinton, no. Obama, no. Sanders, no.

Twelve, "Obsession with Crime and Punishment: Under fascist regimes, the police are given almost limitless power to enforce laws. The people are often willing to overlook police abuses and even forgo civil liberties in the name of patriotism. There is often a national police force with virtually unlimited power in fascist nations."

Trump, check. Clinton, half-check. Obama, half-check. Sanders, no. The half-check for Secretary Clinton stems from her support for President Clinton's crime bill, something else she has called a mistake. Obama's half check stems from his abuse of the Espionage Act[302] to repress leaks of government abuses and unwillingness to relax drug laws.

Thirteen, "Rampant Cronyism and Corruption: Fascist regimes almost always are governed by groups of friends and associates who appoint each other to government positions and use governmental power and authority to protect their friends from accountability. It is not uncommon in fascist regimes for national resources and even treasures to be appropriated or even outright stolen by government leaders."

> Trump, half-check. Clinton, check. Obama, check. Sanders, no. Trump deserves a half-check for bringing his son-in-law into the administration as a close advisor. The Clinton Foundation's foreign donors, who received special treatment, prompted her check as Secretary of State, and Obama received a full check for how some of the stimulus package funds were distributed and how his Wall Street donors were not prosecuted for the fraud that contributed to the Great Recession.

Fourteen, "Fraudulent Elections: Sometimes elections in fascist nations are a complete sham. Other times elections are manipulated by smear campaigns against or even assassination of opposition candidates, use of legislation to control voting numbers or political district boundaries, and manipulation of the media. Fascist nations also typically use their judiciaries to manipulate or control elections."

> Trump, check. Clinton, check. Obama, half-check. Sanders, no. Republican operatives, not Trump, were responsible for the mass voter suppression dubbed Interstate Crosscheck[303] that helped him win the election; but he was the beneficiary

of those efforts. While the Clinton machine appears to have engaged in election fraud during the primaries, that undermining of the popular will could have been undertaken by Republican hackers intending to make her the nominee since Trump was polling closer to Clinton than he was to Sanders. There was election fraud during the Democratic primaries;[304] we just don't know who was behind it. We do know the Clinton machine, including the DNC, undermined Sanders campaign using an array of sleazy tactics, foremost collusion with the corporate media. Obama gets a half-check for not forming a commission to investigate the various tactics the Clintoncrats were deploying against the Sanders campaign.

My tally: Trump, 11 of 14 for now—78.57%. Clinton, 9.5 of 14—67.85%. Obama, 9.5 of 14—67.85%. Sanders, 0.5 of 14—3.57%. It's pretty clear Senator Sanders is an abysmal fascist. If you scored Clinton higher or lower than Trump, you may have information I lack or lack information I have. You may question my doubling the 9th characteristic of fascism, but that would underestimate the threat posed by Obama's "free-trade" agreements starting with the TPP. If my assessment is off compared to the most informed and unbiased person alive by a point or two, the idea that Trump and Clinton are roughly equal on a fascism assessment scale of 0 to 14 reinforces the Bernie or Bust argument. While Trump is an overt proto-fascist, Clinton is a quiet but clear corporate fascist. Neoliberalism is corporate fascism! They were both unacceptably fascistic candidates for President. Writing in the *Black Agenda Report*,[305] Glen Ford claims what the vast majority of American have yet to realize: "Yes, the Democratic Party has been a wondrous vehicle for integration of Black America into the mainstream – of fascism."

The N Word
Neoliberalism, also called the Washington Consensus, is the ideology of what Senator Sanders called the "establishment." Neoliberalism's "very existence as ruling ideology is not even noted by the population at large."[306] Like fascism, neoliberalism has defining characteristics. Paul Smyth argues neoliberalism is the "dominant global ideology of nation states [and] has permeated and trans-

formed international institutions, non-governmental organizations and even to the roots of society and everyday culture."[307] Once this ruling ideology, neoliberalism, "is understood by the public as a tool for corporate and oligarchic pillage, coercion is all the state has left."[308] Anis Shivani explained:[309]

> ...neoliberalism is not classical liberalism, or a return to a purer version of it, as is commonly misunderstood; it is a new thing, because the market, for one thing, is not at all free and untethered and dynamic in the sense that classical liberalism idealized it. Neoliberalism presumes a strong state, working only for the benefit of the wealthy, and as such it has little pretense to neutrality and universality, unlike the classical liberal state.

Neoliberalism is not a brand new ideology. Originally, it was an economic philosophy that emerged in the 1930s among European liberals, and it was an attempt to provide a "Middle Way" between the laissez-faire of 19th Century classical liberalism and socialism. It involved "the priority of the price mechanism, free enterprise, the system of competition, and a strong and impartial state."[310] In the United States neoliberalism got its footing in the 1970s under President Carter,[311] and it was embraced by Presidents Ronald Reagan, Bill Clinton and Vice-President Al Gore. The "godfather" of this version of neoliberalism was Charles Peters, a journalist who published "A Neoliberal's Manifesto."[312]

Keep your pencils handy; this is another interactive exercise. I'll offer my assessment; you mark yours in the margins. First a disclaimer. Because Donald Trump has little governing record and he frequently contradicts himself, it is impossible to know if some of these characteristics are his or not. Therefore, instead of a "check" or a "no," I use question marks again to indicate something that's unknowable at this point. Like the list of fascistic characteristics, this is another list to serve as threats to be on the lookout for during the Trump presidency and Democratic Party primaries going forward. As with the list of characteristics of fascism, exert a fierce objectivity in your own assessments.

One, Privatization: Turning public services over to private, for-profit ownership is believed to increase efficiencies of the services and enable the market to regulate almost everything and commodify almost everything.

Trump, check. Clinton, check. Obama, check. Sanders, no.

Two, Corporate-Oriented "Free-Trade" Agreements: Think NAFTA and the Trans-Pacific Partnership. Salient features of these agreements are low tariffs on imports and the "investor state dispute tribunals" in which corporations have their profits protected by included sections of the agreements, what I called corporate protection rackets in my Philadelphia speech.

Trump, ? Clinton, check. Obama, check. Sanders, no.

Three, Wall Street Campaign Funding: Financial capital is used to help elect supportive candidates and influence political parties and other institutions.

Trump, no. Clinton, check. Obama, check. Sanders, no. Trump's "no" can be doubted because of the advice he's seeking from Wall Street by nominating one of them as Treasury Secretary, but he didn't use much of their money to get elected.

Four, Self-regulated Markets: Corporate activities are to be deregulated in order to allow greater flexibility and profitability of their operations. Going even further, President Obama's "free-trade" agreements (TPP, TTIP and TiSA) would have allowed the corporations themselves to regulate their activities in the states within the agreements.

Trump, check. Clinton, check. Obama, check. Sanders, no.

Five, Limited State Power: States must remain out of economic activities including not only direct provision of services (Medicare for all is an example) but even government spending to decrease unemployment.

Trump, ? Clinton, no. Obama, no. Sanders, no.

Six, Corporate Property Rights: Corporations maintain and expand the ability to exclude others from the uses and benefits of their property.

Trump, half check. Clinton, check. Obama, check. Sanders, half check. Neither President Trump nor Senator Sanders threatens corporate rights to property, and they both oppose the "free-trade" agreements which are how those rights were to be expanded. The right to property is the only right corporations should conceivably have. Rights are for every human individual within a rights-based social order but not for organizations. Organizations have privileges that can be revoked for illegal activities. They also have certain constitutional rights due to narrow, illegitimate, Supreme Court decisions.

Seven, Free Flow of Capital: The world is the wealthy investor's oyster. Free, unregulated movement of money for the purpose of investment, trade or business production wherever a corporate actor wants to make money by investing in business activities.

Trump, check. Clinton, check. Obama, check. Sanders, no.

Eight, Flexible Labor Markets and Open Borders: Corporations have the freedom to outsource jobs to low wage countries, import low wage labor for manual labor and squeeze labor as much as possible.

Trump, no. Clinton, check. Obama, check. Sanders, half check (for supporting labor from Latin America, but not supportive of outsourcing American jobs).

Nine, Cutting Taxes for the 1%: Referred to as "supply-side economics," the intention is to provide the maximum amount of capital to the wealthy in order to stimulate investment in corporations and/or the markets.

Trump, check. Clinton, no. Obama, no. Sanders, no.

Ten, Coercive Economic Restructuring: Used in the aftermath of an economic crisis to force developing countries to cut social spending and human services in exchange for debt reduction and loan guarantees.

Trump, ? Clinton, check. Obama, check. Sanders, no.

Eleven, International Economic Imperialism: Regime change and disruption for often elected but uncooperative leaders of foreign countries by the most powerful state(s) of the economic system.

> Trump, ? Clinton, check. Obama, check. Sanders, no. A number of reasons have been put forward as to why Trump bombed a Syrian air base and called for regime change in that country, but it's not clear economic domination is one of them.

Twelve, Economic Growth at All Costs: Concerns about ecological destruction are sidelined to keep the economy as a whole and corporations as sub-systemic parts growing for ever greater profitability.[313]

> Trump, check. Clinton, check. Obama, check. Sanders, no.

Thirteen, Wealth Equates with Virtue: From One Party Planet, "In an unspoken moral hierarchy, financial wealth and business success equates with success in life and moral virtue."

> Trump, check. Clinton, check. Obama, check. Sanders, no. It appears that racial justice for Obama amounted to people like him getting ahead rather than focusing on the economic rights of minorities as groups.

Fourteen, Competition Among Self-Interested Parties is the Only Way Society Can Be Ordered: "Survival of the fittest through eternal competition [among] self-interested parties is, practically speaking, the only law upon which society can realistically be ordered."[314]

> Trump, check. Clinton, check. Obama, check. Sanders, no.

My tally: Trump, 7.5 of 14—46.43%. Clinton, 12 of 14—85.71%. Obama, 12 of 14—85.71%. Senator Sanders has a score of only 3.5% because the democratic socialism he practices is an anti-neoliberal ideology. Trump may end up being more neoliberal than he seems at this point. Roger Harris writes, "What we are seeing is Trump, not reversing Obama, but intensifying the neoliberal project. We should expect more aggressive privatizations, deeper tax cuts for corporations and investors, further militarized police, and greater deregulation for the financial sector." Further militarization of the police is a characteristic of fascism, not neoliberalism. The two major parties gave voters a choice between a fascistic neoliberal and an increasingly apparent, neoliberal fascist. Is it any wonder so many voters stayed home on Election Day?[315]

While Trump does not (yet) appear to be a full-blown neoliberal fascist, those question marks are likely to be resolved over time, and all of the evaluations of Trump are subject to change. It is possible, perhaps likely, President Trump will be swayed into full-blown neoliberal fascism by the time those folks of the "deep state" he has appointed as members of his cabinet are done advising him. We hope he keeps his promises and follows up on his Inaugural Address promises. Either he's a radical moving the Republican Party toward a new nationalism by keeping those promises about respecting the independence of nations, or he's just a con man saying what he thinks people want to hear only then to function in cooperation with the establishment's "deep state" agendas of global enforced deployment of neoliberal agreements specifically and their overall preference of a foreign national leader's ideology: neoliberal capitalism. They call it "regime change," but imperialism is how the establishment in both major parties has functioned since WWII. Wall Street and other corporate campaign donors have captured the Democratic and Republican parties. On social issues like gun safety and abortion rights, they keep their bases at one another's throats, but on basic economics and fealty to Wall Street's "free-trade" agenda especially, they function as a political duopoly,[316] two parties that function as one.

The neoliberal order imbues a world economic system of competing private empires (subsystems called transnational corporations). The United States enforces the system of transnational, corporate subsystems all seeking to extract resources to make money and grow in order to make more money and grow more. That system long precedes neoliberalism, and it's called capitalism. The owners get wealthier and wealthier while many of the rest of us work more for less money if we can find a job at all after transnational outsourcing and greater deployment of robots. I address that economic order in the next chapter.

Climate Change

The Trans-Pacific Partnership had a provision allowing automatic approval of liquefied natural gas export facilities.[317] Secretary Clinton didn't express opposition to that dangerous arrangement of the TPP either. Her support for fracking would have expanded the exporting and pipeline infrastructure of ever-increasing releases of methane into the atmosphere, just like Trump will, only internationally. I hope Trump agrees the American market is large enough and self-reliance is better than placing the gas we're extracting on the world market. It will last longer as a short-term bridge to the change in the energy sector human survival depends upon. There must be a transformation from fossil fuels, and we're running out of time if it's not too late already, if there is going to be anything close to the preservation of our current, green climate. We are still standing on the edge of the next American Revolution which is needed because we're also standing on the edge of climate preservation. Extreme extractions of energy can be stopped by sufficient resistance from citizens using direct actions and curbing consumption, but we also need sustainable energy sources to become competitive in the market place. Sustainable energy entrepreneurs need to thrive and help drive the required transformation of the energy sector.

Trump is going to accelerate climate change faster than Secretary Clinton would have, but her support for hydrofracking of gas and oil most certainly would have accelerated climate change as well. Unless there is an unforeseeable breakthrough in energy technology Trump allows to unfold in the marketplace, there is no almost no hope of preserving the Earth's climate to sustain millions, much less billions of people for much longer than the short run. There was a reason we used #JillOrDoom on social media during the last month of the campaign. The two major party candidates did not represent a tough decision about greater "evil"; the American people were offered the choice of two poisons: death by nuclear war with Russia (with loss of jobs, self-government and sovereignty[318] along the way) or death by warming planet if nuclear war with China doesn't do the job first.[319]

Democrats Reform or Die

Every Democrat, who supported Hillary Clinton during the primaries, a candidate who was under FBI investigation at the time, with all of her baggage, her neo-conservative, hawkish foreign policy and her agenda to advance, neoliberal globalization, shares some of the blame for making this general election a choice between two poisonous pills. Bernie or Bust had the full intention of helping Clinton get defeated in support of Jill Stein, but the vote count information indicates Secretary Clinton lost the election because she was the neoliberal status quo in what turned out to be a change election.

Neoliberal Democrats are conservatives who support abortion and gay rights, and their support of corporate globalization makes them a threat to the American experiment of democratic self-government. Neoliberals are attempting to impose corporate self-government by way of "free-trade agreements" on all levels of the American federalist system that will prevent our representatives from regulating corporations how they see fit. People have been protesting trade organizations and globalization for years, but my interest was sparked by my former editor at *The Amendment Gazette* after he called the TPP "Citizens United on Crack"[320] as I explained in Philadelphia. The type of government Americans have is under threat from corporate globalists who largely share the characteristics of neoliberalism. We intend to help neoliberal Democrats lose national elections until the Party unites behind real progressives.

The transnational, corporate desire for a uniform set of rules they need to abide by is understandable. It's called harmonization among states of corporate regulations via "trade agreements." If that is to be considered for the benefit of transnational corporations, the process of writing those regulations must abide by the Constitution. The Commerce Clause tells us Congress should be the body doing the regulating of commerce with other nations, not the Executive Branch or the corporations themselves. If the trade agreements are only about tariffs and currency manipulation, a straight majority vote and signature by the President should be sufficient for enactment. If the agreement includes a systemic, legal transformation like the TPP, then 2/3 of both houses of Congress and ratification by 3/4 of the states should be required. Allowing our democratically established laws to be opposed in private tribunals, where corporations can sue us (we the people, our government), and our taxes (or the national debt) increase just when our government defends our laws in their "tribunals" and there is potentially much, much more taxation or debt when the corporations win their cases, would be a corporatization of our system of lawmaking. This is, simply stated, unacceptable. Our system of government is under assault by these neoliberals of the Democratic Party establishment and their allied neoliberal Republicans.

These trade agreement tribunals are unidirectional. We, our government, can't use them to sue the corporations. Those private legal provisions should have been considered an amendment to our Constitution as well since they corporatize and override our judicial order. The 45th President says he wants to renegotiate NAFTA. Forcing corporations to purchase private insurance and ditching the one-way investor-state dispute settlement chapters would be a big step away from anti-republican and undemocratic control obtained from previous "free-trade agreements" put into place to benefit the power elite of the world's large, transnational corporations. If Trump is the fascist many of us on the left believe him to be, he'll protect corporate power. If he's just a con-man, then he'll govern like a neoliberal using the TPP as the model for bilateral (two state) agreements and/or incorporate many of the ideas of the TPP into and advance the geographically massive Trade in Services Agreement. If he keeps these trade tribunals unidirectional, then he's just a nationalistic neoliberal and deserves two "checks" on the 9th characteristic of fascism. In other words, Trump may turn out to be a fully neoliberal fascist.

Trump has refused to put his business interests into a blind trust and govern as a man. By keeping control of his corporation in the family, the 45th President is literally running the nation as a corporation. That can't end well for the United States; but this chapter is not attempting prophesy.

Hack or Leak?

Were the DNC and Clinton campaign manager John Podesta's email accounts hacked by Russians as the CIA and the FBI[321] claim? Julian Assange, who if anyone should know, claims the emails were leaked from inside the United States, inside the organizations. If Podesta's email account was not hacked after a phishing scam that acquired his password, then there is still extensive Clinton machine/media collaboration under way to hide the truth about the source of these emails. As a skeptic of the CIA claims, my inclination is to believe Assange and Murray.[322] Unfortunately, most people will believe whomever they want rather than to relentlessly investigate the identity and motives of the source(s). In a post-truth, "alternative facts" and "fake news" media environment, knowing the actual truth takes a good deal of effort.

The Veteran Intelligence Professionals for Sanity state:[323]

> The various ways in which usually anonymous spokespeople for U.S. intelligence agencies are equivocating – saying things like 'our best guess' or 'our opinion' or 'our estimate' etc. – shows that the emails alleged to have been 'hacked' cannot be traced across the network. Given NSA's extensive trace capability, we conclude that DNC and HRC servers alleged to have been hacked were, in fact, not hacked.

Levitsky and Ziblatt fret because "leading Republicans — including the president-elect — endorsed the view that the Democratic candidate was not a legitimate rival" because why exactly? Is Hillary Clinton or any other rival above the law? If the establishment is attempting to delegitimize Trump's presidency[324] by creating fake or misleading news stories about Russian involvement with our election that the legacy, mainstream media and many people on the left from Michael Moore and Keith Olbermann to Bill Moyers and Michael Winship,[325] are parroting, then they are as great of a threat to democracy as is Donald Trump, if not more-so. Many liberals seem to have amnesia; the CIA has a record of lying.[326] I agree with Paul Street when he wrote "Blaming Russia is Irresistible to the Democrats" in *Truthdig*:[327]

> The "Moscow stole it" narrative is a fancy version of "The dog ate my homework" for a dismal dollar-drenched Democratic Party that abandoned the working class and the causes of peace, social justice and environmental sustainability long ago.

There's a range of possibilities from Putin having commissioned hacking of the DNC to help elect Trump to Matt Taibbe's view that "outgoing Democrats … using an over-interpreted intelligence 'assessment' to delegitimize the incoming Trump administration and force Trump into an embarrassing political situation: Does he ease up on Russia and look like a patsy, or escalate even further with a nuclear-armed power?"[328] We don't know if the WikiLeaked emails were obtained from hackers or from inside leakers; but in his last press conference, President Obama referred to the "DNC emails that were leaked."[329] Mark Weisbrot notes "The media coverage makes for an entertaining circus, especially the acrobatics of various political leaders as they flip-flop on issues of Cold War and peace and who should be stupid enough to believe intelligence agencies, on faith, after they have lied about so many things from Iraq's alleged weapons of mass destruction back to the Gulf of Tonkin resolution and the Vietnam War."[330]

It's entirely possible the intelligence community and WikiLeaks founder Julian Assange are both telling versions of the truth. The CIA may have evidence showing Guccifer 2 was a Russian agent, and he set up his own website to dump what he found after he or they had hacked the DNC and/or Podesta email accounts.

Whether the DNC and Podesta emails were leaked by an insider or hacked by a Russian operative or both ("one hacking operation does not preclude another"[331]), the intelligence community and the corporate, mainstream media views are the Russians manipulated the elections by exposing the Clintoncratic machine for having manipulated the primaries. Because of WikiLeaks we know the CIA's UMBRAGE group is able to misdirect attribution of their own cyber-attacks and hacking efforts by leaving behind the "fingerprints" of the groups the techniques were taken from.[332] It's possible a rogue agent in the CIA hacked the DNC's email account.

Russian manipulation of U.S. elections is bad. Domestic manipulations of U.S. elections are not really news or of concern to Clinton's supporters in the media. All manipulations of U.S. elections are threats to democratic order, and they should be treated as such by citizens and the media alike. We support the creation of two independent special prosecutors, one to investigate Russia's ties to the Trump campaign and the other to determine why exit polls were so far off from the reported vote totals in the Democratic Party primaries.

Finally
In Nevada, where Jill Stein did not get on the ballot and there is no write-in option, I would have left that ballot line blank if I lived there. If I were some-

how compelled to fill it, to vote for Trump, Clinton or the Libertarian, Governor Johnson, I would normally reserve the right to private ballot and not convey my choice to anyone. In the context, however, of this story, that would be pure cowardice. If I had to choose among a Libertarian, who supported the TPP, a neoliberal neo-con with public and private policy positions and neo-fascist Trump, I would have chosen the candidate who would not implement the TPP, Donald J. Trump. Luckily, Jill Stein was on the ballot in my state, and I sleep well knowing I voted in accordance with my progressive values and the most dangerous, major party candidate of my lifetime was defeated. Hillary Clinton was very experienced with imperialism, using military might for regime change and trade rule enforcement and advancement.

When Clinton lost the general election, American democratic order dodged one bullet and took an arrow in the back. Levitsky and Ziblatt are right; Trump is a threat to what's left of our democratic order. We the people are going to have to fight to demand opposition to his regressive Court nominees and policy initiatives just as we would have had to fight like hell to stop the TPP in Congress had another neoliberal won the general election because that "free-trade agreement" was an even greater threat to democratic self-government than anything Trump has proposed to date. Many of the very people, who don't want Trump "normalized" in any way have been complicit in the normalization of the neoliberalism of the Clintons, Obama and the rest of the establishment Democrats. Trump is very bad news; Hillary Clinton would have been worse in very important ways.

Chapter 11
What's Next?

"Those who do not have the ability to make power elites afraid do not succeed."[333] ~Chris Hedges

Legitimate Elections

The American system of voting is dangerously flawed if not flat-out broken. Before any discussion about our plans for the future can proceed, we must address the risks of using electronic voting machines. Many of Sanders' supporters are convinced Sanders was robbed by somebody manipulating the results in certain counties around the nation. Election fraud and systematic voter suppression make a mockery of "democratic" order.

Electronic voting is vulnerable to vote-count manipulation at several points in the process. What is the partisan make-up of the voting machine manufacturers? Can they be trusted to write clean programs with no manipulation of the outcome? Testimony from a software coder makes it clear the answer is no.[334]

Are the machines themselves vulnerable to tampering by voters? Yes. What about the electronic transmission from the polling place of voting machine totals to the central, tabulating computers? Yes, that data can be intercepted and modified. And the central county computers that do the tabulation of vote count from the individual machines; are they vulnerable to hacking? Yes. Electronic voting machines are a terrible idea. [335]

In a YouTube video called "Fraction Magic – Detailed Vote Rigging Demonstration," Bev Harris, author of *Black Box Voting*, demonstrates how a hacker with the "master key" can access what are called GEMS programs containing voter data and change them, to set the outcome as some desired percentage! The GEMS program is installed in 25 states, 616 jurisdictions including some in Florida, Pennsylvania, Wisconsin, and Michigan. Who wins elections, local, state and national, in those jurisdictions is not up to the voters; it's up to the people with access to the GEMS files.[336] If you believe there are legitimate election results in the United States, you need to watch that demonstration. It's chilling. Even if the election systems are more secure than it seems, who administers the computers involved?

With two weeks remaining in his second term Obama placed election infrastructure on the list of "critical" systems protected by the Department of Homeland Security. States alone need to administer elections and carefully share the effort to protect their election systems from intrusion with the federal government by choice. If access to states' electoral network is required by the federal government, this "critical systems" designation is another threat to our electoral systems.

Many of Sanders' supporters believe Bernie was robbed of the primary, including the RAP committee members, and indeed he was. Election Justice USA did extensive analysis of the Democratic primary results[337] and established:

> ...an upper estimate of 184 pledged delegates lost by Senator Bernie Sanders as a consequence of specific irregularities and instances of fraud. Adding these delegates to Senator Sanders' pledged delegate total and subtracting the same number from Hillary Clinton's total would more than erase the 359 pledged delegate gap between the two candidates. EJUSA established the upper estimate through exit polling data, statistical analysis by precinct size, and attention to the details of Democratic proportional awarding of national delegates. Even small changes in vote shares in critical states like Massachusetts and New York could have substantially changed the media narrative surrounding the primaries in ways that would likely have had far reaching consequences for Senator Sanders' campaign.

The obvious culprits behind this election fraud are participants in the Clintoncratic machine, but we don't know who actually rigged and/or hacked the machines to deploy fractional voting if that is how it was done. Republicans had reason to rig the Democratic primaries too, and so did the Russians. They may well have preferred to have Trump against Hillary, and who can blame them for that? If I could put money on it, I'd bet the Clinton machine via of either voting machine manufacturers rigging the software they use, GEMS files manipulation by the people with the master key were responsible for Sanders' primary election defeat or both. However, if the Democrats could do that, why wasn't that done on Nov. 8th? Perhaps someone changed the master key to the GEMS folders, or Republican hackers did a better job changing the outcome than Clintoncratic hackers.

Even exit polls are corrupted according to Richard Charnin, one of the top election fraud researchers. On Redacted Tonight VIP, Lee Camp interviewed[338] him about the 2016 Democratic Party primaries. He claimed:

> Bernie Sanders has probably done better than the unadjusted [exit poll] numbers that we're looking at, and the discrepancies that we see, because they've already been adjusted, and from my experience, they're adjusted in one direction. Ultimately, they're going to be adjusted to match the vote of the establishment candidate.

Our American system of "democratic" order is not trustworthy because the work of building a voting system was outsourced from the state governments to private corporations.

If the election system is being rigged, then there is no democratic order. Revolt Against Plutocracy is ready to work with other organizations such as No More Stolen Elections[339] to help abolish all electronic voting machines, scanning machines and tabulating computers in the United States. No doubt hand-counting of millions of paper ballots will delay knowing the results of close elections for a day or two, maybe longer; but that's a small price to pay for having trust the outcome of every election has not been rigged at some point. Andrew Levine is right: "Electoral reform ought to be at the top of every pro-democrat's to-do list."[340] Anyone can take immediate action by calling your representatives in state government and telling them to fix the electoral system by returning to hand-counted, paper ballots.

Trump probably won the 2016 election more so from mass voter suppression software called Interstate Crosscheck than any Russian influences. Investigative reporter Greg Palast has researched this extensively, and he explains how it works in detail in his documentary The Best Democracy Money Can Buy.[341] If you'd like to read about it online, search for "The GOP's Stealth War Against Voters."[342] Stopping GOP operatives from this massive voter suppression effort won't be easy. The safe thing to do is to re-register to vote on time before each election. Changing party affiliation is a perfectly legitimate reason to change and update your voter registration. Because names can be deleted from voter lists right before an election, it is, unfortunately, no guarantee your name will be on the list of voters when you attempt to vote. If you are denied the right to vote after following party rules, contact the local media and let honest journalists and/or columnists know about it.

Stopping the corporate control of the Democrats is, in part, a simple matter of pledging to the revolution: #RevolutionOrBust. Pledge to never vote for a neoliberal ever again. Wall Street showed their hand with that tabled for now "free-trade agreement," the Trans-Pacific Partnership. Establishment Democrats threaten democratic order every bit as much as Donald Trump does, perhaps more-so.

Free trade is either low or zero tariffs on imports and a prohibition of state manipulation of currency values. That's it. That's free-market capitalism. The TPP would have fundamentally transformed the domestic system of corporate regulation from democratic self-government in the United States to corporate self-government top to bottom, from the national to the local levels of government. That's neoliberalism, the ninth characteristic of fascism on steroids. The more Trump adopts the 14 characteristics of neoliberalism, the more we'll agree he doesn't really have an ideology beyond advancing his quest for wealth, power and fame. He'll probably fit right in with the neoliberal, pro-life hawks by the end of his term, something I do not mention in the Trump section of the Conclusion.

Political Equality for All Citizens

RAP's agenda remains the same: political equality for all citizens. One person, one vote is a necessary but insufficient condition for a democratic order. Campaign finance deregulation as decreed by the Supreme Court has created a system of government of the rich people. That is plutocracy. Political equality for all citizens would require an overhaul of our campaign finance system under Article 1, Section 4 of the Constitution. Congress and state legislatures have the power to regulate the manner of holding elections, and that included campaign finance until the Supreme Court usurped our representatives' power to contain the influence of big money in politics. It did so first in 1976 with the *Buckley v Valeo* decision, again in 2010 with the infamous *Citizens United v FEC* and again in 2014 with *McCutcheon v FEC*.

The relationship between big money in politics and resulting legislation and policies is one of legalized corruption. This is what we understand Bernie Sanders referred to when he spoke of "establishment politics." Politicians in office should be serving the public or national interests, not the private interests of corporations. In order to abolish legalized corruption and plutocracy, the American people need to equalize money in politics, to make every citizen a donor of equal value.

We are not under any illusions the current Congress will act to legalize democratic order in the United States when the plutocrats control all three branches of government. Therefore, no lengthy elaboration of political, financial equality is necessary here. To summarize:

> Our creative compromise is a **synthesis of "public" financing and a voucher program**. Political equality means not just one person/one vote but also one person/$X.00 maximum available for political donations. No one should be allowed to give more money to candidates, parties and PACs than $X.00, and the value of X would be determined by compromise in legislation. For Americans who do not make enough to pay $X.00 in income or capital gains tax, their voucher could be supplemented or funded by a **tax, not on citizens**, but on American-based transnational corporations.[343]

The entire system of campaign finance could be funded by one good quarter of Exxon/Mobil profits alone. Funding a system of democratic order would serve as a stark reminder to the large corporations the people rule in a democratic order, not the plutocratic overlords based in the corporate sector. A small tax on transnational corporations is a cost of doing business in a democratic order.

The value of X in this agenda would be up to Congress to decide for themselves and the Executive Branch. Such a system would require a constitutional amendment to overturn the illegitimate Court doctrines that money given or spent on political campaigns is protected under the First Amendment. If the Framers of the Constitution had intended the spending or donation of money to be protected as a right, they would have included it in the Bill of Rights. Political equality for all citizens would require representatives to focus on what their constituents want rather than special, private interests with lobbyists and wealth. It would solve the problem of money in politics without taking much out of the system by having "X" match the 2012 levels of spending for federal office, about $50.00 per citizen per year.

This principle applied by law would not lead to some progressive ideal. Americans will still be divided as much as the neoliberal elites pretend to be over social policies. Progressives and conservatives are opponents, and we're about equally numbered. Moderates and liberals together make up the largest plurality, so lawmaking would continue to require compromises.

#NotMyPresident

The anti-Trump rallies that popped up around the country right after the election were premature and—according to Professor Cohen—"infantile."[344] Where were the protests after it was revealed how much the DNC worked to sabotage Senator Sanders' campaign and ensure Clinton was the nominee? Michael Hudson summarizes[345] our view of this opposition to the new President before he had even taken power:

> The anti-Trump rallies mobilized by George Soros and MoveOn look like a preemptive attempt to capture the potential socialist left for the old Clinton divide-and-conquer strategy. The group was defeated five years ago when it tried

to capture Occupy Wall Street to make it part of the Democratic Party. Its attempt to make a comeback right now should be heard as an urgent call to Bernie's supporters and other "real" Democrats that they need to create an alternative pretty quickly so as not to let "socialism" be captured by the Soros and his apparatchiks carried over from the Clinton campaign.

Because the superdelegates chose to lose the election, for better or for worse, Trump, a neo-fascist, is our president. We will work with liberals, radicals and principled conservatives to stop specific agenda items of his, but we won't fall for the faux and, until proven, manufactured "outrage" over Russian hacking that may not have even taken place (more on that below).

Busting the Establishment Democrats

I knew making the case for attempting to deploy leverage again would be difficult for the current committee to agree on. All of us are angry with the Democratic Party. We are Greens now. However, we have come to a decision, and I want to share the original text pasted from where it was copied on our wiggio communication board. By sharing the back and forth over this, the most contentious decision the committee has yet to make, I tell the story transparently in order to help past and future "busters" understand the reasoning.

> **@BernieOrBust:** I have the drafts of 10 chapters of Bernie or Bust nearly completed. The last chapter, "What's Next?" has to be a committee decision. I'd like to break this down into three sections: Fighting Trumpism, Move to Amend, and Busting 2020.
>
> I'm disinclined to make an ongoing, organizational effort to fight Trump except in specific circumstances mostly because I'd like to get back to my regularly scheduled life. To do a lot of emailing would require some fund-raising. We're down to around $500.00 left in our account, and we need to hang on to most of that for when we get fined by the FEC for our late report.

Busting 2020 is likely to be the topic of hot discussion since we're mostly fed up with the Dem. Party. However, our innovation, the "or bust" strategy we brought into this year's primary and general election, will only work in the Dem. primaries. Think about it: the country knows about "or bust" now. We'd have a HUGE advantage by 2019 compared to where we started (from scratch) in 2015. Maybe no one will be worth supporting this way; that's a decision we'll make in 2019. Right now we need to decide if we're open or perhaps even committed to using leverage again in the primary season of 2020. We may have enough influence, especially since it's clear we're not "or bluff," to pick the nominee of the Dem. Party in 2020. When I write "pick," I mean demand of course. Our record, this potential to demand a major party candidate, is not something I'm inclined to walk away from. Leverage is our revolutionary strategy.

It's Dec. 15th. I'd like to get a consensus by the committee on whether or not we will attempt some version of "or bust" again in 2020 by Jan. 1st. There are six of us on the committee now. Four of us need to agree on what we'll do in 2020.

Charlie: I've thought about this some, and I honestly cannot now say (here at the tail end of 2016) WHAT I think, either way, about making a decision in the present about committing to any version of "or bust" in 2020. It's just too far away for me.

Tom: I believe the time we have been waiting for has arrived. Personally, I've been waiting for it for a very long time. What you can say about Trump and his incoming administration is that it is absolutely transparent. And, everyone is awake to some degree or another now. There is no disguising the "bad guy" or the evil policies that have been going on under the partnership of neoliberal and neocon. Even the sleepiest among us know more about Trump's incoming administration than they ever knew about Obama's.

RAP has, in my opinion, arrived at the moment when it will make the biggest difference. People are becoming "activists" in huge numbers as a reaction to this "shocking" election of an orange orangutan. Even the anti-Trump protests, though misplaced, hint at a swell of millions across this country that heralds only the first wave.

I could not imagine this election turning out so incredibly well. The corrupt Democratic Party exposed to the world for what it is, and a president-elect and his administration are so clearly defined as the target.

The Republicans won't be taking money from fossil fuel companies as a "pay to play" and then trying to push their agenda through congress. No. The secretary of state IS the actual CEO of Exxon and the head of the department of Energy is Rick Perry who once vowed to get rid of the department and is actually on the board of directors Energy Transfer Partners! The conflict of interests and their motivations will be crystal clear.

Revolt Against Plutocracy now has the most well-defined target and purpose that it could have ever had. I think we should start from there.

Also, it doesn't matter who runs for office. But, I believe the criteria should be two-fold:

1. never support a democrat - that just gives power and perpetuates a corrupt party. No matter how well intentioned the person running is.
2. The progressive agenda, solely, should have our loyalty.

This is something that we should have learned well from this election. Never again should we give ourselves and our cause to a person or personality. Or to a party.

@BernieOrBust: Tom, there is a logical conflict between your two points. On one hand, never support a Democrat. On the other hand, support a progressive no matter what.

What if Sanders runs again as a Democrat in 2020? What if another genuine progressive runs as a Democrat? I agree with #2, but it's in conflict with #1 if a real progressive throws his/her hat into the ring as a Democrat.

The biggest problem I would have would be if Sen. Warren were to run, but again we can make the decision on whom to support in 2019.

The point is our revolution (not Bernie's) deployed leverage this year. I think we should be open to doing so again if there is a progressive we can support. We don't need the slogan for now; we just need to decide, 4-2 at least, whether we MAY deploy leverage again in 2020.

I think we'll have the influence next time that we wanted, but didn't have, on voters and superdelegates this time. I'd like to state in "What's Next" that we plan on deploying our strategy again if, and only if, there is a progressive running we deem worthy of our support.

This is not a "silence is consent" decision. I would like to hear from Sabrina, Niko, Charlie and Areej. Let's discuss this and get consensus by month's end.

Charlie: I think I've already indicated this by implication, but I'll try to make it more clear: I am not ruling out our using leverage ("or bust") in 2020.

That said, there are no circumstances in which I will ever support [Elizabeth] Warren for president.

Tom: My fear is that compromise will eventually lead us to the current state of affairs - the lesser of two evils. It was a slow and insidious turn until one day we found ourselves with a corrupt insider duopoly which rejected Bernie. And the magnitude of the dysfunction is in Bernie's own rejection of himself and the desperate American families he represented.

@BernieOrBust: I had a conversation with a local, like-minded Bernie or bust supporter today. He made a couple of valid points. 1) the candidate would have to be at least as progressive as Warren. 2) We would not do this if someone as progressive as Warren is not a candidate. I will make it clear if it's a choice between Warren and Senator Jeff Merkley of Oregon; Merkley would get the nod because he endorsed Sanders. This would be by way of hypothetical examination of possible candidates.

As for compromise, we simply won't. That's why Patrick left; he wanted a negotiation/compromise stand with the Clinton machine between the DNC and the general election. We did not.

Charlie: I will never support Warren, and I'm saying I strongly recommend that RAP never support Warren. She has shown herself to be a traitor to progressives.

Sabrina: I think #Busting2020 is powerful. I too believe this is a time for pulling back, watching, creating strategies, and consistently building on all that has been done - but without those people like @BernieOrBust, who are still managing to give more of their time than is good for them, having so much on their shoulders.

I am and have been for quite some time, a member of Move to Amend. You certainly have an easy acceptance of this from me.

As for Trump, I agree that if there were to be any major efforts in this area, it should involve focusing on specific actions, events, and not on his entire political existence. Action just for action's sake isn't the kind of attention to best benefit this movement.

With the amount of recognition the "or bust" movement has garnered, if continued, it could become the best strategy for maintaining a control on the behavior of corrupt politicians, period. As I have been watching from the shadows these last months, it has seemed to me, that the Green Party has too many of the problems associated with the current parties. True control of, by, and for the people, in my opinion, MUST come from the outside. I don't believe this strategy needs to only focus on the DEMOCRATIC Party, it can be applied against ANY establishment politician when there is a viable, Grassroots style politician able and willing to run against the incumbent/establishment option.

I support Charlie in his stance on Warren 100%.

Tom: I think Sen. Warren has shown what type of politician she is. Her late arrival to the events happening at Standing Rock proves this and leaves no doubt that she is an opportunist and firmly ensconced in the establishment bubble of the privileged.

I'll have to be forthcoming as well as Charlie. My own admission is that I don't think I'll be supporting Bernie in the future as he has shown what type of politician he is as well. He left us hanging and joined with the Democratic Party to ensure that the progressive agenda was abandoned – an agenda that is sorely needed by the American families languishing in desperate and life-threatening conditions. I cannot state that emphatically enough.

He could have run with Jill Stein. She offered. He refused. Perhaps, we still would have gotten Trump, but, a progressive third-party would be well into adolescence by now and not just a twinkle in someone's eye.

I say this with respect.

Sabrina: Agreed. Bernie and Warren are both tarnished by their obedience to the Democratic Party. Once a politician has compromised their integrity to the level that Bernie and Warren have, faith should never be placed upon them again.

Yes, had Bernie run with Stein, we may have received Trump, but a fight to regain the freedoms we have lost and to create a true representation of the People won't be won through a single encounter; we were prepared to have to keep fighting even if Bernie had become President.

@BernieOrBust: I expect this to be a contentious discussion, and I hope we can disagree with respect. I am disinclined to ever support Warren after her refusal to endorse Sanders. It was our petition, after all, calling on her to do so.

Bernie could have run as a Green, but he said he would not be a spoiler from the very beginning. I don't believe his integrity on this matter should disqualify him from future consideration. However, I don't think he'll run again in four years; and this isn't about picking a candidate. I'm trying to frame our plans in broad, generic ways (to let the establishment know we're not going away).

I want to use Warren as a marker; we will not support anyone who is not as progressive as she is. We will not (it's apparent) support her specifically, but anyone we do support (endorse is too weak of a word to encompass leverage) will have to be as progressive as she is, only with convictions.

I certainly would support Sanders if he runs again, but we're not picking a candidate here. We're framing our future strategy.

All we need to decide is will we deploy the movement building strategy of leverage in the Democratic Party primaries if, and only if, there is a progressive candidate we can find consensus to support?

My position is yes, we should do this again if there is someone worthy. I'm a Green now, but it doesn't matter. I was a Republican when this idea first came up. Party membership is moot at this point. I agree with almost everything Sabrina wrote in her #Busting2020 post, but I doubt a progressive will run as a Republican. I can write that we could support a progressive Republican, but in all likelihood, the #Busting2020 strategy will be executed in the Dem. Party. We will get the nominee we want, or next time we will bust the Democrats. (We came within 9,700 write-in or Green votes in PA of claiming responsibility for doing so this time.) Our threat of four more years of Trump will be something Democrats won't be able to ignore next time. We could be responsible for either a progressive in the White House or the end of the world (if Trump is re-elected).

As to what "or bust" might mean, that's something else that can wait until 2019 to decide (if there is a United States by then). Green? Socialist Party? A party we don't know about yet? If we agree on using leverage, the candidate and the "or bust" option will be decided later. Right now I want to determine if we have consensus on Candidate X or bust...or not.

Charlie: Yes, I am for "candidate X or Bust" in 2020 (but ONLY, of course, if candidate x is a genuine progressive).

@BernieOrBust: Three of us support a provisional (progressive) candidate X or bust 2020 strategy. If Sabrina, Niko or Areej agree with that, I will include the intention to try again in "What Next?" unless someone puts up a block in which case we'll discuss the intention more.

I will also outline our agenda as part of that chapter to make the process behind political equality for all central to our electioneering strategy. That's how I'll introduce Move to Amend as a fraternal organization.

I'm going to make an argument that Senate Dems need to learn from Republicans and obstruct Trump's worse tendencies using filibuster voting. We will use our list of busters to encourage that behavior, the closest condition to a Blue Senate available.

Charlie: And I want to make clear (as I hope that @BernieOrBust will do in his book) that I'm entirely open to any possibility of a progressive running for the Republican nomination.

Tom: Charlie, I don't really know how that is possible. How can you have a progressive republican? progressive = democratic socialism which means "big government" which is what, in my opinion, we need.

Charlie: Tom, Please note that I mentioned the possibility of a progressive running for the Republican nomination. I didn't say that such an unlikely candidate would himself or herself actually be a Republican.

@BernieOrBust: The problem with a throw-back, progressive Republican is almost no Republicans would support him or her.

Charlie: Of course. But I still want us to be open to the possibility.

@BernieOrBust: Agreed. If there's no dissent, I will add that. Also, I spoke with Niko on the phone today. He supports progressive candidate X or bust 2020, so I need to hear from Areej. No pressure to conform Areej; either we have unanimity on repeating this strategy or one committee member disagrees with RAP in order to focus on building an opposition party and never getting involved with the two major parties again.

The sentiment is mixed on our Facebook page. A good number of commenters want nothing to do with the Democratic Party again.

Areej: My apologies I had some insane couple of weeks of finals. I don't think being involved in the two major parties is a good idea. I don't support it for many reasons including: Losing is not the worst thing that can happen to these DNC party operatives, misunderstanding what incentive structure the Democrats have would be a great mistake, our job now is to educate people to leave the two party trap.

Second, how progressive is progressive, Keith Ellison? He's now is considered progressive; I have the same views as Sane Progressive (Debbie Lusignan) if I want to see in details how people are so easily manipulated. We either believe that we can build an outside party outside of the two parties which work for corporations and by definition have a massive conflict of interest with the people, or we don't and this is mere negotiation with corporations to throw crumbs our way. We can't afford round two of Trump 2020 with our grassroots efforts being WASTED on the Democrats. Every penny, and second needs to go into reforming/building Greens this time. Please let me know what you think.

@BernieOrBust: I sensed you would not be happy, and I want you to make your case. My love or hatred for a party is irrelevant. We're here because we used the system to either elect Trump or get a progressive into the White House. Five of us agree, let's try using leverage again. We have made a name for ourselves, and in 2016, Bernie was right to run as a Dem. The media would have ignored him if he hadn't, and he'd been blamed for Trump instead of the FBI and Russia had he not tried what he did. The poll our partners commissioned in June indicated Bernie would be a "spoiler" with a narrow Trump victory over Clinton if he ran as an independent or Green. [That was before the WikiLeaked emails and Clinton speech to bankers.]

2020 could be altogether different, but leverage, if the right progressive runs, can only work in a major party. If no acceptable progressive steps up, then we'll do what we can for the Greens who are "responsible," mathematically, for Pres. Trump. Bernie or bust is not. (I posted than on our Facebook page last week.) You're terrified of Trump. That's HUGE leverage.

Anyone can be a partisan, major or minor party. We're revolutionaries out to deploy leverage again. Convince me any left party can win in 2020, and I may change my mind. The oceans are dying. We don't have time for Party-building, so we are using the partisan system to leverage our candidate into the White House. Bernie or bust was understood as accomplices of Bernie in a hostile takeover of a major party. Trump actually pulled that off. Had there not been election fraud on the Dem. side this year, Bernie would have as well. Bernie didn't win big the last super Tuesday, so the party with the superdelegates is both more difficult and has fewer people to convince of how serious we are about "or bust." They paradoxically make leverage potentially more difficult and easier if we let them know much earlier next time.

No one anywhere on Earth has the experience we have deploying leverage.

We plan on being hated. We're going to threaten a two-term presidency for Trump, and if you do really good work building the Green Party or uniting all of the progressive parties for an American Syriza in 2020, mathematically you'll help re-elect Trump by dividing liberals from progressives. Leverage is the one strategy that can unite, but we're being insistent: no neoliberals. We are in revolt against neoliberal tyranny if we agree on that side project [which pervades this text].

If we do not undertake this unique strategy, we're just another public interest group with a super PAC. I'm not crazy about K. Ellison, but he's the best being put forward [at that time]. Sanders had an imperial foreign policy view on some issues, but we embraced his "revolution" and attempted to impose him on a party. I think Ellison is an interesting test. If Bernie is not successful reforming the party like everyone before him since the Clinton era, then we'll back only a progressive insurgent expressing a commitment to defeat the neoliberal [order]. We want to be able to claim responsibility for helping re-elect Trump if the Dems nominate another neoliberal. As one comedian put it on The Nightly Show, we're going to "blow shit up" if we don't get our way. Keep in mind, "or bust" will end up being that 3rd party anyway. We're not going to repeat our mistakes. That's job # 2 of Bernie or Bust: Lessons learned…

Tom: @BernieOrBust, I can't believe you are trying to scare us with Trump. That is what we are fighting against. Voting out of fear. Voting for the "lesser of two evils." You have the same message as the corrupt democratic party: "winning is the most important thing" and once our horse is in office, then, we'll make those big changes.

NO.

I rejected that when the hillarybots told me how scary Trump is and I rejected it when Bernie told me that. This is not about "winning." It's about building a movement that is loyal to the progressive agenda and not to the establishment politicians that reside in both the democratic and republican party.

With respect, I have to wonder where your head is.

Working within the system means that NOTHING will change. Nothing will be accomplished. Except for a short-term victory that might make people feel good - but, the corrupt establishment two party system is still in power. And, then, we've accomplished nothing unless this is about a short-term victory.

I have to ask you what your motivations are @BernieOrBust?

Charlie: Tom, I still need to re-read @BernieOrBust's most recent message, but I doubt he's trying to scare US. Leverage, though, does have very much to do with inspiring fear in Democrats—so that they'll do our bidding, so to speak (ASSUMING there's a genuine progressive we'd support who would run – at least for purposes of election — as a Democrat).

Please read @BernieOrBust with a charitable spirit.

Tom: I was too strong in my opinion. But, I just can't stand to see us make the same mistake over and over again. Wasn't this election a final wake up call?

When does it end? When do we break off from our addiction to this corrupt two party system? When is the right time? Never?

Let's not make the same mistake that Bernie made.

Or, really, this whole election, a onetime chance to really change course, will fall away and the safe status quo will continue on.

It's safe. But, I wonder how committed people are if they fall back to safe. I thought we were all awake now, and let's talk leverage. We have it now. We don't need to go running back to the corrupt two party system and beg for a place at the table.

It was RAP and many other political groups and social media that defeated the status quo and kept Hillary out of office.

We have a strategic position now. We need to use that and keep going with it.

And now, you are talking like Bernie - work within a corrupt system for "leverage."

I'm sorry, but, I won't follow you there. We need to have the courage to push forward with what we've gained.

@BernieOrBust: We never felt Bernie made a mistake running as a Dem. for reasons I already laid out. We are either going to deploy leverage again or not. If we do it again, we will be building on lessons learned and the database that's in place. If we do not deploy leverage again, then what are we? One of hundreds of public interests groups [with a PAC].

We will help keep neoliberals out of office, at least Democrats in the White House. Leverage fits nicely with a Revolt Against Neoliberal Tyranny (RANT), [a divisive] project [acronym being discussed on another wiggio thread].

I think "nominate a progressive or we will work to defeat your candidate" is a more radical and revolutionary strategy than simple support for a 3rd party that will be no more likely to win in 2020 than one was in 2016. There is pragmatism behind leverage. With leverage, we can help a progressive get into the White House. Without deploying leverage again, we can what? Help the Greens get to 5% which will divide the left and help re-elect Trump or Pence.

We know what happens if leverage fails in 2020; we will support the 3rd party candidate. If it works next time, we help get a progressive into the White House. Tom asked what motivates me. Being successful by getting a progressive into the White House and saving humanity from climate change motivates me. In our two-party mental prison, how does that happen without leverage?

If things change between now and 2019, we can adapt; but I want to spell out our tentative plans for the next election in the last chapter

Areej: I just want everyone to reflect on how much effort was sunk in to Bernie's run. With the sabotage that occurred, what DEMAND did Bernie have in way of reforms to set the stage for a possibility of an incumbent to run within the party. You speak about leverage as if we have it, there is no leverage. You CANNOT convince an individual party operative to sacrifice their criminal career which depends on corporate donations.

The one message that people have gotten (the majority of people) is that only a more centrist candidate might have beaten Trump, and be terrified even some more from a leftie candidate Sanders. As I told @BernieOrBust, I understand I'm in the minority with this opinion and I'm remaining as a critic with the hopes of diverting undeserved, ineffective time and effort of some future Democrat savior (ones that are half decent are dwindling anyway, assuming Bernie doesn't run), and focus our efforts in building the green party. If 4 years are not enough, then the impossibility of forming an effective third party should be alarming and telling more than ever, about the nature of American democracy (i.e. we really have none).

This next 4 years should be focusing on challenging absurd laws that prohibit vote counting, and taking some of these laws all the way to the Supreme Court. In addition, we should focus on recruiting new blood into the Green Party. It's disappointing that Green party (or a formation of a brand new party) is not going to get the attention it deserves and then gets blamed in October of 2019 for being disorganized because enough people followed another pied piper Democrat. Action is to have the guts to do what's REALLY required of us and take a step that others are too scared to do to achieve what's needed, before this country devolves into right wing fascism. It's on its way.

Tom: I believe that Areej and I are pretty much in agreement and on the same wave length.

I do believe that many progressives are having the same problems as the neoliberals in learning the right lesson from the election.

In trying to make this into a two party contest and using leverage to "beat" the other party, we are locking ourselves into the same corrupt system that we should be fighting against.

When I first started supporting Bernie, I thought the most important thing was to get a progressive into the White House. I learned this election that there is something far more important. And that is to break this corrupt two party system down. We've already begun to do that.

The Democratic Party is dead. I have no doubt about this. And the dems will lose BIG in the mid-terms. There will be no doubt then from anyone that it is, in fact, dead.

So, logically, why would we be committing to working within a system that doesn't exist anymore except in name? Shouldn't we be working to build the Green Party?

Where are the disaffected progressives going to go? Back to the party that destroyed their dreams of having a progressive in the white house? I don't think so. They'll be looking around for a place to go.

If Bernie had won, we could have looked forward to a mid-term election where many progressive democrats would have been elected. After Bernie's betrayal, that's not going to happen.

Two things can happen: 1. the progressives again stay home for the mid-terms, OR 2. We can get progressives excited about the mid-terms and bring them to the Green Party. And work to get Green Party candidates to run for mid-terms. And maybe we could work to get progressives out to vote for the mid-terms, and vote for those Green Party candidates.

Also start to build a strong third party for the next presidential election.

Charlie: Tom says: "… logically, why would we be committing to working within a system that doesn't exist anymore except in name? Shouldn't we be working to build the Green Party?"

1. We AREN'T committing to doing any such thing. We (as RAP) are not part of the system, or at least I don't view as such. Rather, we work as a PAC not officially affiliated with *any* party. (Indeed, PACs can't legally be officially affiliated with any given party anyway, right?) WE dictate as an independent entity. I've always liked that about us.
2. There's no reason why any one or all of us as individuals cannot also work to build the Green Party. Indeed, I am now (as of a number of months ago) a member of the Minnesota Green Party. That's not mutually exclusive with our individual involvement with RAP and RAP initiatives.

@BernieOrBust: I'm not certain where Tom has come down at this point. We promote and help build the Green Party between now and 2019. Then, if and only if, there's a real progressive running in the Dem. (or the unlikely Republican) primaries, we execute our plan: Candidate X or Green. (BTW, it won't work in the Republican primaries because no progressive would have support from the Republican base. In theory it's worth mentioning, but from a practical perspective, it's just not going to work against an incumbent President supported by a largely, reactionary Party base.)

If it works, we have a candidate for the White House we can support and can win the election. If it doesn't work again, we have "or bust" Green candidate we can support and cannot win the election (unless [Patrick's] RANT is wildly successful getting the American people to turn against neoliberals and fascists alike).

I keep coming back to this: if we don't build on our experience and attempt this again in 2020, we're just another public interest group with a PAC. Almost nobody is blaming us (or giving us credit) for Clinton's defeat. In four years, we should be in position to take credit for either a progressive in the White House or the defeat of another neoliberal. Our disdain for the Dem. Party is moot. Again, we're not partisans; we're revolutionaries.

Five of us are on board with this approach. Tom, does "Ok. Understood." mean you're on board as well? With four of us supporting leverage in 2020, it's going to happen. I want to report if this is a unanimous decision or not. If not, then it's going to affect the ending of Chapter 4, "Treasurers Dropped Like Flies," and Chapter 10, "What's Next?"

Tom: I was just addressing the misguided (imo) view that the democratic party is worth saving. It is not. It is the antithesis to RAP, RANT and the progressive agenda. It would be a HUGE waste of time and effort to try to work with or within the democratic party.

Third party should have the focus. Self-fulfilling prophesies about third party being unviable or perceived to be unviable are just another way to say that we have to accept the "lesser of two evils."

That is not true and that type of thinking leads back to another Trump presidency.

But, yes, I'm onboard.

@BernieOrBust: We're not working in the Dem. Party; Sanders is doing that. I wish him well with that undertaking. We're not working with the Dem. Party if we back a progressive running as a Dem. We'd be backing the candidate and his/her agenda.

Meanwhile, we build the Green Party. If we don't do that, it never will become viable. Writing in *CounterPunch*,[346] Andrew Levine wrote, "I did try to convince myself and others, as I have before, that this time, there was a chance that the Greens would break out of the margins, and therefore that voting for their candidates could serve a more useful purpose than merely indicating disgust. Of course, this didn't happen; it never does."

For the purposes of deploying leverage in 2020, the Green Party doesn't need to be viable; it just needs to be enough of a threat for "or bust" to be taken seriously by Democrats.

We're majority on board for deploying leverage in 2020 if we can at that time agree on a candidate to support. I think this has been a useful and helpful discussion. I appreciate the heat and intensity that accompanied the respect for our differences.

Senator Warren

Ironically, the standard-bearer for the progressive we want to support in 2020 is Senator Elizabeth Warren, but we want a candidate with a profile in courage. When people were standing up for revolution in 2016, Warren sat during the primary in her own state waiting to see who would come out and then endorsed Clinton. In a column addressing how the corporate media is setting the public up for another corporate Democrat in 2020 by fearmongering over Trump, Caitlin Johnson notes[347] the Democrats will:

> …try to offer us an Andrew Cuomo. This will be unacceptable. If that falls flat, they'll try to offer us Elizabeth Warren. This will also be unacceptable. Warren will be another Obama, saying all the right things while selling America's lifeblood to the highest bidder and helping to deepen the chokehold of the Walmart economy. Despite her aptitude with Twitter and making viral videos wagging her finger at indifferent billionaires who will suffer no consequences for their crimes, Warren has wound up on the wrong side of every major progressive acid test she's been given,[348] from Bernie to DAPL to the DNC scandal to Hillary's warmongering. She's another smooth-talking neoliberal in progressive's clothes, just like Obama was. Not acceptable.

I don't know if I'd categorize Warren as a neoliberal. A major consideration as to whether a politician is a neoliberal can be derived from their donors. Go to the Open Secrets website[349] and find out who contributed to the person's election. If you see Wall Street banks listed, the candidate is a neoliberal. Warren has no such contributors, so we deem her more a spineless progressive than a neoliberal. She's not even willing to vote against Trump's nominee for HUD,[350] Ben Carson! Paraphrasing Anonymous, we will not forget Warren's cowardice; we will not forgive her for it.

Since this discussion, Areej resigned from our committee. Like many revolutionaries, she wants no part of the Democratic Party going forward. We support her intention to build the membership of the Green Party in the coming years. Many of the folks commenting on our Facebook page express deep disdain toward the Democratic Party after what the DNC and other Clintoncrats did to Sanders. On a post titled "The True Enemy of Progress Isn't the GOP, It's the Democratic Establishment,"[351] Larry Snider wrote:

> I am going to go #ProgressiveOrBust …for the remainder of my life. I am now a #TealGreen. I am more than happy to help Brand New Congress and Justice Democrats if there candidates will put Main Street leaps and bounds before Wall Street. If they lose their primary then I will not be voting for the corporatist in the general. Instead I will be campaigning for and donating to Green Party candidates. Hopefully the infrastructure will be there for us to help GP candidates remotely. Three cheers for #ProgressiveOrBust2018…Neoliberalism has perverted the Democratic Party, possibly beyond repair. The time for incrementalism has passed. Drastic times call for drastic reforms. If the Democratic establishment will not become the people's party, than we will have to make our own political party. The Green Party is open and if people are willing to work we can help build it up. No one will do it for us, we must become the change we want to see.

We surveyed our pledge-takers during the course of writing this book. 94% of them agree to deploy leverage again in 2020 if we support the right progressive. We will not deploy leverage on behalf of anyone who endorsed Hillary Clinton in the primaries. If the Democrats nominate Hillary Clinton again or anyone who endorsed her or any other neoliberal in 2020, we will do our level best to help defeat him or her by supporting a real progressive with our PAC and our online, revolutionary army. There will be a progressive in the White House in 2021, or we'll help defeat the Democratic Party, "busting" the nominee by supporting the progressive party of opposition with highest membership at that time. #ProgressiveOrBust

We never started a Bernie or Bust page or group on Facebook, but there were quite a few of them. I asked an administrator of the Official Bernie or Bust group, Brayden Portillo, what types of posts were censored; and he messaged me they only deleted pro-Clinton posts. He agreed it could have been ABC, Anyone But Clinton that I had declaimed on The Tim Black At Night program, or #NeverHillary, an idea that misses the point of committing to a candidate "or bust." Next time leverage is applied, a clear explanation of the strategy needs to be clearly described, as much as it's in the movement organizers' control, at the moment of voter pledge. "Or Bust" will be specific and define a revolutionary, mass movement the media will still distort.

Stopping and Supporting Trump

Sabrina articulated our view precisely. We cannot predict every policy proposal and bill Trump will propose that we will oppose, but we certainly wanted to prevent President Trump from getting a nominee in the Supreme Court. Eventually, Trump would slam a nominee into the Court when Congress is on break, a recess appointment. Don Hazen wrote,[352] "Many are arguing that since McConnell and the GOP refused even to consider Merrick Garland, Obama's nominee for Scalia's seat; refused to act on more than 80 of Obama's federal district court judges; and upped the ante by saying they would never allow a Hillary Clinton nominee to be considered by the GOP-controlled Senate, it is now time to play the game like the conservatives." Trump's SCOTUS nominees should be filibustered and stopped by Democrats[353] if they want to get re-elected. We used our mailing list and revolution or bust "army" to let Senate Democrats understand that message, and we hope other organizations will join us. Democrats, who collaborate with Trump's plutocratic, corporatist, anti-human rights nominees for SCOTUS judges with anti-worker, anti-consumer agendas, are not worth keeping in office; and there are plenty of them.[354] #ObstructOrBust was our hashtag, but the filibuster option for Supreme Court nominees has been dropped by Senator McConnell.

Vice-President Pence is to the right of Trump. Like Dick Cheney and Dan Quale, he provides assassination and impeachment insurance for the President. We do not advocate the impeachment or removal of or harm to come to the 45th President. On January 10, 2017 I posted a *Washington Post* column[355] by Richard Cohen entitled "How to remove Trump from office." It advocated for Vice President Pence and members of the Trump's cabinet to make Pence the President by declaring Trump unfit for office under the Twenty-Fifth Amendment. I asked on our Facebook page how many people wanted Pence rather than Trump as President, and by a ratio of 45 to 1, our supporters preferred Donald Trump to Mike Pence.

When Trump is doing something we support, whether it's a domestic policy (legislation) or a foreign policy initiative, we will express support for it. In "Standing on the Edge of the Next American Revolution," I argued for a new foreign policy, "National self-determination." In his inauguration speech, President Trump said, "it is the right of all nations to put their own interests first."[356] These ideas are in alignment with my own and in opposition to the record of the American establishment since at least WWII. Trump's cruise missile attack on Syria on April 6, 2017 demonstrated he will not abide by the claims made in his Inaugural Address. Another example would be his willingness to work together with Russia to defeat our common enemy and promote trade between our nations. Unfortunately, by bombing the Syrian air base, Trump has turned what he called an "asset" (a good relationship with President Putin) into a lost opportunity and a dangerous escalation of tensions between the United States and Russia. 100 days of President 45 had not passed, and Trump had already reversed himself on a long list of campaign and inaugural promises. He's conducting foreign policy more like a globalist. President Hillary Trump, Inc?

Professor Stephen F. Cohen, Professor emeritus of Russian studies at Princeton University and New York University presented the pre-Syrian missile attack framework:[357]

Trump brings to the Presidency a businessman's way of thinking. Businessmen don't go looking for friends, they go looking for partners, people who have the same interests they have. In my opinion, there's nothing except this Cold War mania in the U.S., nothing objective, and the demonization of Putin in the U.S., which has become an institution - there's no practical national interest reason why Trump and Putin should not become national security partners.

It means political people, who understand how dangerous this new Cold War is, did not vote for Trump, but will support him if he pursues a policy of trying to find cooperation with your President, President Putin. But will those people come forward? They don't want to be called names either. So this is a struggle in my country. You've got struggles in your country. Our struggle here is that if Trump does this, pursues what used to be called detente with Putin, we need to support him.

Our willingness to support some of Trump's initiatives and oppose others aligns with Sanders' positions of supporting and opposing the 45th President.[358] Rep. Dennis Kucinich[359] and comedic political commentator and Bernie or Bust supporter Jimmy Dore also support this strategy.[360] While there will be opportunities to organize opposition to specific agenda items and Court nominees online and on the phone, the Trump administration provides the impetus to form stronger communities of mutual support and opposition to his fascistic authoritarianism[361] offline as well. Going to meetings and gatherings to resist Trump and the neoliberal alternative is arguably essential going forward.[362] To be crystal clear, we opposed Trump during the election; and we still do. All we are willing to cooperate with are his peace and disarmament initiatives vis-à-vis Russia and his trade agreements if and only if they are not burdened by the characteristics of neoliberalism. Mixing targeted tariffs with free-market capitalism would be a reprieve from the neoliberal, international, corporate coup Obama and Clinton were hell-bent to advance starting with a version of the TPP. With President Trump changing positions on so many issues he campaigned on, it's possible the globalist establishment he's surrounded himself with will end up advancing neoliberal trade agreements.

There can also be no getting around party-building. Unless you're physically unable or unwilling to make the time, it's time to build a party of opposition to the neoliberal economics of Clinton, the libertarian economics of Governor Johnson, Clinton's neo-conservative foreign policy and Trump's brand of fascism, something we can fully and accurately evaluate now that he is in power. If President Trump should end up governing as an authoritarian tyrant taking away people's rights on a much larger scale than Obama did, we will cease all willingness to support him in any way. We will not oppose Trumpism without framing progressive, non-neoliberal, alternatives to his regressive and fascistic policy proposals. Doing so only plays into the hands of the establishment who will frame themselves as "better than" Trump. That's only true on social issues, so don't buy it next time the Democrats have a primary: #ProgressiveOrBust. A growing progressive party of opposition to neoliberalism will make that slogan more effective. All Democrats need to know their neoliberal candidates will not be supported by revolutionaries in the general election.

Climate Preservation

Like Secretary Clinton's plans to expand hydrofracking, all indications are Trump's policies will accelerate climate change even faster than hers would have. Like soldiers on a battlefield surrounded by the enemy, we can either surrender to the catastrophe coming our way or fight to the death for a sustainable energy future. It is, to a limited extent, in our hands.

The fight for climate preservation will have to be statewide and local efforts rather than national. The water protectors at Standing Rock serve as courageous models for climate action. Activists will have to put their bodies on the line in the coming years. We also need to cut our energy consumption dramatically. A 50% reduction of per capita energy consumption would provide Americans with a quality of life equivalent to that in France and Japan.[363] This will mean pushing local governments to act to provide better mass transit systems, authorize sustainable energy projects, etc., as well as personal sacrifices such as vacationing locally and otherwise cutting back on energy usage. Reducing Christmas displays and turning them off right after Dec. 25th is one of hundreds, perhaps thousands of ways Americans can cut back on the amount of energy we consume. Climate preservation comes down significantly to personal behaviors because the national government is going to do little if anything to slow climate change. No issue separates liberals and progressives from neoliberals, conservatives and corporate fascists better than climate change. Neoliberals and conservatives will frack us over for the fuelish purpose of putting off what is urgent.

In theory, the idea of voluntarily cutting consumption to reduce our carbon usage should appeal to liberals and progressive alike; but there's another reason the broad American left would want to unite to consume less. The economy depends upon demand for goods. If there is low demand for new goods, we'll slow the economy down during Trump's time in office. This, in turn, could lead to a voter backlash against Trump and Republicans in time for the 2018 midterm elections. I'm not suggesting people go without necessities; just make what you have last longer. If you truly **need** something new, buy something; but otherwise save or invest your money until Trump and the right are driven from office. As climate change combatant Bill McKibben puts it,[364] "… one goal of our fight must simply be to break the power of Trumpism and all that it represents." One doesn't need to share this entire book to spread the idea of fighting Trump and climate change by consuming less. Just share the idea of a consumer boycott for new merchandise on social media.

If sufficient materialism becomes a movement, unemployment will increase which Trump will claim to be "fake news" or just "a lie." This strategy is not about America winning or losing; it's about curtailing consumption primarily to preserve the climate and secondarily to make sure Trump isn't successful boosting the economy. Because scale matters, merely curbing your consumption and figuring out how to curb energy use is not enough. Talking to people you know about this and sharing this strategy to individually undermine Trump's chances of accelerating a slow-growing economy online will help this strategy become effective. It'll take millions of liberals and progressives consuming less than before January 20, 2017. We all can rewrite the zeitgeist one tweet, one post, one conversation at a time: curb consumption—stymie Trump. It's not only about helping Trump fail (controlled slowing of the economy); it's something everyone in a developed country can do. Cut back. Purchase only what you need, not what you want. Some people are addicted to shopping, but they should not be ridiculed. Ask the person what they could do to harm Trump by, essentially, slowing down, taking foot off gas, turn out the lights, forgo spending money you don't have to until Trump is gone. If need be, purchase a high mileage, used car or second hand clothing. There are dozens if not hundreds of ways to oppose Trump from getting under his skin to making calls to your congressman to oppose the President's policies and Supreme Court nominees. Everyone needs to have their congressperson's and Senators' phone numbers on their cell phones.

We need a new green deal using government spending to stimulate enterprise. Inventors need to figure out how to re-use captured carbon and sell it in the marketplace. International forums can mandate what the business sectors from neoliberals to Trump will not: ships must run on compressed hydrogen by a reasonable date in the future. Onboard storage of hydrogen by 2025 and onboard production of hydrogen from water need to be mandated by 2050. These are survival demands upon the commercial transportation sector. The mandates can be lifted only if a better alternative to fossil fuel power system is invented and developed. National defense and government spending on vehicles could help lead the transition to a post-fossil fuel energy sector, but none of this is going to happen under Trump

The world came together and solved the problem of ozone depletion. Chemicals were banned, and that technology was replaced by another. The 45th President and his Congress are not going to solve the problem of climate conservation. Resisting corporatism, embodied by a corporation and a president as one (President Trump, Inc.) may slow the fossil fuel machine down, but a neoliberal Democrat in 2020 cannot be the alternative. Unless Americans individually decide to consciously reduce energy consumption and a movement of climate conscientious around energy conservation becomes pervasive in the United States, the acceleration of global warming may be too great to handle regardless of our post-election cooperation, technological advances or mandates by 20 whenever. The world can solve the problem of climate change, but we're going to have to buy time for now by consuming less energy in the meanwhile. Maintaining the unnecessary hyper-materialism of our corporatized economic and social order will spell doom for coastal cities around the world.

Trump has already reversed himself on a number of issues, and it's possible he will be more horrific than he sounded as a candidate. He has admitted there is "some connectivity" between human activities and climate change, but nobody on his cabinet reflects that sentiment.[365] Trump has appointed a climate change skeptic, Scott Pruitt, to administer the Environmental Protection Agency; and he has not stepped back from his promise to cut environmental regulations that he argued during the campaign are an unnecessary burden on US corporations. We can hope for the best, but we need to prepare for the gravest dangers Trump will pose to the climate in part by making changes in our lifestyles.

It is possible and even desirable having a person like Trump in the White House will motivate more Americans to take actions to cut energy consumption and join the fight against fracking, pipelines, etc. "We're going to need demonstrations more frequent and even larger than those that helped stop Washington's war on Vietnam."[366] All of these will consume energy getting to and from the demonstrations, so citizens need to be open to efficient innovations when it comes to protests and opposition efforts. Getting involved with climate preservation lifestyle may be part of creating a voter backlash against him in 2018, but activism is the antidote to the utter despair[367] many people feel after the election of a climate change denier. After acknowledging the desperate situation the Earth's climate is in, Chris Hedges insisted, "We have a moral imperative to stand up ... for life. The consequences of doing nothing insure ... the extinction of the human species."[368]

Recommendations

1. Make sure you're registered to vote by changing your party affiliation from one of the two (normally) neoliberal parties to the Green Party or an even smaller progressive party and get involved to build that party of opposition. The Green Party is not strong enough to win major elections at this time. It's up to revolutionaries, democracy advocates, climate activists and other progressives to change that. If "or bust" is going to mean anything Democratic voters and especially superdelegates will need to be concerned about in terms of winning elections, a growing party of progressive opposition to corporate-funded neoliberal "puppets" must be on their short list. After the pri-

maries, you can vote for anyone you want. Just as in 2016's round of primaries, registering as a Democrat—or in a parallel universe or another time to Republican—or not, will depend on whether or not there is a progressive candidate running you deem to have a low enough number of fascistic and neoliberal characteristics and a sufficient skill set as an organizer and a leader.

2. State activists are making progress getting state legislatures to pass resolutions to Congress asking them to pass an amendment to overturn the Citizens United and all other related decisions. We encourage people to participate, give a little of your life to legalize democratic order, by joining Move to Amend and helping out if you live in a state that has not yet passed a resolution to Congress. At some point, the pressure will be applied to get Congress to act, but that's not likely for at least two to four years. Getting America on track to a democratic order will require abolition of the Supreme Court-established doctrines that 1) money is speech and 2) corporations are protected by constitutional rights. If the Framers had intended the spending or giving of money to be included as a fundamental right, they would have added it to the list. The regulation of money in politics is covered in Article 1, Section 4 of the Constitution. Congress and the states shall regulate the manner of holding elections. Speech cannot be curbed in any way, but money spent on it (the volume of the speech) can be regulated as originally intended.

3. I asked our supporters to build lists of email addresses, people to whom they can forward our political, call-to-action messages. While there will always be a need for offline organizing, we can do a lot online with the right tactics. Build lists of people you know. Have a list? Trade it with another from a progressive you know. Someone reached out to me in the course of writing this story, and I've traded around 70,000 email addresses I've built over the years, mostly from peti-

tions, with him. Some of them come from people who took our pledge. We promised we would not do that without first asking our pledge-takers' consent in an online poll.[369] Just start with your own contacts and build the list(s) over time. These can be used to stop Trump's worse inclinations and Court nominees for now and to help elect a progressive in the next election.

We polled our pledge-takers on this, and most of them support exchanging their addresses with other revolutionary groups. This email tactic will be deployed to build our online army in the years to come.

Keep in mind, some free email services limit the number of messages sent in a week. For most people, a dozen or two would be a great start. There are ways to harvest your email account for everyone you've ever emailed. It takes time, but this is a key tool of the revolution. Instead of organizational "spam" people get, you can reach out to many as an individual and communicate one to one. Be sure to use BCC for addressing emails to stop or promote policy making in Congress and state legislatures whenever reaching out to more than one person at a time. During elections, these can be used to help elect candidates. It works.[370]

If you are not part of the solution, you're part of the problem. If you have not, please join our revolutionary movement. If you never took the Bernie/Jill/revolution or bust pledge, or if you took it, unsubscribed and have decided to plug back into our "or bust" network, please go to citizensagainstplutocracy.org and take the voter pledge. However, if you have unsubscribed from our mail list, you'll need to use a different email address.

4. After you're finished reading this, please share *Bernie or Bust* with a friend or relative. We won't build the revolutionary movement we need if this book sits around gathering dust.
5. If election integrity is important to you, register and get involved with No More Stolen Elections:
https://www.nomorestolenelections.org/
6. Cut your consumption (see the Conclusion).

One Party Planet

7.   Search for, find and read One Party Planet.[371] The corporate
media does not only manufacture consent for what the establishment wants from the people, it manufactures their reality,
a bogus, pro-corporate understanding of the world we live in.
Military interventions half way around the world are allowed
to be understood as matters of "national security." Other ex-
amples could fill a book.

One Party Planet is free, and it conveys an independent description of our
world order that is not difficult to understand and, just as important, provides
a framework of a way to think about how a progressive revolution can transform the international corporate world order into something just and sustainable. Before the author describes the neoliberal world order, he has a section
explaining how he knows what he is describing. Near the end of the pamphlet,
the author cites the need for systemic thinking, but he doesn't explore systemic
transformation.

Think of every transnational corporation as a subsystem functioning
within the larger system, the neoliberal world system. The transnational corporate subsystems have inputs (supplies, human and raw materials, etc.), an
output (a service or product) and feedback in place to order new supplies of
what to put into the business. That feedback can be changed in order to cut
sub-systemic (corporate) costs and a range of other reasons. Changing the neoliberal system into something sustainable may be a matter of changing the
rules and the information fed back from output to input within those transnational corporations.

Trump's neo-fascism and Clinton's neoliberalism made revolution the only
sane option, and that will continue to be the case whether or not her name is
attached to the Party establishment. Wall Street's agenda, the corporatization
of everything, must be opposed as much to change the status quo as to preserve
certain aspects of the status quo. Trump threatens our civil liberties; Obama
and Clinton threatened to transform our system of governance from democratic self-government to corporate self-government. To defeat the job-out-
sourcing, corporate globalizing, neoliberal candidate, the American people,

including a number of Bernie or Busters outside of the RAP committee, chose the only alternative many of his voters believed could defeat Clinton.

Internationalizing corporations, or in Marxist terminology, expropriating the expropriators, is not necessary for systemic transformation. The analysis offered in One Party Planet is not class-based; it's a systems-based analysis. The corporation or more precisely, transnational corporations are the subsystems of the "unit" the author analyzed, a capitalist-state world system propped up by neoliberal ideology. The central banks are other, special case subsystems. The neoliberal order is a world system made up of these subsystems. The neoliberal agenda is nowhere simultaneously more difficult to directly understand on one hand and more clear, once explained by trade lawyers and activists on the other hand, as are the so-called "free-trade agreements" Obama's trade representative was negotiating. The three trade agreements Obama was rolling down the fast track were fundamentally un-American, anti-democratic and constitutionally dubious menaces to democratic order, our rights, U.S. sovereignty and to every elected representative in the United States. Neoliberals are coming to displace American workers and our system of government, shape our understanding of their world and abolish or create the rules and regulations that curb the worst excesses of corporate greed. We need a revolution, not just to transform our politics from oligarchy into a democratic order, but also to preserve the legal order (democratic, self-government) we have in place! Smaller, local corporations are the engine of new employment, and they are not the parts of the world order we're concerned with.

Richard Moser writes about a revolution 100 million people could support. Full disclosure: he donated generously to our CAP PAC. He writes, "Transformative movements recast and reconstruct cultural materials from the past and present to create a new world out of the world we have inherited."[372] A post-neoliberal world order will stem from the world we have. A world system of transnational corporations and states is in place. We can transform it by changing the rules, but first revolutionaries have to win a national U.S. election not once but repeatedly, like the Jefferson-Madison-Monroe run early in our republic and similar to FDR's nearly four terms in the 20th Century. The U.S. is the core state of the world system. If a revolution can succeed here, it could ripple around the world at various rates of change. It could put Brexit to shame and change the course of history away from neoliberal, corporate domination. Moser adds, "By using the ideas of transformation and reconstruction we can better envision the process of historical change as the play between continuity and discontinuity or between tradition and innovation."

Writing on his website[373] and with no coordination with RAP, Moser argues, "The experimental approach of the inside/outside strategy,[374] alertness to transformation [and/or] reconstruction as modes of revolutionary change, universal values as rhetorical framework and political ideal,[375] and the recognition that our ideals and strategies must, of necessity, speak to a hundred million people[376] and more, are four parts of a work in progress." That is RAP's approach in a nutshell. We'll operate inside/outside of the Democratic Party as long as it remains functional. We perceive transnational corporations and central banks as subsystems to transform into service organizations, hold human rights, including, especially the right to vote, as our moral core and hold political equality for all citizens as our political ideal. Bernie's campaign, running on the platform he did, which we largely support, can, of necessity, earn support of over a hundred million people. His campaign inspired millions of Americans to get involved and made political revolution against the neoliberal establishment mainstream and a real possibility. RAP intends to build on that legacy. We are not a campaign for the White House; we're building a movement for peaceful revolution to get a worthy progressives into the government. #ProgressiveOrBust is our revolutionary demand going forward.

Our revolutionary movement is a necessary revolt against neoliberal and fascist tyrannies. I'm not just referring to what Bernie called establishment politics, establishment economics and corporate globalism. We add to that list every political candidate with a score of 30% or more on the list of 14 characteristics of fascism or the list of 14 characteristics of neoliberalism. Our revolutionary movement intends to reverse the drift toward American fascism and "empire." Our mission is to deploy innovative strategies and continue using any and all legal tactics to secure the next American revolution that the people, the nation, the world and the planet desperately need if coastal cities are to survive the next century and the human race is to survive another 1,000 years.

See FAR or Else: Revolution Can't Go on Vacation Under Trump

After the Woman's March in Washington DC and hundreds of sister marches around the world, neoliberal Senator Van Hollen said, "We need to harness that energy in the weeks and months ahead. The Senate's going to be the main battleground; we need people to sustain what we saw on Saturday and fight the battles."[377] Many Democrats agreed, but allowing neoliberal Democrats to "harness" the opposition to Trump must be resisted every bit as much as Trump's reactionary agenda and Supreme Court appointees. It is their neoliberal political philosophy that created the backlash which helped get Trump elected in the first place.

A former RAP committee member, John Rachel, has been working for four years on the idea of having populist candidates sign a contract with voters that obligates them, if elected, to actively support more than 4-6 of 11 policy positions large majorities of American voters support. For example, raising the minimum wage to $15/hour is supported by 63% of voters; and it's the first policy position listed. After a good deal of discussion, brainstorming and multiple rounds of voting, we decided to call these candidate agreements Contract For American Renewal (CFAR, pronounced "see far").

In 1994 the Republicans took the House of Representatives for the first time in decades using their Contract With America. In 2018, we're attempting to use a Contract For American Renewal to help left/populist Democrats with their primaries ("C-FAR"). If the CFAR-signing Democrats do not win their primaries, leverage activists will continue to build a decentralized movement of voters pledged to vote only for CFAR third party candidates where they are on the ballot and for CFAR write-in candidates where there is no CFAR candidates on the ballot ("or Else"). RAP is using #CFARorElse to build momentum for a left-populist wave election as backlash against Trump and to advance the political revolution Senator Sanders sparked.

#CFARorElse is an ambitious new movement intent on immediately following upon the innovative Bernie or Bust strategy for the midterm elections. Indeed, CFAR or Else aspires to become "Bernie or Bust on steroids," intending to expand Bernie or Bust's electoral mission from Bernie vs. Hillary to left-populists vs. neoliberals generally. In growing beyond its initial movement, CFAR or Else hopes to benefit from the large existing pool of Bernie or Bust pledgers and sympathizers and grow into an effective, electoral leverage movement.

Leverage (or Else!) will be applied on behalf of the left-populist candidate for U.S. Senate or the House of Representatives. It is not something RAP can directly organize, so we intend to build an army of leverage activists and teach, guide and tutor them to duplicate Bernie or Bust strategy and tactics at the local/state levels. CFAR or Else is revolutionary approach to using major party structures as Sanders tried to do. Whereas he didn't want to divide the left, we made it our point to do just that in order to nominate the only candidate who would have united the Democrats for President. The "or Else" side of the CFAR or Else double-edged sword intends to use third party CFAR candidates, who are on the ballot and, CFAR-signing write-in candidates as spoilers to aid in the defeat of the neoliberals who win their primary contests. #CFARorElse may accurately be thought as a #WarOnNeoliberals.

Depending on how safe the seat in Congress is it won't take a lot of voters pledged to vote for a CFAR candidate. Leverage can be a few hundred voters in close elections and tens of thousands pledged voters where the Democrat or Republican holds a gerrymandered safe seat. In such contests, the only likely accomplishment will be to build a list of regional voters on the left. That's the beginning of the key section in a network of networks that leverage activists can acquire and use to help left-populist candidates get elected. Building leverage can build influence if it's done right.

The reason for organizing (CFA)Renew(al) or Else right now is simple, and is substantially explained by prize-winning journalist Glenn Greenwald of the Intercept. Massive resistance to Donald Trump's openly extremist presidency is inevitable, but it matters enormously what movements or organizations seize the leadership role in that resistance.[378] The revolutionary left must take the lead in forming the key issues for the 2018 midterms. By 2020, the party dynamics may be much different, but for the next campaign season, the Democratic Party is still be best bet, perhaps the only chance, for opponents to neoliberalism to succeed in elections for Congress. The left can use the Party rather than the other way around, and congressional races don't have superdelegates in the way.

In our U.S. political system, only candidates from the two major parties routinely have a shot at winning high political offices, like the presidency, Congressional seats, or state governorships with rare exceptions. As Norm

Solomon wrote, "Those who scoff at using the Democratic Party as an electoral tool to oust the Trump-Pence-Ryan-McConnell GOP have no other credible electoral tool to propose."[379] Therefore, it's simply inevitable that mainstream media and most voters will perceive the Democratic Party as the chief opposition to Republicans controlling government, under a Trump presidency or any other Republican one. But as Greenwald rightly notes, the Trump administration's unprecedented extremism makes the political stakes of a potent, principled, successful opposition especially high. Whatever the public's knee-jerk, unthinking perception that Democrats are the bona fide resistance to Trump, a Democratic Party so corrupt, unpopular, and tone deaf to the desperate need for internal reform is simply not equal to the resistance task.

How can a party so despised by voters that it just lost to a repulsive Trump and openly extremist Republicans plausibly package itself as a viable alternative? Without reforms so sweeping they amount to a top-to-bottom Democratic Party housecleaning, it simply can't.

Needless to say, the unfitness of today's corrupt Democratic Party to form a viable, let alone potent, opposition to Trump has drawn attention from pro-Sanders party progressives. Facing large segments of eligible U.S. voters deeply distrustful—even openly hostile—toward the political establishments of both major parties, they feel poised to package themselves as the legitimate, urgently resistance to Trump, and as the alternative that can replace Trump and Republicans politically. And if any of these reform-from-within groups (Our Revolution, #DemEnter, Brand New Congress, and Justice Democrats, to name a few chief players) showed the least sign of taking "political revolution" seriously—above all, the notion that political revolution is a peaceful civil war waged until oppressive enemies are definitively toppled from power—we might safely leave the anti-Trump resistance in their hands. As Naomi Klein, writing in the immediate wake of Trump's shocking election, diagnosed, "The Democratic Party must be definitively wrested from corporate neoliberals, or it must be abandoned."[380] While it's premature to judge, none of the new reform-Dems-from-within organizations seem the least bit interested in such a stark identification of their political enemies, nor can one imagine them making the faintest gesture toward abandoning the Democratic Party should their remorseless enemies keep their power. They will be very unlikely even to make the rather trivial "abandonment" of voting Green in the general election should their handpicked progressive candidates lose their primaries. Applied leverage is an antidote to all this money in politics and helps level the playing field against the establishment.

Since all the new reform-from-within organizations seem intent on playing by the neoliberal's rules—rules that define party progressives as second-class citizens[381] and gag their faintest criticisms of a neoliberal elite that constantly bashes them[382]—an outside-the-party movement is urgently needed to lead the anti-Trump resistance. CFAR or Else, pledged not merely to vociferous criticism of corporate neoliberals, but to hunting them to political extinction,[383] was formed to step into the revolutionary breach created by majority disgust with both Trump and the neoliberal Democratic Party establishment. Like Bernie or Bust, we will use congressional district-organized voter pledges to only support CFAR candidates at the "ballot box" as our chief tool of serious opposition. In a forceful extension of the Bernie or Bust pledge, we will organize voters not merely to refuse a single candidate, but to deny their votes to neoliberals under any circumstances. In the course of promoting our pledge, we intend to provide relentless political pressure and contractual litmus tests of how serious reform-from-within organizations are about waging civil war on neoliberals. While we're officially "skeptical but not dogmatic" about attempts to reform Democrats from within, we lean strongly toward supporting Greens and other third parties that are sources of serious neoliberal fighters. Also, we feel that if the reformers from within have any hope of success at all, it will be due to pressure from our uncompromising revolutionary stance against neoliberals.

Until a lot more Americans escape the two-party mental prison and reject the Republican/Democratic corporate duopoly, CFAR or Else gives liberal and moderate Democrats the option of winning against the Republican side of the establishment behind a candidate who can C-FAR. The problem is that "progressive" is a label the establishment Democrats have co-opted.[384] How can we tell if a candidate is a neoliberal? Did they support Hillary Clinton or the fast track bill? If necessary, follow the money, and find out who the large donors are. If PACs, are they public interest PACs or corporate interest PACs? Research could be required because many corporate PACs and organizations have names that seem to be in the public interest. Backing a left-progressive

Democrat required this kind of research until the CFAR was introduced to RAP. We knew Bernie Sanders' record and agreed with the lion's share of it. All CFAR or Else organizers need to do is get left-populists candidates to sign a CFAR. Candidate contracts simplify the task of determining what candidate to support in the primaries because neoliberals won't risk signing one, at least not a CFAR.

While some observers may deem a CFAR or Else strategy as a "Tea Party of the left," we make a distinction between their commitment to take over the Republican Party and our willingness to see the Democratic Party die if it remains a neoliberal party. Whether progressives can execute a hostile takeover of the Democratic Party and reform it into a party of opposition to neoliberalism and fascism or the Party is destroyed by a long string of election losses for establishment candidates is a matter of indifference to us. "Or Bust" and "or Else" can be interpreted as busting up and destroying one of the two parties of Wall Street.

The way to get the under-funded progressive elected as the nominee in the primaries is to make sure to reach as many Democrats as leverage activists can by speaking up at public debates, handing out quarter-sheet flyers at Democratic Party events, letters to the editor, door to door pamphleteering using walking lists to find registered Democrats, etc. to inform them the only candidate you'll support in the general election is the real progressive. Political philosophy trumps party, and climate preservation compels the urgent acquisition of political power. We need a strong party of opposition to fascism and neoliberalism, but until progressive, third party candidates can win elections, applied (communicated) leverage is the revolution's best shot of taking power. We will provide best practices, tips, suggestions and tutorials for helping CFAR candidates on the tutorial tab of our activists website: https://cfarmovement.us.

Think of this approach as an inside/outside strategy. Leverage voters will #DemEnter and #DemExit as a matter of routine. This would have to be organized and coordinated in large part by vetted local activists RAP enrolls on the activists website above. Fundraising could be channeled through a national PAC, local progressives could form their own PACs or a combination of the two tactics. An individual can only spend just under $1,000.00 of their money on political activities without forming a Political Action Committee. Revolutionaries may not want to form a PAC, but collusion and money spent organizing may require registering for one on the FEC website. (When in doubt, activists can ask the FEC for an "advisory opinion.") RAP will provide guidance on PAC formation on the website above as this next stage of applied leverage advances. Most of the time used on a PAC involves data entry, and there are shortcuts for small donations.

Revolution Against Neoliberals

Neoliberal, corporate fascism and fascistic neoliberalism are destroying the planet's carrying capacity. Please help us change the world by joining our movement today. If you're already part of our "army," ask someone you know to join us. Half of Senator Sanders' supporters would be enough voters to demand Democratic Party primary outcomes favoring the CFAR candidates.

Take the voter pledge near the bottom of citizensagainstplutocracy.org.

Donations to our PAC will be used to cover operating costs and contract with individuals to promote our Revolution or Bust pledge online between presidential election cycles. They will be deeply appreciated.

We have also started a YouTube channel in order to express our views on a variety of political matters and to make sure we get the facts out about what we are attempting to achieve going forward. You can find it by searching on YouTube for "Revolt Against Plutocracy." Please subscribe to it, if you haven't already, before starting the Conclusion.

Conclusion:
#RevolutionOrBust

"So save your hysterical concerns about Trump for others and either commit yourself to building a revolutionary movement or get out of the way."[385] ~Amaju Baraka, 2016 Green V.P. candidate

Necessity for Revolution

A revolution to take power from increasingly fascistic neoliberals that their mainstream media allies either collude with or don't consider dangerous and anti-democratic, is *essential* for climate preservation and for the legalization of democratic order in the United States. We need a rapid mobilization on the scale of WWII coupled with market initiatives to transform the energy sector from coal, gas and oil to green energy: sun, hydrogen, tidal, geothermal, etc. That's not going to happen unless the climate change planks of the Green Party platform are adopted as emergency measures very soon. This will definitely not happen under Trump, so climate preservation is primarily up to us with the level of materialism we choose to consume. If Clinton had supported climate preservation before profit and opposed hydrofracking to accompany her proposed spending on climate research, she would have been for this reason alone slightly less dangerous than Donald Trump in our view.

The threat posed by neoliberal, so-called "free trade agreements" can't be overstated. The transnational corporate actors are attempting to impose their rules and regulations upon our representatives at all levels of government and assert their property rights against theft. If "harmonization" of corporate regulations across borders is even desirable, that should be up to Congress because the Commerce Clause of the Constitution should be followed. There is little constitutional about either the fast track law passed in 2015 or the TPP. The danger is that Trump is exactly what Governor Romney suggested he is, i.e., a con man and a fraud. The hope is Trump does not take on more of the characteristics of neoliberalism now that he's in power. His supporters and opponents need to make certain his bilateral agreements are not rebranded versions of the TPP. If he is the economic nationalist he ran as, then the corporate protection rackets called "trade tribunals" must go. There is no reason the anti-globalism left and right cannot set aside their differences and work together to hold President Trump to his campaign rhetoric on trade.

Trump's rust belt working class support saved the United States from a series of corporate coups des lois [French for laws: a series of sudden changes of U.S. legal order into a corporate system of governance]. (This is the agenda of the corporate globalists.) They should be thanked for helping preserve what's left of American sovereignty and democratic self-government and not insulted. Trump will otherwise reverse social progress the old fashioned way, by nominating far-right judges to the Supreme Court like Neil Gorsuch and cutting federal programs designed to solve problems.

It's possible enough opposition had built up against the TPP for it to not pass in Congress, but Obama would have done all he could in his last lame duck session to make a series of deals again. He was rather good at that. There certainly would have been a fight with most people not really understanding how much would have changed under the promising label, "free-trade agreement." Clinton told a reporter she would not use her power as President-elect to discourage congressional Democrats from voting for the TPP. While we appreciate President Trump for pulling out of that agreement, his neo-fascism is a terrible price to pay for dodging that bullet. So far, the resistance is affecting the implementation of some of his Presidential Directives. If the vast majority of voters were not mentally locked inside a two-party system, Governor Johnson or Dr. Stein could have won the election, but on the other hand Secretary Clinton could have been the primary beneficiary of Trump voters choosing the Libertarian option more than they did. Ironically, the two-party mental prison may have saved the United States legal order from neoliberal corporatization. Until a Trump trade agreement is available for review, there is no way to tell if Trump will end up being just as dangerous in this regard. Corporations do not need their private, international, corporate profit protection racket-like tribunals. They can buy private insurance against losses as a result of doing business in Vietnam for example. The communist country that pushed out the American empire was one of the 12 nations included in the TPP.

Foreign Policy

The revolutionary movement will contribute to more right-wing victories whether it is the Green Party, the Peoples Party or the Progressive Independent Party[386] once they gain enough support to divide the liberal-progressive American left. Unless the Democrats become completely defeated and dysfunctional during the next few years, the electoral leverage of CFAR or Else gives liberals the opportunity to support genuine, not fake[387] progressive Democrats for electoral success and real change. Either American liberals can wake up, walk away from neoliberal candidates and support progressives for genuine change to protect the public interests over the corporate interests; or the Republicans will be in the White House for a long time. While loss of the neoliberal Democratic Party would be a good thing, Republican fascists or neoliberal Democrats will probably lead to a violent repetition of history as the American "empire" clings to world-wide power. I wish President Trump the very best luck if he really wants to leave other countries alone. His willingness to authorize a military operation in Yemen that had been initiated during the Obama administration demonstrated he'll be as bad if not worse than President Obomber[388] if he continues to operate in this vein. Bombing a Syria airfield after a chemical attack on civilians without proof of the source of the attack indicates just that.

Empires are usually crushed eventually by counter–imperial violence. A rare exception was the peaceful collapse of the Soviet Union. The United States supports international, corporate empires called transnational corporations that grow and grow, and they are protected by the largest and most imposing military power on Earth. National security doesn't require more weapons or Pentagon spending. The American people can protect real national security and leave the world alone, but that would leave a so-called "vacuum of power."

The U.S. could lead the world under the rule of international law and universal, national independence along with some of the maxims of power. In foreign policy, it's possible to be a dove and a hawk at the same time, but not usually with the same issue. If the U.N. would become better at peace-keeping and policing of world order, national security would still mean spending money on nuclear strategic deterrence up to the last day if and when they are all decommissioned. Even then, national security will require research and engineered upgrades for warehoused delivery systems and warheads. A cessation of those efforts is virtually impossible to verify, so even complete disarmament won't stop a level of nuclear arms upgrade and readiness.

So-called "homeland security" safeguards against terrorist threats will need to continue for centuries after this conflict of violent Islamic jihad against American occupation of mostly Muslim countries is resolved. Our drone strikes, other terrorizing violence against Muslims and invasions of their nations will not soon be forgotten. Revolutionaries ignoring these security imperatives will not and should not win elections to national office. There's a big difference between national security and world security.

The nuclear weapon straightjacket the major powers are wearing is going to require a careful, secure, measurable and verifiable reduction of weapons, not an arms race both major party candidates supported, apparently, as it turns out. Hopefully more people will pay attention to this concern as nuclear war could wipe humanity out much, much more quickly than accelerating climate change will. The only reason we might need more nuclear weapons is because of Russia. China has a small fraction of nuclear weapons compared to us, but Russia and the U.S. are in rough balance. If Trump is smarter than he seems to be, his nuclear weapons tweet may have been an initial bargaining stand for nuclear arms reduction negotiations. If not, the America people will need another nuclear freeze movement. President Trump has the potential to put a lot of problems on the plates of liberals and progressives alike. On the other hand, President Reagan got along with Chairman Gorbachev and helped end the Cold War. We hope Trump and Putin will do it again. Peace with Russia would improve our strategic security. Cooperation over common problems can build trust over time. The Democrats have created a climate of fear over Russia's "involvement" in the 2016 election that's shameful and reactionary.

Money In Politics and Lewis Powell

#RevolutionOrBust is a personal, political commitment to politicians who solve problems, not those who cause problems or those who ignore them. The neoliberal, pro-corporate political center is corrupt, beholden to wealthy donors, and that corruption has been legalized by Supreme Court-imposed campaign finance anarchy. The financial manner of holding elections that has been unleashed by the Supreme Court has legalized what used to be commonly held understanding of corruption. It is not quid pro quo corruption, but working in government on behalf of private, for-profit interests. An infamous Supreme Court decision, *Buckley v Valeo*, changed that legal understanding of corruption *and* protected money as speech. The Court is not likely to reverse that 1976 7-1 decision, so the people will have to demand such a reversal if plutocracy and oligarchy are to be abolished and democratic campaign finance established. Getting big money out of politics to establish democratic order requires a constitutional amendment demanded by the people. That's a key issue of agreement we and most American people have with Senator Sanders.

Buckley v Valeo was written "in curium" meaning we don't know who changed the meaning of corruption in American law. However, a member of that Court, Judge Lewis Powell, had written a secret memo to the U.S. Chamber of Commerce[389] that has set off a series of changes in education, law and government that renders the struggle between people and the corporate interests virtually impossible for citizens to win. Individuals have many interests, but corporations have only three: survival, profits and growth in that order. The doctrine of corporate constitutional rights was not begun by Judge Powell, but he wrote a narrow, 1978 decision allowing corporations to spend money on campaign ads during ballot measures. His secret memo of 1971 unleashed what has come to be called neoliberal globalization. Judge Powell's influence coincided with neoliberalism taking hold in the United States in the 1970s. Defeating the entrenched establishment with all of their deep-pocketed, corporate connections of support will require awareness by 100 million Americans, rural and urban, young and old, black and white, religious or not about how threatening and dangerous are the corporate coups being attempted by neoliberal supporters of so-called "free-trade agreements." The Breitbart wing of Trump's support should be in alignment with progressive opposition to the NAFTA and TPP-type agreements that threaten jobs and American sovereignty.

Senator Sanders' legacy will either be that of another progressive who failed to secure the nomination of the Democratic Party or one of legitimizing peaceful, democratic revolution. That means, not just a change of the party holding power, but using that power to make the significant changes required to legalize democratic order. That change of party could, in theory, derive from within a corrupt party or from outside the two major Wall Street parties. If American history is any guide, we need a progressive president as soon as possible and a third party to serve as an organizing structure to win elections. New parties take multiple election cycles to take hold, and the two-party, establishment controlled system makes it nearly impossible to get the attention required to build a large base of support. I argued in Chapter 1 revolutionaries need to make the Internet "their revolutionary machine," and Senator Sanders wrote the "Internet offers revolutionary prospects."[390]

My Role

Actual administration of any movement will be more effective if that work is done as a committee. I should have either asked for help with what I needed to do to get Bernie or Bust on television or raise more money to contract for the video production I don't have the skills to do myself. On top of a full-time job, I took on too much work which in turn inflicted damage to my marriage. I have said "I'm sorry" to my wife more times than I can count. The RAP committee made the decisions, but I did all of the administering of the strategy including all email communication with pledge-takers. Remember the quote by Anonymous in Chapter 1? "It starts like an itch ... our spouses reject us." I know I write for other people when I convey our efforts and online time in support of revolution have been very stressful on personal relationships. This is a civil war, and our friends and family members have to understand the future of not only democratic order in the United States, but of the human race as a whole are at stake.

A better division of labor and greater voluntary collaboration would have made deployment of the "or Bust" leverage strategy more effective. When I needed to ask for help getting our ads on the air, I failed on a personal level. The failure was not of any subsequence since the establishment was determined to stop Sanders. It wouldn't have mattered without a very expensive ad campaign to successfully burn through Clinton's regional firewall. Without a famous and trusted name on our committee, we couldn't begin to raise the millions of dollars needed to do that.

Bernie's Book

In *Our Revolution*, Sanders' book about his campaign for President, he calls "the limitation of our imaginations" a "serious crisis" in his Conclusion.[391] We agree but reiterate, before jumping ahead with what seems like a great idea, do the necessary research first. Not every idea anyone can imagine is a good idea. One of the conditions on whether leverage will be applied or not could become the extent to which progressives run the Democratic Party for national office. Revolt Against Plutocracy is a committee, and we can always change our decisions. For 43% of our pledge-takers, the decision to use leverage again depends on the candidate. RAP will poll them to make the decision who to support in 2020 with us. Our revolution is democratic, civil war against neoliberal Democrats in and out of office, racists, fascists, and neoliberal Republicans in that order. Hopefully, the choice the American people are offered will be as obvious in 2018 midterms and 2020 as it was in 2016.

Major party primary season leverage will work best when the progressive option to the neoliberal parties has enough support to make the threat credible. With Hillary Clinton as the candidate, the 1% of the vote attained by Jill Stein was not enough for the Democrats to lose the election because most Green Party members wouldn't cast vote for anyone for President without a Green candidate and a third of those who were still willing to vote would have supported Trump.[392] Third party growth in the coming years is needed to break the corporate, major party political duopoly. Remember, Clinton was so bad, even the sexist and bigoted Donald Trump could beat her. If half of Bernie's supporters would register with the Green Party, revolutionaries could wage a more effective #ProgressiveOrBust strategy in 2018 and 2020 in collaboration with Revolt Against Plutocracy. Until Interstate Crosscheck ceases to function, re-registering to vote at the latest period before the cut-off date in your state is a good idea.

Why not register as a member of the Green Party? They are the only party addressing climate change in a manner that could slow, stop and preserve the climate of the 20th Century. The Greens are the largest party of opposition in the United States. If a climate preservation movement doesn't slow the expansion of fossil fuel extraction, refinement and use during the next four years, it may be too late to slow global warming by 2021. 2016 may have been the last shot we had for the energy sector transformation we need to survive as a civilization or perhaps even as a species. Becoming a member of the Green Party will help bend the arc of history toward survival, but that alone won't preserve the climate. #ProgressiveOrGreen is a tool the Green Party can embrace as Jill Stein did by inviting Sanders to join at the top of their ticket and telling our rally,[393] "our hearts are with [Bernie Sanders], our hearts are with you; whatever happens … we're going to continue this movement;" or they can disavow the leverage strategy. It doesn't matter in our planning. Our loyalty is to progressive revolution, not to any party. Should a new party arise and show momentum, it could become the primary vehicle for peaceful revolution.

Revolutionary Consumption: Targeted Spending

Global warming changes normal strategic thinking. We're out of time. The world needs a progressive American administration now and a revolution like that of 1800 to give it time to finish the transformation of the energy sector. We need a green new deal or a rapid market shift to sustainable energy. Bernie was right in the debates with Clinton; climate change is our biggest national security threat. We've fought and won wars before. Governments have been fighting terrorism for many years, but the threat to life, property and well-being posed by climate change is unprecedented and planet-wide. A mass extinction is already underway. Technologically speaking, ignoring the scientific, climate consensus is an unnecessary risk. We can address this problem and create lasting jobs, but not without a revolution in thinking and consuming first.

Corporatists—whether neoliberal, libertarian or fascist—will not save the world because that would threaten the corporate profits and survival in the energy sector of the economy. Writing in *Counter Currents*, Rupert Reed and Deepak Rughani point out, "Our lifestyles ensure that we aid and abet destruction, without ever consciously choosing it for ourselves."[394] Therefore, we all will have to cut back on our carbon footprints as much as we can learn to. From what we eat to whether, how and why we drive a vehicle, with Trump in power, it's on people to learn how to cut back and do voluntarily what corporations don't want: reduce unnecessary consumption. The national government is not going to fix this under either Trumpism or neoliberalism, so we need to buy less, travel less and do with less until humans get an appropriate climate change response figured out and transformed. It should not take more than a generation or two of "sacrificing" our current levels of consumption. Instead of an Arab Spring or an American Autumn, we need a carbon footprint diet. A revolution in buying habits can help preserve the climate. There's a lot to this. Do not go out and buy an electric car, for example; but, only when you need a new vehicle, make your next car a high mileage, electric or hydrogen/hybrid car. There's no rush to buy something new when you have something that works for now. Just use it less. For poorer people, this is easier because they already only spend for their needs, but for people with the means, buying an unnecessary upgrade is indoctrinated by our corporate-crafted culture: consume, consume and then consume some more. It won't be easy to shake off these spending habits for the greater good, but it's necessary.

Economist Joseph Schumpeter described the history of technological advance as "creative destruction."[395] Producers of merchant ship sails lost their jobs and businesses when the steam engine came along, and the producers of steam engines lost or retooled their jobs and businesses when they were replaced by the internal combustion engine. If a movement of reduced consumption grows and takes hold, it could cause a devastating economic crash which is not the objective. Therefore, optional spending should target the market of sustainable energy systems for the home. Rather than saving too much money, which drains capital from the economy, home owners can advance the transition from fossil fuels by purchasing solar panels, rooftop mounted windmills, etc. This would stimulate one sector of the energy market and depress the fossil fuel sector. People who rent are not in position to make such purchases, but they can curb spending, cut consumption and replace gas guzzlers with higher mileage, used vehicles when needed. It's important to stress, the aim is to slow, not crash, the U.S. economy.

This sounds easy, but conversations with spouses on spending considerably less on what we want until Trump is out of power can become heated. "I need a new Iphone; I'm out of memory." "Is there an Ipod lying around? No? Donald Trump thanks you" could start a fight. A movement to keep the economy on the edge of recession will need a website to share best practices on energy use reductions, making the effort household-wide, memes, printable leaflets and a home page explanation of the strategy along with a record of the last three GDP reports on a side panel. I've recorded three videos of explanation, but it's really quite simple: we are not letting Trump make America "great" (economically) to intentionally harm his Party's chances in 2018 and his or V.P. Pence's chances of re-election in 2020. As a bonus, we may preserve the climate long enough for a real progressive in the tradition of FDR like Bernie Sanders to take power of government and address both the levels of carbon and the methane escaping into the atmosphere threatening at least coastal cities around the world. If Trump gets the economy growing faster and gets re-elected, submerged cities will be a matter of when, not if. Submerged cities will just be the beginning as climate shifts toward Desert Earth. Addressing the existential threat of climate change, Noam Chomsky has stated,[396] "if there are ways out of this, it's going to be not easy." Changing from consumers needing instant gratification to savers of the climate is going to be "not easy," but what other options do we have?

What About Terrorism?

We share Jill Stein's understanding of the problem which she conveyed at our rally.[397]

> Where did this terrorism thing get started? In Afghanistan ... Charlie Wilson's war ... We created the international jihadi movement, and boy did it backfire ... Let's put it to bed. We started this monster; we can put an end to it by depriving it of its food, of its funding and its weapons. Dropping more bombs and ... shooting up terrorists only creates the next cycle of terrorism.

9-11 was backlash against President H. W. Bush's war against Saddam's Iraq and the basing of American troops in Saudi Arabia during and after Operation Desert Storm. Progressive author Caitlin Johnstone cuts through the state propaganda in her Newslogue column "Newly Released Letter From 9/11 Mastermind Shows How Interventionism Causes Terrorism:"[398]

Any critical thinking about why terrorists do what they do has largely been marginalized from public discourse to the point where Americans don't even really think about it anymore beyond "They're just crazy" if they're a Democrat or "Islam just sucks" if they're Republican. Which isn't much better than "They hate us for our freedom," because it assumes the exact same Bambi-eyed innocence under unprovoked attack from irrational monsters. It's something we're not meant to think about because that's "humanizing" and "sympathizing with" the people who commit these heinous crimes, but the new release of an 18-page letter[399] to President Obama from the alleged mastermind behind the 9/11 attacks builds on an ever-increasing mountain of evidence that the best thing Americans could possibly do to protect themselves from terrorist attacks is demand their government espouse a non-interventionist foreign policy.

Attacks against Western countries will continue for a period after the "war against terrorism," however it is resolved. Leaving Muslim countries alone would significantly shorten that time frame.

Write-In Strategies

Using a write-in strategy to support a candidate not campaigning in order to get a vote in the next House of Representatives requires a best case scenario in terms of its numerical make-up. An Operation Deny 270 should be used to purposely divide support for the largest party if and only if the number of potential supporting members in the next House of Representatives could add up, counting incumbents and—at most—75% of all challengers who support the write-in candidate for President in that election. In 2016 they were called Berniecrats even though those candidates for Congress included independents, a few Green candidates and a write-in candidate or two. Denying 270 electoral votes remains a potential option depending upon the circumstances of the candidate and his or her potential support in the post-election Congress.

A willing write-in candidate is another option available depending on who that is. Seven states do not permit write-in options to voters, so it would require a strong 43 state strategy. Support for a progressive willing to run as a write-in candidate for President could be an option going forward, but the more progressive candidates take votes from the largest progressive party, the more they undermine the potential of that party attaining 5% of the popular vote and formal minor party status or even a plurality of the vote count. The choice of writing in or voting third party could be made based upon how close the polls indicate the write-in candidate or a progressive, third party candidate is to a plurality of support. There are multiple paths through revolution and a myriad of ways for the establishment to get around or just to stop them. No one has ever claimed revolutions are easy.

Obama

During the primaries last year, I saw a video by progressive commentator, Benjamin Dixon.[400] He advised Sanders' supporters to focus on Clinton and be respectful of Obama as he was and remains greatly admired. With the election behind us, it's time to put the kid gloves away.

Late in President Obama's farewell address,[401] he quoted George Washington's final address. "Self-government is the underpinning of our safety, prosperity and liberty, but from different causes and from different quarters much pains will be taken to weaken in your minds the conviction of this truth." A neoliberal President, who shepherded three attempted, international regimes of corporate self-government (via "free-trade agreements") at every level of government, has gall to quote a Founding President on democratic self-government. Paul Street has noted on Truthdig, "Obama is a master at using words to blind supporters to his deeds."[402]

Neoliberal globalization is an existential threat to democratic self-government. Obama was conning Americans because he sure as hell must understand the difference between legislators writing corporate regulations and corporate lawyers and executive officers writing and then negotiating for corporate regulations (in 12 countries initially). Obama, perhaps even more than Trump, is the real con man. Bear in mind, "Standing on the Edge of the Next American Revolution" was published during Obama's second term. It's ironic and frightening to have the backlash to neoliberalism and the post 9-11 drift toward fascistic authoritarianism be a President even more fascistic and authoritarian than Bush or Obama. People are frightened and economically marginalized, and they voted for an unknown but successful businessman who seemed to be on their side of free-trade agreements and jobs. Trump is not just part of Obama's legacy, but the legacy of neoliberal control of the Democratic Party from President Clinton on.

America needed a progressive revolution to preserve ideals of liberty and justice for all along with the climate before it was too late in 2016. The President did nothing about voter suppression strategies and apparent election fraud during the primaries. In 2020, it has got to be #ProgressiveOrBust because neither the neoliberals nor the anti-science, corporate fascists are willing to undertake the necessary transformation of the energy sector of the economy. Libertarians are even less reliable on the crises of accelerating climate change.

Think Nationally, Act Locally

Look to participate in offline community organizations. We've recommended involvement with Move to Amend, but many other options are available if you happen to live in one of the 18 states that have already asked Congress to amend the Constitution to overturn the *Citizens United* and related decisions. Those 18 states are California, Colorado, Connecticut, Delaware, Hawaii, Illinois, Maine, Maryland, Massachusetts, Montana, New Jersey, New Mexico, New York, Oregon, Rhode Island, Vermont and West Virginia, Nevada plus the District of Columbia. The key word of this section is to act. Use the Internet to coordinate and plan, but it's no alternative to community involvement. Trump claimed his victory was one for the people; it's up to progressives to work with other people as he betrays that claim to build opposition to both his unconstitutional and reactionary policies and neoliberal priorities, especially from those within the Democratic Party.

We need to have a civil, not violent, war against the establishment and their allies in the media. If you're mobile and able, go to meetings. If not, plug in online. A civil revolution involves civic participation. The Internet and snail mail remain about the only hope peaceful revolutionaries have to circumvent corporate media's interpretation of the world propagated as news and commentary. We need to build from the grassroots and create the revolution we need. Our system both demands that happen non-violently and prevents it from happening peacefully due to the huge costs of running for national office. Local empowerment is still available under Trump, but it won't happen unless people act to organize. "Federal policy change in the next four years doesn't depend on Mr. Trump but on whether our representatives support or oppose him," a guide entitled "Indivisible"[403] says. "And through local pressure, we have the power to shape what they consider possible." Protests can slow Trumpism, but opposing him alone won't solve the current problem of increasing greenhouse gases. Neoliberalism is just as much of a threat to sustainable climate conditions as Trumpism.

Trump, A Wake-Up Call

If Secretary Clinton had gotten elected, there would have been no Women's March. Liberals would have continued their slumber as they were under Obama's neoliberal presidency. Trump's presidency is motivating people to act, to protest, to call Congress and to start building structures of opposition to his fascistic authoritarianism. If Trump's opponents do not recognize the threat posed by neoliberalism and help build organizational structures to challenge the priorities of corporate profit and growth, they will only serve to play into the hands of the neoliberal elite. American citizens, revolutionaries or not, cannot allow that to happen.

Trump's presidency should be a clarifying moment for the creation of a new revolutionary movement to transform the American system from an oligarchic, corporate "new world order" to a democratic republic. His executive orders banning immigration from seven primarily Muslim countries sparked protests across the nation, but if the resistance movement doesn't effectively oppose neoliberalism too, curb consumption and stem Trump's regressive policies, our time as a species on this planet will be cut short by our own unwillingness to undertake the changes in lifestyle and sometimes hard work needed for progressives to both secure power at the ballot box and occupy the streets. We can do what we can to carefully slow the economy down by taking personal responsibility for consumption and buying habits regimented by decades of corporate advertising. We can also use Trump's presidency to build a genuine, unified movement of opposition to him.

We still have it in our power to begin the world over again, but it'll require *sacrifices* of time, effort and new stuff (revolutionary consumption) Americans are not used to making. Because Trump has at least pretended to be in denial about the greenhouse effect carbon has on the atmosphere and probably doesn't worry about the accelerating warming of the Earth, the 45th President's opponents, regardless of ideology, have a common interest in curbing his authoritarian impulses and ultimately defeating him. This includes a lifestyle decision: buy just what you need and make do with what you have because the federal government is going to unleash fossil fuel extractions and pipelines even more than it did under President Obama. Congress has been captured by corporate interests since at least 2014, and now the President is literally a corporation!

Speculation doesn't belong in a conclusion, but Trump's unwillingness to give up his business to serve the nation may be an intentional tactic to transfer his office to a right-winger he trusts, i.e. Vice President Pence, a socially conservative neoliberal. Trump will have achieved a good bit of what he sought: his name on the wall of history, a right-wing Supreme Court judge while maintaining the brand name he refused to release and will continue to market someday as an ex-president. Of course, a Republican House of Representatives would have to impeach him under the "emoluments" clause of the Constitution which bars government officials from receiving gifts from foreign powers or for obstructing justice if that is why he fired FBI Director Comey, and that's unlikely.

If President 45 is such a grave threat, and we believed that would have been the case regardless of whether he or Clinton had won the election, then the need for liberals to work for progressive Democrats—rather than corporate-funded Democrats—should be clear. When progressive Americans refuse to support neoliberal Democrats in the general election, either Trump will be strengthened in Congress or registered Democrats will decide to support progressive candidates allied with Senator Sanders. That, in a nutshell, will be "Progressive or Bust" going forward. We're turning left or right because we refuse to continue down the road of neoliberal, corporate globalization.

President Trump is the consequence of decades of neoliberal, corporate policy making. Neoliberalism is the disease; Trump is a symptom. Democratic socialism is one antidote to both. His opponents without a clear alternative set of policy options—not just to Trumpism but to neoliberalism as well—are part of the problem. The increasingly fascistic character of America under Bush, Obama and now Trump is not acceptable. We need a different foreign policy that has a clear distinction between national and world security. We need a political system that equalizes the financial influence of all citizens. We needed the revolution the DNC, then the superdelegates along with the establishment media collaborated to block. However, because Senator Sanders framed his candidacy for President as a "political revolution," a movement of both opposition to Trumpism and a citizens war against neoliberalism is more likely now.

Resisting Trump alone only plays into the hands of those behind the malevolent neoliberal order. Unless liberal Democrats, union members, environmentalists and progressives understand Trump is the symptom of the disease (the neoliberal agenda of corporate globalization and economic imperialism), the broad American left will continue to lose elections.

Revolutionary Media

Mainstream media shares the understanding the U.S. is a stabilizing power in the world and "free-trade" is OK if not great, so they will be the enemy of the revolution. If an opposition were strong enough by 2020 to win a national election in a four-way contest, leverage wouldn't be needed. We believe a liberal-progressive alliance in the Democratic Party is the best chance at this time.

Our direct media are emails, websites, trustworthy news sources, door to door leafleting, talking, and to a limited extent (they are owned by corporations with political interests), social media. We are the media. Trustworthy, revolutionary news and opinion sources are Jimmy Dore of *The Young Turks*, *Tim Black At Night*, Chris Hedges of *Truthdig*, *Let The Madness Begin*, *Democracy Now*, *The Intercept*, Abby Martin of *Empire Files*, Caitlin Johnstone with *Newslogue* or *Medium*, Michael Sainato, *Observer*, the *Black Agenda Report*, *In These Times*, *The Benjamin Dixon Show*, *CounterPunch*, The Real News Network (RNN) and, of course, *Redacted Tonight* hosted by Lee Camp. The last of these is a comedy show which conveys better information about "the system" than anything you'll hear on mainstream media. While the list is not exhaustive, it's a good start.

The National Association for Media Literacy Education is a good resource for learning how to analyze and evaluate news stories. Their website argues in order for people to become "responsible citizens … individuals need to develop expertise with the increasingly sophisticated information and entertainment media that address us on a multi-sensory level, affecting the way we think, feel, and behave."[404] We cannot agree more.

On Leverage

Our trans-partisan, inside/outside strategy of electoral revolt against the establishment will remain active to let Democrats know in all national elections, we are #ProgressiveOrBust. Party affiliation is of secondary consideration, a tactic to deploy until a third party can successfully challenge Democrats in elections. Half of the traditionally Democrat Party progressive base should be enough to provide the leverage needed. It's not hard work; we're just changing parties to either compel reform of the Wall Street-backed neoliberals or escort them to the dustbin of history. With the selection of Clinton-supporting and Obama White House recommended Tom Perez as the Party Chairman, the establishment retains control of the Democrats.

So why bother supporting progressive candidates running as Democrats? It depends on the congressional district. If a popular progressive is running either as an independent or progressive party candidate against the establishment Democrat, "or bust" messaging on social media would not be needed. Changing parties to vote for the progressive in the Democratic primary would help convey the leverage strategy to Democratic Party loyalists, but why bother if a strong progressive candidate running outside of the political duopoly is just as likely to win? The CFAR or Else strategy for congressional races can have exceptions based on local conditions.

A progressive running as a Democrat has the best chance of getting elected at this stage in the revolution. If the establishment Democrats get crushed again in the 2018 midterms and thereafter as they did in 2016, it would set back social progress faster than the neoliberals. If Trump is re-elected because the Democrats nominate another Wall Street-backed candidate many revolutionary progressives have pledged a refusal to vote for, and he doesn't become a "free-trade" neoliberal himself, national self-determination and sabotaged, illegitimate, "democratic" self-government will be protected from international, corporate rule-making. It's one thing to have an elected president deregulating business activities; it's quite another to allow the corporations to write their own rules during secret negotiations when an up–or–down vote with no amending of "free-trade agreements" (fast track) is the law of the land. The Trans-Pacific Partnership and the Trade in Services Agreement should be a wake-up call to Americans. Two elements of the establishment's agenda are another cold war with Russia and so-called "free-trade" agreements. Liberal establishment pundits will vigorously disagree, but those elements remain the reasons Trump is not as dangerous as the neoliberal Democrats who support those two agenda items along with hydrofracking and continued, extreme extraction of fossil fuels such as mountain top removal to extract coal and deep water drilling for oil and gas.

Why bother working to reform the corrupt, Wall Street-backed Democratic Party at all? Until a progressive party of opposition to both fascism and neoliberalism can win three–way or four–way contests, supporting one will certainly divide the American left and help elect neoliberal and fascistic Republicans. That is precisely the promise of "or bust." CFAR or Else is the most likely manner at this juncture of history with which progressives can actually win primary elections.

When the members of the Democratic National Committee elected a Clintoncrat, Tom Perez,[405] as Party Chairman and voted against a ban on corporate donations on February 25, 2017, they sent a message to progressives. The Democratic Party will remain a wholly-owned subsidiary of Wall Street banks and the rest of corporate America. The establishment learned nothing from their loss to Trump, and the Democrats will continue to lose to Republicans unless Party members themselves reject neoliberals in the primaries and choose progressives instead. If they do not, Trump will be re-elected; and the Democratic Party will be en route to the dustbin of history right next to the Whig Party where they will belong.

A strategy that threatens the re-election of Trump seems at odds with the strategy of revolutionary consumption. Trump is dangerous, but another neoliberal like Senator Cory Booker (D–NY) would not be much better for climate preservation and more frightening, still, in the case of Clinton. We do not need to be the world's policeman, judge, jury, prison guard and executioner, a modern day "empire." Congress would declare war on any nation pouring terror from the sky on American families in the form of Hellfire missiles launched from robots flying above. The foreign policy of neocons like Clinton, the neoliberal like Obama or the "bomb the shit out of them" nationalist like Trump's advisor, Steve Bannon, will produce backlash against the West and Americans. The United States needs to and can safely, militarily withdraw from the Middle East. Our wars there are causing more problems for American's safety and security than they are solving. This demand isn't a purity test;

the people need to get control of the military profit-making corporate complex which contributes to both regional instabilities and climate change as most ships and all tanks and aircrafts run on fossil fuel. Peace and climate preservation are going to require an American revolution to take power from the neoconservatives, fascists and neoliberals. Liberal and moderate Democrats must decide if they want to defeat Trump behind a real progressive or lose again in 2020 by nominating another neoliberal "free-trader" and/or warmonger. Revolution isn't a "purity test." It's a necessary struggle for peace, sustainable prosperity and climate preservation. Revolution is not a choice; it's necessary for human survival and further evolution.

If the left takes on a range of strategies every presidential election cycle, we'll never win. Revolution trumps party loyalty. Our inside/outside strategy of electoral revolt against the establishment will remain active to let Democrats know in all national elections that the movement remains #ProgressiveOrBust. Unlike previous efforts to reform the Democratic Party, we're giving them an existential choice. It either becomes a party of labor, climate preservation, peace and human rights; or we'll do our level best to help kick it into the aforementioned dustbin of history.

Although #CFARorBust is at the formation stage of development as this is being written, we're already seeing tweets and other feedback from establishment types about "purity tests." Progressive or Bust is a peaceful struggle against neoliberals and fascists. Progressives can differ over policy proposals without having their "purity" questioned. The only "purity" voters need to be concerned with is whether or not your candidate has accepted big money from corporate interests, and is, therefore, beholden to them.

We are now #DemExit; we are members of the Green Party. We will #DemEnter again but only if called for. If the liberals in the Democratic Party side with the neoliberal establishment, we'll then #DemExit again. Until a progressive, third party is strong enough to win three–way or four–way contests in national elections, the Green Party at this particular stage of American history can serve as an instrument of leverage (our fallback position) when neoliberals win their Democratic Party primaries. This strategy will only last as long as needed to either destroy the neoliberal, Democratic Party or to compel its reform into a progressive party as it used to be before the 1970s.

If Bernie Sanders and someone like Rep. Tulsi Gabbard (D–HI) were to start a new party, that would render leverage obsolete and in all likelihood lead to the re-election of Trump unless the Libertarians put forward a strong enough ticket to also divide the right. Unless the Democratic Party collapses between now and 2020, it could serve as a vehicle of progressive change just as Senator Sanders attempted in 2016.

#RevolutionOrBust

No book about unresolved current affairs or struggles can be truly "complete." In order to keep this history a reasonably quick read, there were facts not mentioned and arguments not made or completed. Hundreds of whole books have been written about foreign policy and terrorism, and I covered the topics in a few paragraphs. These topics and counter-revolutionary media/establishment collusion are worthy of book-length explorations and arguments. For now, what's contained in these pages will have to serve as conversation starters and, more important, provide an understanding of election leverage.

Peace, human rights, sustainable prosperity and climate preservation are possible, but not without another American revolution. It is not enough to have a hundred thousand or even a million voters understand the need for revolution and the strategy of leverage to get progressives into power. When 50 to 100 million American voters comprehend the only sane option to the militarism, a growing police state, the unendurable exploitation of resources and global warming associated with fascism and neoliberalism, a peaceful revolution will become unstoppable. We're running out of time. Now you have completed this story and manifesto, please share it with a friend, family member or stranger. If you're willing and able to advance the revolution even further, consider purchasing more copies to use as birthday, graduation and Christmas gifts. Thank you.

AFTERWORD

"It is easier to forgive an enemy than to forgive a friend."[406]
~William Blake

In May 2017, the Revolt Against Plutocracy took a contentious 3-2 vote as to whether or not we'd endorse the Draft Bernie movement[407]. Former committee member, Charlie Hobbs, made it clear he would resign from the committee if we endorsed that movement.

Although Charlie was a workhorse of the Bernie or Bust movement, I would have gladly accepted his resignation because many people conveyed to me on Facebook that he was rude, mean and/or threatening. One example I noticed was a post from Charlie on a Facebook group page asking people to donate to our PAC, which was good. However, he ended his fund appeal with something to the effect of donate to our PAC "or else." Or else?

Once Tom and Niko had conveyed to me they supported RAP endorsing the Draft Bernie movement, I was scheduled to speak on the weekly Draft Bernie conference call.[408] Charlie had been given administration rights on our two Facebook pages, Revolt Against Plutocracy with over 32,000 followers, which I started in 2014, and Jill or Bust with over 16,000 followers that was started by one of our volunteers. As I was preparing my notes for the Draft Bernie conference call, it occurred to me to demote Charlie so he couldn't cause any problems.

While I was on the conference call, he did just that. He removed me as an administrator of my own Facebook page, and Facebook would do nothing about this theft of my page. He deleted a good deal of posts, videos, etc. on the page, renamed it and blocked me from posting comments on it. I started a new page called Revolt Against Plutocracy. Another lesson learned.

If you use Facebook, please like and follow the new RAP page if you have not already. Thank you. https://www.facebook.com/RevoltAgainstPlutocracy/

ACKNOWLEDGMENTS

This movement and book would not have been possible if not for the patience of my wife Torie. She went to bed and woke up alone while I plugged away on my computer for months on end. I am indebted to Revolt Against Plutocracy co-founder, contributor to and editor of this book, Patrick Walker, a brother in revolution. Without his collaboration there would not have been a Bernie or Bust pledge movement. I want to thank my actual brother Robert for his invaluable, voluntary editorial work on this book and the good folks at Dorrance Publishing Company.

The growth of the Bernie or Bust movement was no accident. It occurred because dozens of online volunteers helped promote the Bernie or Bust pledge on Facebook, Twitter and on news websites. Considering the innovative and pioneering nature of this strategy, it's quite remarkable so many people grasped the value of leverage and helped build it by driving traffic to our website. They were the core of this movement. I want to thank each and every person who took the Bernie or Bust pledge. They made Bernie or Bust a movement, and they will help us select the progressive candidate we'll support with leverage again in 2020 unless Senator Sanders makes a clean break from the corrupt Democratic Party and joins a third party.

Members of the Revolt Against Plutocracy decision-making committee deserve special recognition. Current members Niko House, Tom Ulcak and Sabrina Giesler are genuine and committed revolutionaries. The contributions of former RAP spokespersons YahNé Ndgo and Gregory Haddock will never be forgotten.

We are grateful to our allies in the media: H.A. Goodman, Tim Black, Debbie Lusignan (The Sane Progressive), Michael White and Will Gaillard

(Let The Madness Begin), Robert Brown (Freedom in Fire), Jimmy Dore (The Young Turks), Reno Berkeley and Shaunee Flowers (Inquisitr), Michael Sainato (Observer), Cliff Rover (CNN iReport), Brogan Morris (Salon), Shane Ryan and Walker Bragman (Paste Magazine), Matt Turner (Novara Media), Amanda Girard (U.S. Uncut) and Lee Camp (Redacted Tonight). Dawn Papple (Inquistr) was very helpful to my getting the timeline in the #OpDeny270 chapter accurate.

We appreciate musicians Kor Element and the Ultimate Rage for writing and performing their two songs titled "Bernie or Bust" at our rally in Philadelphia.

Obviously, there would not have been a Bernie or Bust movement had Senator Sanders not framed his candidacy as a political revolution. Whether or not he makes another run for the White House, the revolution he sparked will continue come hell, high water or both. For that, we are eternally grateful to him.

@BernieOrBust
Ithaca, NY
March 7, 2017

End Notes

Introduction

1 https://youtu.be/_ptu4TBEVPo
2 https://youtu.be/YE5Ha52PBVg
3 https://citizensagainstplutocracy.wordpress.com/2017/01/07/bernie-or-bust-survey/
4 http://www.realclearpolitics.com/video/2015/08/06/trump_i_will_not_pledge_to_endorse_republican_nominee.html
5 http://www.aeinstein.org/
6 http://www.slate.com/articles/news_and_politics/politics/2016/11/the_people_who_look_at_trump_and_don_t_see_a_racist.html
7 http://www.alternet.org/election-2016/how-democracy-ends?
8 https://youtu.be/O8V9YKUrlYA
9 http://www.revolutiontelevised.org/episodes/bernie-or-bust/

Chapter 1: Revolution Before Bernie

10 http://kingencyclopedia.stanford.edu/encyclopedia/documentsentry/where_do_we_go_from_here_delivered_at_the_11th_annual_sclc_convention/
11 https://youtu.be/PKZKETizybw
12 http://www.truth-out.org/opinion/item/331:unequal-protection-how-corporations-became-people-and-how-you-can-fight-back
13 http://www.truth-out.org/opinion/item/375-unequal-protection-the-deciding-moment
14 https://youtu.be/qCV1Ea5tdOY
15 http://www.amendmentgazette.com/
16 http://www.amendmentgazette.com/how-spending-money-became-a-form-of-speech/
17 http://www.amendmentgazette.com/2014/02/04/interview-ben-cohen/
18 http://www.amendmentgazette.com/2015/09/23/martin-kirk-interview/
19 http://therules.org/we-live-on-a-one-party-planet/
20 http://www.amendmentgazette.com/2014/09/16/chris-hedges/
21 https://youtu.be/ecQ0PtIrENM
22 https://scholar.princeton.edu/sites/default/files/mgilens/files/gilens_and_page_2014_-testing_theories_of_american_politics.doc.pdf
23 http://www.amendmentgazette.com/2015/01/01/sparking-third-american-revolution/
24 http://www.ushistory.org/us/20.asp
25 http://www.amazon.com/American-Revolution-1800-JeffersonDemocracy/dp/1609949854/ref=sr_1_1&tag=thomhartmann
26 http://www.amendmentgazette.com/2014/06/05/principled-conservative-congress/
27 http://www.amendmentgazette.com/how-spending-money-became-a-form-of-speech/
28 http://www.amendmentgazette.com/what-is-citizens-united/
29 http://www.amendmentgazette.com/2014/04/06/mccutcheon-decision-will-increase-corruption-threaten-the-republic/
30 https://www.popularresistance.org/
31 http://thinkprogress.org/climate/2014/09/16/3567322/this-changes-everything-naomi-klein-capitalism-climate/
32 https://youtu.be/zORv8wwiadQ
33 http://www.amendmentgazette.com/2014/06/05/principled-conservative-congress/
34 http://www.huffingtonpost.com/charles-ferguson/the-financial-crisis-and-_1_b_782927.html

35 http://www.heritage.org/federalbudget/national-debt-skyrocket
36 http://daviddegraw.org/peak-inequality-the-01-and-the-impoverishment-of-society/
37 http://thinkprogress.org/economy/2014/12/12/3603194/dodd-frank-cromulent-phil-gramm/
38 https://firstlook.org/theintercept/2014/10/07/key-democrats-led-hillary-clinton-leave-doubt-endl-ess-war-u-s-doctrine/
39 http://www.newworldencyclopedia.org/entry/American_Empire
40 http://www.alternet.org/civil-liberties/blaming-government-its-surveillance-programs-ignore-plut-ocrats-behind-curtain-who?
41 http://ivn.us/2014/12/11/congress-quietly-passes-bill-allows-feds-unlimited-access-private-comm-unications/?
42 http://alochonaa.com/2014/12/17/american-protests-against-the-militarized-police-state/
43 http://www.aopa.org/News-and-Video/All-News/2014/May/28/CBP-to-be-more-judicious-in-stopping-GA-aircraft-after-AOPA-applies-pressure.aspx
44 http://www.theamericanconservative.com/articles/drones-against-the-fifth-amendment/
45 https://www.opendemocracy.net/crime-of-being-poor-class-and-criminal-justice-in-america
46 http://www.waronwhistleblowers.com/
47 http://home.cc.umanitoba.ca/~altemey/
48 http://www.amendmentgazette.com/are-corporations-people/
49 http://www.amendmentgazette.com/2014/10/17/shift-interview-jeff-clements/
50 http://theantimedia.org/time-lapse-video-shows-massive-amount-people-protested-police-brutali-ty-today/
51 http://newdeal.feri.org/wallace/haw23.htm
52 https://www.youtube.com/watch?v=37Dvt2EqXF4&feature=youtu.be
53 http://www.slideshare.net/ChangeTheRules/one-party-planet
54 http://www.amendmentgazette.com/2013/08/02/feudalism-then-and-now/
55 http://www.truthdig.com/staff/chris_hedges
56 http://wagingnonviolence.org/feature/meet-stellan-vinthagen-head-first-university-program-civil-resistance/
57 http://www.alternet.org/activism/should-protestors-embrace-violence?page=0%2C2&akid=12570.256714.9cENjM&rd=1&src=newsletter1028563&t=2
58 http://www.commondreams.org/views/2014/12/11/what-makes-nonviolent-movements-explode
59 https://www.brainyquote.com/quotes/quotes/j/josemarti225375.html
60 http://www.amendmentgazette.com/2014/05/27/ontology-101-money-speech/
61 http://www.solarhydrogentrends.com/
62 http://www.amendmentgazette.com/2014/05/27/ontology-101-money-speech/
63 http://www.goodreads.com/quotes/64634-we-have-it-in-our-power-to-begin-the-world
64 http://members.shaw.ca/jeanaltemeyer/drbob/TheAuthoritarians.pdf
65 https://youtu.be/bjdcanXK4zo

Chapter 2: From Revolution to Bernie or Bust

66 http://www.azquotes.com/quote/472736
67 https://www.facebook.com/RevoltAgainstPlutocracy/
68 http://www.huffingtonpost.com/charles-ferguson/the-financial-crisis-and-_1_b_782927.html
69 https://www.facebook.com/TrueBlueDemocratsAProgressiveRevolt/
70 http://www.politico.com/story/2009/04/inside-obamas-bank-ceos-meeting-020871
71 For example, Patrick's pro-Warren piece at http://www.opednews.com/articles/Leftists-Awake-Warren-s-by-Patrick-Walker-Class_Climate_Economic_Exploitation-141201-501.html
72 https://citizensagainstplutocracy.wordpress.com/our-revolution/
73 http://www.blackagendareport.com/bernie-sanders-sheepdog-4-hillary
74 http://www.salon.com/2014/07/27/my_party_has_lost_its_soul_bill_clinton_barack_obama_and_the_victory_of_wall_street_democrats/
75 http://www.counterpunch.org/2015/06/12/what-bernie-sanders-supporters-can-learn-from-howard-

deans/

76 http://www.opednews.com/articles/Frankly-Koch-Brothers-Des-by-Patrick-Walker-ACLU_Climate_Death_Death-Penalty-140118-76.html
77 http://harrypotter.wikia.com/wiki/Dark_Mark
78 http://www.opednews.com/articles/Vincent-Bugliosi-and-The-P-by-Michael-Collins-Bush-Admin_Iraq-War_Vincent-Bugliosi-150610-190.html
79 http://www.globalissues.org/article/105/effects-of-sanctions
80 http://www.democraticunderground.com/1002477149
81 http://nbcpolitics.nbcnews.com/_news/2013/06/06/18804146-obama-continues-extends-some-bush-terrorism-policies?lite
82 http://www.huffingtonpost.com/2012/10/23/climate-change-presidential-debate_n_2004067.html
83 http://www.counterpunch.org/2015/03/27/the-logic-of-lesser-evilism/
84 http://www.opednews.com/articles/Bernie-s-No-Sheepdog-Prov-by-Patrick-Walker-Bernie-Sanders_Bernie-Sanders_Climate_Democrat-150526-77.html
85 https://citizensagainstplutocracy.wordpress.com/
86 https://www.change.org/p/senator-warren-and-the-progressive-caucus-endorse-senator-sanders-for-president
87 https://citizensagainstplutocracy.wordpress.com/2015/08/12/the-two-fists-of-revolt-against-plutocracys-revolutionary-strategy/
88 http://www.nationofchange.org/news/2015/12/06/climate-judge-hansen-profiles-clintons-democrat-criminals/
89 http://www.counterpunch.org/2015/12/18/whitewashing-hillary-by-redwashing-progressive-critics/
90 http://www.nationofchange.org/2015/11/15/sanders-correctly-rattles-sabers-at-the-climate-change-enemy-part-1/
91 http://www.nationofchange.org/2015/11/22/clintons-updated-tammany-hall-destroying-democracy-and-climate-too/
92 https://citizensagainstplutocracy.wordpress.com/2015/12/04/the-thugs-are-taking-over-pledge-is-effective-tool-of-revolt/
93 http://www.washingtontimes.com/news/2016/oct/13/emails-show-cozy-relationship-between-media-and-cl/

Chapter 3: Movement Building and Adaptation

94 https://www.brainyquote.com/quotes/quotes/d/dwightdei101562.html
95 http://www.huffingtonpost.com/h-a-goodman/10-reasons-im-only-voting-for-bernie-sanders-and-will-not-support-hillary-clinton_b_8508172.html
96 https://youtu.be/i5Ul1HslyxQ
97 https://youtu.be/jc769f7Xt9Q
98 https://youtu.be/h5T7Xlyaieo
99 http://www.businessinsider.com/donald-trump-begins-debate-with-a-threat-2015-8
100 http://www.nytimes.com/politics/first-draft/2015/08/28/bernie-sanders-warns-democrats-they-may-not-win-in-2016-without-him/
101 www.culturemix.webs.com
102 https://citizensagainstplutocracy.wordpress.com/faq/
103 http://movement99.org/
104 http://www.peopleforbernie.com/
105 http://www.counterpunch.org/2015/08/03/ere-not-sandernistas-reinventing-the-wheels-of-bernies-bandwagon/
106 http://www.counterpunch.org/2015/07/31/bernie-and-the-sandernistas/
107 http://www.counterpunch.org/2015/07/29/the-wheels-are-off-the-bernie-sanders-bandwagon/
108 http://thehill.com/blogs/ballot-box/presidential-races/242321-sanders-i-like-hillary-clinton
109 http://www.counterpunch.org/2015/04/17/the-last-chance-to-derail-the-clinton-juggernaut/

110 http://www.sanders.senate.gov/newsroom/must-read/sanders-an-expanding-military-budget-taxp-ayers-cant-afford-boston-globe

111 http://live.huffingtonpost.com/r/archive/segment/5592dc51fe3444b1450001b9

112 http://www.counterpunch.org/2015/07/15/chris-hedges-on-bernie-sanders-and-the-corporate-dem-ocrats/

113 https://ratical.org/ratville/CAH/fasci14chars.html

114 https://www.facebook.com/ProgressiveExaminer/

Chapter 4: The Treasurers Dropped Like Flies

115 http://www.goodreads.com/quotes/1307967-a-new-challenge-keeps-the-brain-kicking-and-the-heart

Chapter 5: Bernie or Bust Caucus Tactics

116 http://www.goodreads.com/quotes/84834-we-delight-in-the-beauty-of-the-butterfly-but-rarely

117 http://www.nolandalla.com/i-just-got-push-polled-by-hillary-clintons-nevada-campaign/

118 http://www.usatoday.com/story/opinion/2016/02/20/hillary-clinton-wins-nevada-caucus-harry-reid-culinary-union-jon-ralston/80688750/

119 https://www.theguardian.com/commentisfree/2016/mar/07/democratic-vote-hillary-clinton-elect-ion-2016-bernie-sanders

120 https://youtu.be/jSZURgAY86M

121 https://youtu.be/SWI3GX04tbI

122 http://www.inquisitr.com/3136045/informal-survey-indicates-bernie-or-bust-movement-is-not-based-on-privilege/

123 https://www.surveymonkey.com/analyze/browse/VzFom0TN_2F_2Byrc3KrUkUzagKjQCirDO23 Hxd1rdKRlCY_ 3D?respondent_id=4750189981

Chapter 6: Bernie or Bust Primary Tactics

124 http://www.goodreads.com/quotes/7535788-flexibility-is-the-greatest-strength

125 https://youtu.be/qchE5wPsVgo

126 https://youtu.be/aWnD9e1XnQU

127 A coinage by writer Amos Elroy combining "activist" and "entrepreneur." See endnote v.

128 http://www.huffingtonpost.com/amos-elroy/the-new-political-acterpr_b_8926146.html

129 https://youtu.be/BmITItWOiks

130 https://www.youtube.com/user/THEBIGSHOWM3/videos

131 http://m.washingtontimes.com/news/2016/mar/1/hillary-clinton-cant-count-on-bernie-sanders-suppo/

132 https://youtu.be/EXiAn2mzDmc

133 http://www.rawstory.com/2016/03/bill-maher-clinton-and-sanders-fans-attacks-on-one-another-is-gonna-be-the-death-of-liberals/

134 http://dailycaller.com/2016/03/04/dead-broke-hillary-pays-herself-over-250k-from-campaign-coff-ers/

135 https://youtu.be/jvAFLZpBtA0

136 https://youtu.be/RHEbmSfb-kg

137 https://youtu.be/_1mSirA48dM

138 https://scholar.princeton.edu/sites/default/files/mgilens/files/gilens_and_page_2014_-testing_theo-ries_of_american_politics.doc.pdf

139 http://www.realclearpolitics.com/epolls/2016/president/2016_presidential_race.html

140 https://youtu.be/k0CIGtNmIhg

141 *Give Me Liberty: A Handbook for American Revolutionaries,* Naomi Wolf, Simon & Schuster Pa-perbacks, New York, 2008, pp. 216-217.

142 http://www.cnn.com/2016/04/19/politics/new-york-primary-voter-problem-polls-sanders-de-blas-io/
143 http://www.wnyc.org/story/brooklyn-voter-purge-age-clinton-sanders/
144 http://citizensagainstplutocracy.org/2015/12/04/the-thugs-are-taking-over-pledge-is-effective-tool-of-revolt/
145 http://www.thedailybeast.com/articles/2016/05/31/the-poet-laureate-of-bernie-porn-does-not-want-to-talk-to-the-beast.html
146 http://www.salon.com/2016/04/25/why_i_say_bernie_or_bust_if_sanders_isnt_the_democratic_no minee_his_backers_should_by_no_means_pull_the_lever_for_hillary_clinton/
147 http://www.huffingtonpost.com/entry/bernie-or-bust-voters-have-a-home-with-the-green-partys_us_579ec6a9e4b004301c51811f
148 http://www.slate.com/articles/news_and_politics/politics/2016/05/a_letter_to_a_bernie_or_bust_vo ter.html
149 http://www.salon.com/2016/05/15/bernie_or_bust_will_save_us_the_foul_stench_of_lesser_evili sm_has_made_our_politics_useless/
150 http://www.theatlantic.com/politics/archive/2016/07/among-the-pure-at-bernie-or-bust/493094/
151 https://www.bustle.com/articles/153151-bernie-or-bust-is-not-a-silly-argument-for-marginalized-individuals
152 http://www.huffingtonpost.com/entry/message-to-the-bernie-or-bust-crew-your-revolution_us_57975cfbe4b0e339c23f8f02
153 http://fusion.net/story/355707/bernie-or-bust-jill-stein-yahne-ndgo/
154 http://www.rollingstone.com/politics/features/bernie-or-bust-meet-the-emotional-sanders-supp-orters-booing-the-dnc-w430921
155 https://mic.com/articles/146968/bernie-or-bust-where-does-the-bernie-sanders-movement-go-from-here#.HhWxRxTFV
156 http://observer.com/2016/05/bernie-or-bust-movement-grows-as-clinton-polls-tank/
157 http://inthesetimes.com/article/19329/bernie-or-bust-is-real-and-probably-not-going-away-anyt-ime-soon
158 http://www.inquisitr.com/3684880/what-part-of-or-bust-did-you-not-understand/
159 https://thinkprogress.org/bernie-or-bust-holdouts-resort-to-strange-racially-tone-deaf-tactics-cc008b0accce#.vxfevlq5j
160 http://www.attn.com/stories/10238/myth-bernie-or-bust-movement
161 http://www.thedailybeast.com/articles/2016/10/27/even-michael-moore-is-fed-up-with-the-bernie-or-bust-nuts.html
162 Gaffney, "Bernie or bust will save us" (endnote xxvi)
163 https://www.nytimes.com/2016/03/31/opinion/campaign-stops/bernie-or-bust-is-bonkers.html?_r=0
164 https://youtu.be/Djbkwj3qlFw
165 https://www.change.org/p/bernie-sanders-senator-sanders-speak-with-dr-stein-about-a-sanders-stein-green-ticket
166 http://www.commondreams.org/news/2016/07/08/green-partys-jill-stein-sanders-can-lead-my-part-ys-ticket
167 http://www.surveyusa.com/client/PollReport.aspx?g=16a737fe-f202-42b4-965f-e76b137ba826

Chapter 7: Philadelphia: Our Last Stand, Sanders' Last Hope

168 https://www.brainyquote.com/quotes/quotes/h/horationel167954.html?src=t_desperate
169 http://www.juneteenth.com/history.htm
170 http://citizensagainstplutocracy.org/2016/07/28/dem-superdelegates-guilty-of-dereliction-of-duty/
171 http://www.cnn.com/2016/07/11/politics/hillary-clinton-bernie-sanders/
172 https://youtu.be/QgaSX6wyybU
173 https://youtu.be/SWI3GX04tbI
174 https://www.youtube.com/channel/UCxpfmCp2Z9VPTO7eWV6ebzQ

175 http://www.bernforlove.com/
176 https://youtu.be/mandorjrJYI
177 https://youtu.be/BmITItWOiks
178 https://youtu.be/tjGEHIkZ7ss
179 https://youtu.be/1K6jZtx8XmY
180 https://youtu.be/V77tARCQjcE?list=PLXP2fapQcqgAb15LcWpRdUx3H76B2U4Z6
181 https://youtu.be/jvAFLZpBtA0
182 https://youtu.be/V77tARCQjcE?list=PLXP2fapQcqgAb15LcWpRdUx3H76B2U4Z6
183 https://youtu.be/epZuZsEdj-k
184 https://youtu.be/G61uZbMT_Iw
185 http://www.phillymag.com/news/2016/07/27/bernie-supporters-trump-president-democrats-fault/
186 http://www.phillymag.com/news/2016/07/27/bernie-supporters-trump-president-democrats-fault/#LSC60dtBeg3EZ1ST.99
187 Ibid

Chapter 8: From Bernie or Bust to Jill or Bust

188 https://www.democracynow.org/2016/7/26/who_should_bernie_voters_support_now
189 http://www.whoisjillstein.com/who-is-jill-stein/
190 http://www.whoisjillstein.com/the-other-three/
191 https://citizensagainstplutocracy.wordpress.com/2016/08/07/10-reasons-why-no-sanders-supporter-should-vote-for-hillary-clinton/
192 http://m.dailykos.com/story/2016/7/29/1554022/-Election-Justice-USA-Study-Finds-that-Without-Election-Fraud-Sanders-Would-Have-Won-by-Landslide
193 https://citizensagainstplutocracy.wordpress.com/hrcc/
194 https://citizensagainstplutocracy.wordpress.com/2016/07/28/dem-superdelegates-guilty-of-dereliction-of-duty/
195 https://ratical.org/ratville/CAH/fasci14chars.html
196 http://therules.org/we-live-on-a-one-party-planet/
197 http://www.hillaryantisemitism.com/
198 https://youtu.be/fM-bsSMUgAg
199 https://youtu.be/xb_N02-vh8M
200 http://www.dailykos.com/story/2016/2/27/1492247/-In-1996-First-Lady-Clinton-Still-Proud-Of-Conservative-Roots-Backing-Pro-Segregation-Goldwater
201 http://www.greenpeace.org/usa/campaign-updates/hillary-clintons-connection-oil-gas-industry/
202 https://www.periscope.tv/w/1ypJdPoDgMQJW
203 http://www.alternet.org/election-2016/donald-trump-trying-tank-his-campaign
204 https://docs.google.com/forms/d/e/1FAIpQLScQqOmZI2ddRbDzY4J9WELS3dR9grZqg4bhiNc8dsS4Jf-ROQ/viewform
205 https://secure.actblue.com/contribute/page/revolt
206 https://youtu.be/_tjRVMf5Wk0
207 https://citizensagainstplutocracy.wordpress.com/our-goal-democracy/
208 http://www.rawstory.com/2016/09/jill-stein-insists-trump-is-less-dangerous-than-clinton-and-attacks-bernie-sanders-as-a-dc-insider/
209 http://www.politico.com/story/2016/07/terry-mcauliffe-hillary-clinton-tpp-trade-226253
210 http://freebeacon.com/uncategorized/clinton-surrogate-told-supporters-clinton-planned-betrayal-tpp/
211 http://www.truthdig.com/report/item/we_were_warned_about_barack_obama_—_by_obama_20170114
212 http://www.nytimes.com/2008/03/04/us/politics/04nafta.html
213 www.lesserevil2016.com/bio
214 http://www.hillaryantisemitism.com/hillary-nword/
215 https://citizensagainstplutocracy.wordpress.com/2016/11/05/four-candidates/

216 http://dissidentvoice.org/2016/10/in-november-we-choose-between-war-or-peace-with-russia/
217 http://www.gq.com/story/176-reasons-donald-trump-shouldnt-be-president-olbermann
218 http://www.truthdig.com/report/item/the_most_brazen_corporate_power_grab_in_american_history_20151106
219 http://www.jill2016.com/hatersgonnahate

Chapter 9: #OpDeny270

220 http://embols.com/2016/09/25/how-bernie-sanders-could-become-president-with-only-130000-votes/
221 https://theindependentthinker2016.wordpress.com/2016/09/24/how-bernie-sanders-could-become-president-with-only-130000-votes/
222 http://www.inquisitr.com/3527032/could-just-thousands-in-wyoming-or-vermont-hold-the-key-to-a-surprise-bernie-sanders-presidency/
223 ibid
224 http://nypost.com/2016/04/09/bernie-sanders-wins-democratic-caucuses-in-wyoming/
225 http://www.nytimes.com/elections/results/wyoming
226 http://embols.com/2016/09/25/how-bernie-sanders-could-become-president-with-only-130000-votes/ Quoted with permission.
227 http://www.baltimoresun.com/news/opinion/readersrespond/bs-ed-election-letter-20160801-story.html
228 https://youtu.be/e-DOxmMF7HQ
229 https://www.facebook.com/events/204387946661087/
230 tinyurl.com/BoBbustsWriteInScheme
231 http://thehill.com/homenews/campaign/310287-electoral-college-voters-under-intense-pressure
232 https://www.washingtonpost.com/news/post-politics/wp/2016/09/16/bernie-sanders-this-is-not-the-time-for-a-protest-vote/
233 https://www.facebook.com/xomesxo/videos/vb.672891353/10154615904071354/?type=2&theater
234 http://www.sos.ca.gov/administration/news-releases-and-advisories/2016-news-releases-and-advisories/write-candidates-president-and-vice-president-certified/
235 http://www.forbes.com/sites/carriekerpen/2016/07/20/how-to-run-a-successful-presidential-campaign-on-social-media/#7b044bd13f67
236 https://youtu.be/8rpiqyGmQXQ
237 http://www.cnn.com/2016/06/01/politics/bernie-sanders-hillary-clinton-bernie-or-bust/
238 https://youtu.be/CoIDpo3nIOA
239 https://vtelectionresults.sec.state.vt.us/Index.html#/federal
240 http://elections.cdn.sos.ca.gov/sov/2016-general/sov/2016-complete-sov.pdf
241 http://heavy.com/news/2016/11/how-many-write-in-votes-for-did-bernie-sanders-get-presidential-election-results-california-iowa-new-hampshire-pennsylvania-vermont-total/
242 https://www.facebook.com/groups/OpDeny270/
243 https://youtu.be/CYwEOmMTwSw
244 https://www.laprogressive.com/write-in-bernie-sanders/
245 Ibid.
246 https://youtu.be/7f28dVrtEWA

Chapter 10: The Blame Game

247 https://www.brainyquote.com/quotes/quotes/j/johnfkenn101159.html
248 http://www.inquisitr.com/3207171/election-fraud-study-points-to-rigged-democratic-primary-against-bernie-sanders-video/
249 http://cookpolitical.com/story/10174
250 https://www.emptywheel.net/2016/12/11/obamacare-not-comey-effect/

251 http://www.nytimes.com/2016/12/16/us/politics/hillary-clinton-russia-fbi-comey.html?

252 http://www.counterpunch.org/2016/11/15/break-up-the-democratic-party-its-time-for-the-clintons-and-rubin-to-go-and-soros-too/

253 https://youtu.be/PnjlKAEN_hw

254 https://youtu.be/cuPX0iYKmxc

255 http://www.huffingtonpost.com/marty-rudoy/dear-bernie-or-busters-co_b_12892318.html

256 http://www.rgj.com/story/opinion/readers/2016/11/18/letter-bernie-bust-folks-have-busted-their-future/93798772/

257 We do not know if someone is paying to boost an obsolete post about a limited poll and another about or if it's a Facebook glitch, but our page is getting free advertisement

258 http://www.businessinsider.com/hillary-clinton-donald-trump-polls-50-points-2016-9

259 http://nypost.com/2016/11/03/hillary-cinton-even-lies-about-lying-about-her-lies/

260 http://www.washingtonexaminer.com/more-people-see-trump-as-honest-trustworthy-than-clinton/article/2606540

261 http://www.washingtontimes.com/news/2016/nov/3/hillary-clinton-watches-honest-mistakes-pile-up/

262 http://www.realprogressiveusa.com/news/editorial/2016-11-12-hillary-clinton-is-not-simply-a-symptom-of-our-corrupt-system-she-is-a-leading-cause

263 http://www.huffingtonpost.com/entry/2016-election-poll-bernie-sanders-trump_us_58260f7ee4b0c4b63b0c6928

264 https://www.theguardian.com/commentisfree/2016/nov/09/rise-of-the-davos-class-sealed-americas-fate

265 http://enight.elections.myflorida.com/FederalOffices/Presidential/

266 http://www.nydailynews.com/opinion/bernie-sanders-pay-donald-trump-visit-article-1.2885126?cid=bitly

267 http://www.politico.com/2016-election/results/map/president

268 http://www.politico.com/2012-election/results/map/#/President/2012/

269 http://www.commondreams.org/news/2016/12/12/federal-judge-blocks-jill-steins-pennsylvania-recount-effort

270 http://www.media.pa.gov/Pages/State-Details.aspx?newsid=207

271 https://en.wikipedia.org/wiki/Bernie_or_Bust

272 https://www.craigmurray.org.uk/archives/2016/12/cias-absence-conviction/

273 http://www.motherjones.com/kevin-drum/2016/11/why-clinton-lost-bitter-bernie-crooked-comey-and-wounded-working-class

274 https://www.theguardian.com/us-news/2015/sep/08/hillary-clinton-apologizes-private-email-server

275 http://www.truthdig.com/report/item/no_america_it_wasnt_russia_you_did_this_to_yourself_2016 1210

276 http://www.truthdig.com/report/item/sorry_garrison_keillor_keith_ellison_could_have_beaten_tru mp_20161214

277 http://www.slate.com/articles/news_and_politics/politics/2016/12/the_myth_of_the_rust_belt_revolt.html

278 http://www.politico.com/story/2016/12/michigan-hillary-clinton-trump-232547

279 http://www.nydailynews.com/news/politics/king-obama-clintons-no-idea-dems-lost-election-article-1.2916282

280 http://www.huffingtonpost.com/entry/things-i-blame-for-hillary-clintons-loss-ranked_us_58459894e4b0496fbcb0c26d?

281 http://www.counterpunch.org/2016/12/23/89317/

282 https://www.facebook.com/salon/videos/10154466014756519/

283 http://www.counterpunch.org/2016/12/20/it-wasnt-the-russians-hillary-lost-because-she-blew-off-sanders-and-his-voters/

284 http://www.alternet.org/election-2016/post-election-noam-chomsky-drops-trump-bomb-trump-voters-wanting-shake-systempost?

285 http://www.alternet.org/election-2016/will-trump-provoke-serious-conflict-china?

286 http://theduran.com/wallace-asks-hillary-during-debate-impose-no-fly-zone-in-syria-does-president-clinton-shoot-that-russian-plane-down/

287 https://acronymjournal.com/2016/05/10/bernieorbust-throws-down-gauntlet-declaring-trump-is-no-worse-than-clinton/

288 http://www.politico.com/story/2016/12/michigan-hillary-clinton-trump-232547

289 https://twitter.com/realDonaldTrump/status/811977223326625792

290 http://www.newslogue.com/debate/229/CaitlinJohnstone

291 https://www.nytimes.com/2016/12/16/opinion/sunday/is-donald-trump-a-threat-to-democracy.html?

292 https://youtu.be/7xX_KaStFT8

293 https://theintercept.com/2016/12/02/hillary-clintons-corrupt-establishment-is-now-advising-donald-trump/

294 https://WikiLeaks.org/podesta-emails/emailid/927

295 https://WikiLeaks.org/podesta-emails/emailid/5192

296 https://youtu.be/_1mSirA48dM

297 http://ahtribune.com/in-depth/1473-paul-street.html

298 ibid

299 https://twitter.com/realDonaldTrump/status/823174199036542980

300 http://www.washingtonexaminer.com/trump-i-like-right-to-work-better/article/2583977

301 https://www.theguardian.com/commentisfree/2013/aug/06/obama-abuse-espionage-act-mccarthyism

302 http://www.rollingstone.com/politics/features/the-gops-stealth-war-against-voters-w435890

303 http://www.dailykos.com/story/2016/7/29/1554022/-Election-Justice-USA-Study-Finds-that-Without-Election-Fraud-Sanders-Would-Have-Won-by-Landslide

304 http://blackagendareport.com/dem_and_gop_paths_to_fascism

305 http://www.truth-out.org/opinion/item/36376-our-neoliberal-nightmare-hillary-clinton-donald-trump-and-why-the-wealthy-win-every-time

306 http://www.academia.edu/9772078/What_are_the_identifying_characteristics_of_Neoliberalism_D oes_it_qualify_as_a_distinctive_ideology. Many of these characteristics are derived from Paul Smyth's paper.

307 http://www.truthdig.com/report/page2/building_the_institutions_for_revolt_20170115

308 http://www.truth-out.org/opinion/item/36376-our-neoliberal-nightmare-hillary-clinton-donald-trump-and-why-the-wealthy-win-every-time

309 Manfred B. Steger and Ravi K. Roy, *Neoliberalism: A Very Short Introduction*, (Oxford University Press, 2010), ISBN 019956051X, p. 123

310 http://www.counterpunch.org/2017/02/07/trump-in-the-white-house-what-you-see-is-what-you-get/

311 Charles Peters, "A Neoliberal's Manifesto," *The Washington Monthly*, May 1983

312 http://therules.org/we-live-on-a-one-party-planet/ The 12th, 13th and 14th characteristics are derived from that pamphlet.

313 ibid

314 https://fivethirtyeight.com/features/registered-voters-who-stayed-home-probably-cost-clinton-the-election/

315 http://www.huffingtonpost.com/charles-ferguson/the-financial-crisis-and-_1_b_782927.html

316 https://www.sierraclub.org/sites/www.sierraclub.org/files/uploads-wysiwig/TPP-LNG_Factsheet_Updated.pdf

317 https://www.washingtonpost.com/opinions/kill-the-dispute-settlement-language-in-the-trans-pacific-partnership/2015/02/25/ec7705a2-bd1e-11e4-b274-e5209a3bc9a9_story.html?utm_term=.3f860f22fde7

318 http://www.aljazeera.com/indepth/opinion/2016/12/trump-era-beijing-edge-161206093417749.html?

319 http://www.amendmentgazette.com/2012/06/26/trans-pacific-partnership-is-citizens-united-on-crack/

320 http://readersupportednews.org/news-section2/318-66/40874-breaking-fbi-backs-cia-view-that-russia-intervened-to-help-trump-win-election
321 http://alexanderhiggins.com/WikiLeaks-hillary-clinton-emails-leaked-by-pissed-bernie-backer-not-russia/
322 https://popularresistance.org/us-intel-vets-dispute-russia-hacking-claims/
323 https://youtu.be/skQN8zct-ow
324 http://readersupportednews.org/opinion2/277-75/40906-trumped-by-putin
325 https://www.facebook.com/BenSwannRealityCheck/videos/1301123713285909/
326 http://www.truthdig.com/report/item/blaming_russia_is_irresistible_to_the_democrats_20161222
327 http://readersupportednews.org/opinion2/277-75/41122-something-about-this-russia-story-stinks
328 https://www.craigmurray.org.uk/archives/2017/01/stunning-admission-obama-WikiLeaks/
329 http://www.counterpunch.org/2017/01/11/trust-but-dont-verify-us-intelligence-agencies-and-the-new-cold-war/
330 http://www.counterpunch.org/2017/01/13/did-the-russians-really-hack-the-dnc/
331 http://www.zerohedge.com/news/2017-03-07/WikiLeaks-hold-press-conference-vault-7-release-8am-eastern
332 http://www.truthdig.com/report/item/building_the_institutions_for_revolt_20170115

Chapter 11: What's Next?

333 https://youtu.be/IPLtzoTs8ok
334 https://youtu.be/w3_0x6oaDmI
335 https://youtu.be/Fob-AGgZn44
336 http://www.election-justice-usa.org/Democracy_Lost_Update1_EJUSA.pdf
337 https://youtu.be/R6x8Z4NLUAA
338 https://www.nomorestolenelections.org/
339 http://www.counterpunch.org/2016/12/23/89317/
340 http://thebestdemocracymoneycanbuy.com/
341 http://www.rollingstone.com/politics/features/the-gops-stealth-war-against-voters-w435890
342 http://citizensagainstplutocracy.org/our-goal-democracy/
343 http://citizensagainstplutocracy.org/our-goal-democracy/
344 https://www.rt.com/shows/sophieco/366442-trump-promises-foreign-policy/
345 http://www.counterpunch.org/2016/11/15/break-up-the-democratic-party-its-time-for-the-clintons-and-rubin-to-go-and-soros-too/ Quoted with permission
346 http://www.counterpunch.org/2016/12/23/89317/
347 http://www.newslogue.com/debate/305/CaitlinJohnstone
348 http://www.cnbc.com/2017/01/17/elizabeth-warren-no-longer-darling-of-the-left-commentary.html
349 https://www.opensecrets.org/politicians/summary.php?cid=N00033492&cycle=2014
350 https://youtu.be/P4F5lZVv7X8
351 http://www.newslogue.com/debate/306
352 http://www.alternet.org/can-democrats-get-tough-and-save-us-trumps-supreme-court-nominees?
353 http://readersupportednews.org/opinion2/277-75/40960-focus-top-5-reasons-senate-dems-should-block-all-trump-supreme-court-nominees-forever
354 http://www.nationofchange.org/2017/03/04/democratic-leaders-craven-bunch-idiots-bent-self-destruction/
355 https://www.washingtonpost.com/opinions/how-to-remove-trump-from-office/2017/01/09/e119cc36-d698-11e6-9a36-1d296534b31e_story.html
356 http://www.cnn.com/2017/01/20/politics/trump-inaugural-address/index.html
357 https://www.rt.com/shows/sophieco/366442-trump-promises-foreign-policy/
358 http://www.huffingtonpost.com/entry/bernie-sanders-donald-trump_us_5823b640e4b0e80b02cec30b
359 https://www.facebook.com/denniskucinich/posts/10154527639948218
360 https://youtu.be/2d5eSbnm7zs

361 http://www.alternet.org/news-amp-politics/congratulations-america-youve-elected-actual-fascist-president?
362 https://acronymjournal.com/2016/12/21/in-the-age-of-trump-resistance-movements-must-bring-people-together-beyond-the-digital-realm/
363 http://www.counterpunch.org/2016/12/13/the-ascendance-of-trump-makes-broad-based-climate-action-essential-and-achievable/
364 http://readersupportednews.org/opinion2/277-75/41560-focus-with-the-rise-of-trump-is-it-game-over-for-the-climate-fight
365 http://www.cnn.com/2016/11/22/politics/donald-trump-climate-change-new-york-times/
366 http://www.counterpunch.org/2016/12/13/the-ascendance-of-trump-makes-broad-based-climate-action-essential-and-achievable/
367 https://popularresistance.org/isfreedomplazaanalternativetoanti-depressants/
368 https://youtu.be/p6UJBn7dLec
369 http://citizensagainstplutocracy.org/faq/
370 http://www.forbes.com/forbes/welcome/?toURL=http://www.forbes.com/sites/carriekerpen/2016/07/20/how-to-run-a-successful-presidential-campaign-on-social-media/
371 http://therules.org/we-live-on-a-one-party-planet/
372 https://befreedom.co/2016/06/25/transformation-and-reconstruction-the-means-and-measure-of-revolutionary-change/
373 ibid
374 https://befreedom.co/2016/05/28/learn-from-the-bern/
375 https://befreedom.co/2016/06/09/universal-values-are-revolutionary-values/
376 https://befreedom.co/2016/05/25/how-do-we-organize-a-hundred-million/
377 https://www.washingtonpost.com/politics/democrats-see-hope-in-womens-marches—but-wonder-what-comes-next/2017/01/22/577bf2e6-e0ee-11e6-a453-19ec4b3d09ba_story.html?
378 https://www.facebook.com/groups/411345975864813/
379 https://theintercept.com/2017/02/09/tom-perez-apologizes-for-telling-the-truth-showing-why-democrats-flaws-urgently-need-attention/
380 https://www.theguardian.com/commentisfree/2016/nov/09/rise-of-the-davos-class-sealed-americas-fate
381 https://steemit.com/progressive/@caitlinjohnstone/democrats-can-unite-when-centrists-stop-being-crazy-idiots
382 https://trofire.com/2017/02/16/establishment-democrats-beg-bernie-call-off-angry-voters-fat-chance/
383 https://www.opednews.com/populum/page.php?f=Let-s-Hunt-Neoliberals-to-by-Patrick-Walker-Anti-war_Climate_Democratic_Domination-170114-545.html
384 https://popularresistance.org/be-wary-of-the-democratic-wing-of-the-protest-movement/

Conclusion: #ProgressiveOrBust

385 http://www.counterpunch.org/2017/01/05/trumps-neo-fascism-will-be-built-on-neo-fascism-of-obama-and-democrat-party/
386 http://www.pipunite.org/
387 http://www.counterpunch.org/2013/03/15/the-progressive-movement-is-a-pr-front-for-rich-democrats/
388 http://www.mcclatchydc.com/news/nation-world/national/article124842824.htm
389 http://reclaimdemocracy.org/powell _memo_lewis/
390 *Bernie Sanders, Our Revolution: A Future to Believe* In (New York, St. Martin's Press, 2016), p. 446.
391 ibid, p. 447.
392 https://www.facebook.com/salon/videos/10154466014756519/
393 https://youtu.be/OcKgovk5u6c
394 http://www.countercurrents.org/2017/03/21/apollo-earth-a-wake-up-call-in-our-race-against-time/

395 http://www.econlib.org/library/Enc/CreativeDestruction.html
396 http://readersupportednews.org/opinion2/277-75/42421-noam-chomsky-trumps-muslim-ban-is-a-fabulous-recruiting-tool-for-al-qaeda-and-isis
397 ibid
398 http://www.newslogue.com/debate/333
399 http://www.miamiherald.com/latest-news/article131466809.ece/binary/ksmlettertoobama.pdf
400 https://youtu.be/PChJmaDFYgw
401 http://www.truthdig.com/avbooth/item/president_obama_retraces_past_eight_years_farewell_speech_throws_20170111
402 http://www.truthdig.com/report/page2/we_were_warned_about_barack_obama_—_by_obama_20170114
403 https://www.indivisibleguide.com/
404 https://namle.net/publications/media-literacy-definitions/
405 https://shadowproof.com/2016/10/11/labor-secretary-advised-clinton-cast-sanders-candidate-whites-turn-off-minorities/

Afterword

406 http://www.values.com/inspirational-quotes/3125-it-is-easier-to-forgive-an-enemy-than-to
407 https://draftbernie.org/
408 https://draftbernie.org/2017/05/19/weekly-organizing-call-51817/